Steel Rain,
the Tet Offensive, 1968

by john harrison

6/6/2018

To Bob,

I hope your current adventures
are less violent than the ones
we shared in vietnam.

Currahee

John Harrison

PREFACE

This book starts with jump school just before I joined a legendary airborne unit that was training specifically to go to the Vietnam War. Then, it continues with our time in Vietnam itself during the Vietnam War. It turned out we were there for the bloodiest year of the war, including the Tet Offensive of 1968. I have left out my Basic Training at Ft. Polk in Louisiana, Advanced Infantry Training at Ft. Ord in California and Officer Candidate School at Ft. Benning, Georgia, because very similar stories to mine are amply covered in many other books, and in even some very good movies like *Full Metal Jacket*. This story begins a little later than such stories with my first assignment as freshly minted, Airborne, Infantry officer of the 101st Airborne Division.

Many others who served in the Vietnam War and probably in many other American wars will have had experiences similar to ours. After all, American soldiers, Marines, airmen and sailors are all still young Americans no matter when, or where they served. I hope that this book reminds them of the good times, and there actually were quite a few of those for most of us, along with the not so good.

After Jump School, the first stop on this journey to war is at Ft. Campbell, Kentucky, where I joined my new unit. It was literally still in formation as Company A, 3rd Battalion, 506th (Airborne) Infantry, 1st Brigade, 101st

2

Airborne Division. I was a brand new Second Lieutenant who did not realize how lucky I was at the time.

The unit was brand new because the battalion had been formed specifically to go to Vietnam to reinforce the First Brigade of the 101st Airborne Division which was already in country. The 101st Airborne Division had been one of the first American combat units deployed to Vietnam. The plan was that we would become the First Brigade's fourth maneuver battalion. For anyone that knows the division's storied history it will come as no surprise to learn that after we were long gone from Vietnam, it turned out that the 101st Airborne Division would be one of the last American units to be withdrawn from Vietnam, as well one of the first to go.

Our battalion commander was Lt. Col. John P. Geraci. He was on his third war, and he was very good at what he did. In fact he was good enough to be inducted into the *Ranger Hall of Fame* at Ft. Benning, Georgia. Our company commander was Captain Thomas F. Gaffney. He was on his second war, and like Lt. Col. Geraci, Captain Gaffney had already been to Vietnam twice as a Green Beret.

Both men were already incredible warriors, and they passed that experience on to all of us who were under their command. In large measure the fact that many of us made it home is because we served with these two men. All of the other Currahees in the 3/506th Airborne Infantry Regiment, 1st Brigade, 101st Airborne Division owe them a debt of gratitude.

Of course, we did not know then that we would be present in Vietnam during by far the bloodiest year of that long war. Almost 17,000 Americans died in Vietnam during 1968. This bloody toll included several men from my platoon. That is, almost 30% of all of those that were killed during the entire eight years of the hot war in Vietnam died while we were there for our one year tour of duty. Timing really is everything.

However, the odds were not that good for anybody assigned to Vietnam. The numbers say that one in ten of all of the Americans that actually served in Vietnam proper during the war was wounded or killed. That is an incredible casualty percentage, particularly considering that only about 10% of those that served in Vietnam were actual trigger pullers out in the field. Vietnam was nothing more, or less than a very dangerous place to be, for everybody that served there.

We managed to be in Vietnam at Phan Thiet on January 31, 1968 when they recorded the most Americans killed in action for a single bloody day — 245 KIA. We were also in Vietnam when the most Americans were killed in action during a single month — May 1968, 2,415 KIA were lost during that one month. And, for almost all of the war's bloodiest year as well, 1968.

While we were not in action everyday, it was a regular part of our year in country. If there were no VC around Phan Thiet, which was where we were based most of the time, then we were loaded on our helicopters and sent to Dalat, or Song Be or where ever else the VC/NVA had been found in II Corps. It was a fairly rare day when at least of the companies in the battalion was not in combat somewhere in our area of operation. It was an even rarer week when every company in the battalion had not had at least some contact with the enemy during that week.

It was a really big war for America, our fourth largest war to date based on the casualties incurred. This simple fact is too often either ignored or forgotten. For example, the US Marines suffered more casualties in Vietnam than they did during all of World War II. Similarly, the 101st Airborne Division also suffered more casualties in Vietnam than it did in all of World War II. That represents a lot of hard fighting by some of our most elite troops.

In most of the discussions of the Vietnam War, its sheer size, and the ferocity of the fighting, are oft times secondary to the often still angry political discussions about the war. Nonetheless, that fighting was done, that ferocity was endured by America's sons, and by more than a few of her daughters as well, but their story, the real stories of what they actually did in America's service is still unknown, still unappreciated by their country men and women. It remains unreported.

It is very difficult to explain to people who have not been there what you are talking about when you are talking about actual combat. When I got back many people told me that they assumed that I did not talk about my experience because I was ashamed of what I had done in Vietnam. So, I made a conscious effort to talk about Vietnam, because I was not ashamed at all. In fact, I was proud of what my men and I had done there for America.

The truth is though that a lot of people do not talk about their war because they did not really do anything in their war worth talking about. 90% in any war are REMFs (Rear Echelon Mother F——-) and rarely hear a shot fired in anger. I am not putting them down because they are essential to the battle, but it would be harder to answer the question "What did you do in the war daddy?" if you were in Graves Registration, or toilet paper resupply than if you were in one of the combat arms. However, somebody had to be in Graves Registration and most often, it was not their choice.

I mostly told what I call Infantry humor stories at first, and then I noticed that civilians often laughed at the wrong time in the story and that they did not laugh at all at the parts that I thought were funny. At first this disturbed me. Now it does not. I don't know why it doesn't anymore. However, it is the same thing with lawyer, and teacher, stories. While no one laughs at those either, I still tell those as well.

Lots of men have died in war. In my war it was almost 60,000 KIA. Some died bravely, like my Platoon Sergeant James Bunn, some foolishly, some inexplicably like the guy that just died in the chow hall line one day at Phan Thiet during Tet. One minute he was there, the next he was laying on the ground, dead. I never did learn how or why he died.

It is the giving of orders part that makes for hard memories. People are dead because of what you told them to do. The reality is that this is most often a "there but for fortune" experience. I was lucky. My Platoon Sergeant, SFC James A. Bunn was not.

You could say that luck had nothing to do with being shot as Jim Bunn was shot while he was standing up, in a door way, firing an automatic weapon into a house, in the middle of an epic firefight, but you can't say that luck had nothing to do with still being alive after being in the beaten zone of a machine-gun as I was on the same day. However, they are really two sides of the same coin as is set forth in the stories *The Day Smith Died*, and *Cone Of Violence*.

For me, the fact that the most I ever lost in one battle was two men killed was very important because to me it meant that I did my job. Because of that and the incredible men in Second Platoon, although we were often in fierce firefights, we were never ambushed. We were never even really surprised.

All of the rest is just war, and war really does suck. However, you do meet people there like Jim Bunn, a lovely man to know and a warrior to learn

6

from. A true professional soldier who taught me enough to keep me and many others alive.

Would-a, could-a, should-a, will drive anyone that lets them in their mind crazy. Having said that I refight the battle on 2/2/1968 just about everyday, usually in the shower in the morning. The battle we fought that day never changes, for me it still reeks of death. On the other hand on January 31,1968 we fought the battle I called the "*Turkey Shoot*" and the way my platoon fought and reacted to the enemy that day was simply a beautiful, almost a sublime experience. We fought many more battles, but those are the two battles that I think about most.

Each time I think of these two battles I think of Robert E. Lee's statement at Fredericksburg: "*It is well that war is so terrible, otherwise we would come to love it too much.*" War is not worth the price, but it is something. . .

This is my attempt to tell our part of the story. While it is not a history of our unit, nor even of the war in Vietnam itself, it does tell some of the stories, of some of the things that happened to us while we were together in that far off, dangerous, place, working, fighting, bleeding and too often dying for America.

Since these are stories told through my eyes, unavoidably most of the stories focus on me, what I did, what I saw. Even so, I have tried to include as much as I could about the men that I served with, about the men that literally brought me home alive. Still, it is unfortunately true that much of the focus of the book remains on me, but in large part that is inevitable because this is a book about what I remember, what I saw about what we did so long ago.

Nonetheless, this book does contain parts of the stories that everyone that was there in Vietnam before, after and along with us will recognize. We all fought the same war, whether we were there together or not. Unfortunately, we all also experienced the same return from that war as well.

In part it also focuses on me because, as I learned the hard way at the first reunion of the 3/506th that I went to, attributing something to someone other than the person who did it makes the person who actually did it, very angry. It does not seem to matter whether the act attributed is either good or bad, praise worthy or even loathsome. They still get angry. So, unless I am sure, I do not attribute an act to a name.

Originally I wrote these stories as they came to me. I have now placed them in the chronological order as they occurred. A lot of our time in Vietnam is left out for various reasons, but each story here actually happened. Of course, others that were there will have memories that will differ, even of some of the same events. As a practicing trial lawyer I learned that this is normal, particularly if the events are violent in nature. War is about as violent as it gets, so there are multiple true stories about many of these events.

Earlier versions of these stories have all been posted on my web site and have been read by many of those that were there with me. Many that were there have commented on the stories. If their comments revived a memory, then I added that memory to the story that you will see here. They have all been revised and re-written many times. Each time I did it with a view to making them as accurate as I can. However, if there are mistakes here, they are all my mistakes.

In addition, some of the comments of those that have already read the stories appear right before the story starts. Most times these comments set the stage for the story to follow. Sometimes I just think they are funny, and are related to the story in some way.

Some of the stories are funny too, we were American kids after all. When I say they are funny, I am talking mostly about what I call "*Infantry humor*". The non-Infantry readers may have trouble finding something in these stories that is funny to them. Ask an Infantryman, or Marine, they will know where to laugh.

On the other hand, some of them are not funny at all. Either way, each is a stand alone story that can be read by itself. Taken together, they are a big part of the story of our year at war in Vietnam.

The book is dedicated to all of the paratroopers of Alpha Company, 3rd Battalion (Airborne) Infantry, First Brigade, 101st Airborne Division, the famous Currahee, our Band of Brothers of well deserved legend, first in World War II and now from the Vietnam War as well. It is particularly dedicated to the Second Platoon, my platoon, of Alpha Company, who against all of the odds kept me alive in that violent place, and returned me still alive, and with only a few extra pieces back to America. I apologize for the "X's", this was not my picture. You will see it again.

We had a hell-of-a-ride, didn't we?

john harrison
Washington, D.C.

The 2nd Platoon, Company A, 3rd Battalion (Airborne), 506th Infantry Regiment, 101st Airborne Division, at Fort Campbell, Kentucky.

One

This story is about when we were training at Ft. Campbell Ky., before we deployed to Vietnam. As the XO, or Executive Officer of Alpha Company I was the officer called on most often for additional duties. That kept the company commander free to train Alpha Company and, the platoon leaders free to train their platoons. Unfortunately, when I did get a rifle platoon, somebody forgot to tell battalion, so the additional duties continued to arrive for me.

Among the additional duties was one that I actually got to like. I often served as Trial Counsel or Defense Counsel at various special courts martial. That experience is probably what led me many years later to become an attorney. You just never know.

One of the things we were supposed to do as a battalion was make a combat jump when we got to Vietnam. Thus, we trained as a fully airborne battalion on jump status from the beginning. One of the advantages for me, and everybody else that went over originally was that we drew Jump Pay for the entire time we were in Vietnam, a total of $1,320.00 for me. Officers drew $110 a month Jump Pay, enlisted men only received $55 a month. I don't know why there was a difference, but I understand Jump Pay is the same now for both officers and men.

Soon after we returned from Vietnam and I got out of the Army, I bought a brand new Volkswagen Beetle car to use while I finished college at Georgetown University. I wanted a car that got good gas milage, was unlikely to need to be repaired, and was inexpensive to repair when it did need it. According to *Consumer Reports* at the time the VW Beetle was tailor made for meeting those requirements. In a very real sense then, just being on jump status while I was in Vietnam almost paid for my car while I was in college. I think, including tax, that I paid about $1,600.00 for that car.

Because of a dumb first lieutenant we never made that combat blast though. He had left all the plans for the combat jump in his brief case which was stolen from his jeep which he had parked next to an Officer's Club in Phan Rang while he ate lunch inside. I think that all of the Currahees, myself included, have held that against him for all of these years. It is probably a good thing that we never learned who he is because we really wanted that combat blast. (A "*combat blast*" is a fully tactical parachute jump into combat)

This first story tells you a little part of what exiting an aircraft in flight is all about.

C-130 Running Down The Strip

"I never jumped from an airplane when I wasn't scared. I understand why seconds before the green light turned on, every paratrooper on the airplane yelled and screamed "Airborne" before we shuffled down the aisle headed to the door to jump into the skies. This Airborne spirit separates an Airborne soldier from a leg "Non-Airborne". It wasn't about the extra $55.00 jump pay we received. It was about the bloused jump boots, glider patch, and silver wings. Airborne."

Frank Gilbert
Bravo company, 3/506th Abn. Inf.
February 7, 2016 at 6:22 pm

It was the last jump in jump school. As a treat, we the almost airborne, would get to tailgate a C-130. For those NAPs (Non-Airborne Personnel) reading this, that means you walk right out of the back of the C-130, right down the aircraft's wide open tailgate, and then step off into nothingness about 1,000 or so feet up in the air going about 150-60 miles an hour.

Although the ending could have been better, it immediately became my all-time favorite jump. At least until I tailgated a Caribou, which was the same experience, except better.

Unlike in a unit jump where everyone was usually stamping their spit-shined, black, Corcoran, jump boots on the plane's metal deck and shouting: *"Go!, Go!, Go!,"* in jump school the men inside the plane were quiet, waiting for their jump, while the aircraft's turbo prop engines roared. It was quiet enough inside the plane that even over the turbo prop engine's roar, you could actually hear the electric motors work as they lowered the ramp at the rear of the plane. When it was down, we could see the sun swept Georgia countryside of Fort Benning, below as the three planes lined up on the drop zone. We could also see the red light turn on beside the jump master.

"Get ready."

"Stand up!"

"Hook up!"

"Equipment check!"

"O-K.

O-K.

O-K. . .

All O-K."

The jump commands came loud and fast, but there was no command this time of *"Stand in the Door!"* because this was a tailgate jump and we were all already in the door. We were all looking out that huge, gapping, opening in the back of the plane, looking at the land constantly retreating away, far below.

Then came the deceptively simple command:

"Go."

I never had a feeling of height when jumping out of a plane, or with walking out of one as we did with tailgating the C-130. I think my mind looked down at the ground way below me and said to itself something like this:

"No, you're not really dumb enough to do this, are you?"

"No."

"We're not really this high, are we?"

"No."

"You can't be serious?"

"No."

"You're not really going to just walk off the edge of this ramp?"

"No."

"Are you fucking crazy?"

"No o o o o!"

"One thousand."

"Two thousand."

"Three thousand."

"Four thous. . ."

Opening shock felt.

"Chute open. Fully deployed. Panels all there. No tangles. Good."

"God, it's pretty up here. And, it's so quiet. So, still. Wow."

And then you sort of sit in the chute's webbing as you drift, seemingly slowly at first, down to the drop zone. The only thing that was important then was to keep looking around to make sure that you did not run into another trooper in the air. However, it is so beautiful up there, hanging from the parachute, and the view is so incredibly unobstructed that you really do want to look in every direction at the same time, all the time even if you did not have to look out for, and try to avoid a mid-air collision with another trooper.

Although it never happened to me, landing on another chute on the way down is always a risk as well. I saw it happen to at least someone during every mass jump I ever made.

If you land on another chute on the way down, the training is to quickly run off of it before your own chute collapses around you or you get tangled up in the canopy below. If you do not run off quickly enough, the lower chute will "*steal your air*". At that point, you will have a useless collapsed parachute draped all over you that you must get rid of in midair. Then, you must deploy your reserve, if you have time before you hit the ground, which you probably will not have.

If that happens you will not be able to make what the Army calls a PLF (Parachute Landing Fall). You will make instead a, SPLAT. A SPLAT is not a good landing because it is not a survivable landing. It can also be very messy and hard for someone else to clean up.

If you go through jump school, you will never forget how to do a PLF. Several years ago, over 40 years after jump school, I fell off of my daughter's horse and executed a perfect PLF rolling away from the horse's hooves. The first two weeks of jump school are mainly devoted, not to teaching a proper PLF, but to inculcating it into your soul forever. You start by jumping off of one or two foot high platforms and progress from there. It is not as simple as it seems.

The main idea of a PLF is to ensure that you always land on your side, that you never land going forward or backward, and that you always land rolling. You do this by instantaneously twisting your body to put your side in the direction of the fall as soon as you feet make contact, or sometimes even before contact. It must be done absolutely automatically, or it will be too late. You must be able to roll right side or left side, equally well.

I think anyone that has gone through jump school could no more stop his body from twisting to land on his side in a fall and then rolling than he could stop his right foot from slamming down on the brake if a child ran in front of a car. Even if he was not driving, the right foot would still stomp where the brake should be. It would be absolutely automatic, exactly like doing a PLF is for anyone that was ever Airborne. After Jump School, you just can't, not, do it.

Figure 4-3. PLF sequence.

Scarcely tree top height, about thirty-four foot tower height, is where I get a feeling of height. And, that is also where the land stops moving slowly toward you and begins rushing up fast. The thirty-four foot tower, not the 290-foot tower, not in the aircraft either, is also where almost all of the people that fail jump school, freeze. They simply cannot make their foot, make that step out of the tower. It is a psychological thing, and it is the reason for the thirty-four foot tower. It is much better to find out there than in the aircraft.

I was almost at that point, about 50 feet or so in the air, when the other jumper's chute drifted under mine that day; it stayed under me, just out of reach; I could not get away from it even though I pulled one riser frantically trying; it stole my air; it collapsed my chute into a streamer. Bummer.

Being by then forty or so feet in the air left me plenty of time to realize that I must make the PLF of my life as I hurtled down accelerating at the rate of: 16 feet per second, per second. For those with a mathematical mind, that is the equation that expressed my rate of acceleration according to what we had been taught. More practically stated, with the drag of my streaming parachute, it was not quite the same as jumping off of a three story building —but it was close enough as far as I was concerned and the landing was coming up fast.

When you do a PLF they teach you in jump school to count off the parts of your body doing their job sticking the landing:

"Feet."

"Calves."

"Thigh."

"Hip."

"Shoulder."

"YEA!" Perfect.

But, then I went right back up into the air. I bounced back up into the air. They said that I did a belly flop the second time I landed. Not a PLF, but not quite a SPLAT either. My solar plexus was centered over my reserve chute; the one I did not have time to deploy; and that reserve chute was what probably knocked me out, knocked me out cold.

When I woke up I was laying face down on my stomach, another trooper was shaking my shoulder saying:

"God damn sir."

"I never saw anybody bounce that high."

"God damn sir."

"Are you all right?"

"God damn sir. . ."

Slowly, carefully, I reached up and released my tongue from where it was stuck fast to some red Georgia clay. I guessed it had popped out of my mouth when my chest slammed into the ground. Then, I rolled over and pulled one of the two canopy releases holding one set of risers so that the ground wind did not drag me around. Finally, I just lay there for a while and stared at the blue sky above.

The funny thing is, although I always liked jumping out of airplanes and I made probably 15 more jumps, when the Army stopped paying me for it, I never did it again.

Two

As the A Company Executive Officer, and as platoon leader for that matter, I did a lot of things that were never covered in OCS (Officer Candidate School). This is the story of just one of them.

Unfortunately, I had to go to nearby Nashville, Clarksville and Hopkinsville repeatedly to try to get some paratroopers out of trouble that they had gotten into while on leave. Some of these trips were more memorable than others. I always waited until the next day to go pick them up. I did not want them puking in my car on the way back because the trouble always involved copious quantities of alcohol, usually beer.

Spending six months or so teaching young men to fight at the slightest provocation was part of the problem, but I always thought that all that beer was the biggest contributor to these trips. . .

Nashville Bound

"I was not lying." I said.

"But, L-T my mother had already passed." he said.

"L-T" was and perhaps still is the almost universal nickname in the Army for a lieutenant, any lieutenant. If you have served together and you meet again after you are out of the service, you always stay the same rank you were when you last served together.

"Well, how was I to know that? Your mother loved you, probably. Maybe even a lot. So, that part was true, right?" I said.

We were sitting together at a table in a hospitality room in a hotel drinking. It was at a 3/506th Airborne's reunion several years ago and a former Alpha Company trooper was trying to tell me that I had lied to get him and two of his friends out of jail in Nashville when we had been together training with the 101st Airborne Division at Ft. Campbell, KY., before going to Vietnam. With the full benefit of my very expensive Jesuit education from Georgetown University, I was trying to explain to him why, what I had admittedly said to the Sheriff that night to get him and his two buddies out of jail, was not actually a lie. I thought I was doing pretty good in the argument. I was sure I would win.

"Your mother had been very sick from time to time when she was alive. So, that was true, right?" I said.

"She was dead L-T, not sick. You lied. You know you lied. Admit it." He was smiling.

He thought for sure that he had me at last. His big smile said that as clearly as if he had said the words.

One of my jobs as an XO, or the executive officer of an airborne rifle company had been to take care of troopers that managed to get into trouble with the law. Besides going to nearby Hopkinsville and Clarksville for me this often involved going to Nashville. It is the closest large city to Ft. Campbell, and it had an almost unlimited number of bars filled with cold beer, country music and lots of good looking young women. I would visit with either the police or with the Sheriff, depending on who had custody of the miscreant, to try to get them released without being officially charged with a crime.

I got the call from the Nashville Sheriff's office almost every weekend while we were training. It usually came first thing on Sunday morning. If there had been such a thing then, they surely would have had my number on speed dial.

Sometimes, if it was not too bad, I could handle it over the phone, but sometimes I had to go down and actually talk to the Sheriff personally. Although I would not say we were friends, we had gotten to know each other really well in a very short period of time.

The Sheriff was an old fashioned southern patriot. There really is no other way to describe him. He wanted to be talked into letting my guys go. He knew that we were a D-1 unit on our way to Vietnam as soon as we finished our training cycle at Ft. Campbell and he respected that. However, because of his job, he also needed what he considered to be a real reason to let the guy go. That was the hard part, coming up with a new, a new real reason each time. Sometimes just promising harsh Army justice was not enough.

23

"Officers shouldn't lie L-T." the trooper said again.

Even though it sounded a lot more like *"Ossiffers"* I still knew what he meant. His voice made it clear that he had started drinking much earlier that day than I had.

"Well, your mother had been sick at some point in her life, and she was worried about you. After all you were in the Army and you were on your way to Vietnam; there was a war going on there. She was probably worried about you, right?" I said.

"I already told you L-T—she was dead. She died before I even enlisted. You don't worry much when you're already dead." he said.

"Well, her being dead and all might have been part of the reason the fight started. It might have been the reason you enlisted. You had lost your mom, you were sad, you were angry, that could have even been the reason you threw that fellow into the window at the bar, and then hit the other one with a chair. So, what I said might have been true, right?" I said.

"They were legs, L-T. That's why the fight started. Joe called one of them a 'fucking leg' and then one of them threw a punch." he said.

"See, when I said that they started it all. I was right. They threw the first punch. It was not your fault. You were just defending yourself, right?" I said.

24

"Before that, I did sort of say something to their girl friends about how they're dating a bunch of pussies. That probably didn't help either." he said.

He smiled broadly at the memory. He was enjoying this. He really liked the memory of that night, the memory of that fight.

"Well, they were legs. So, they were pussies. You both were only telling the truth about them. They had no right to be angry, and if you had just won that damn fight and then gotten out of there before the cops came I wouldn't even have had to come get you." I said.

"We were winning until I said to Joe: 'Watch this shit!' Hey, don't you go changing the subject. You're tricky." he said.

Did I mention that we both had been drinking. Although I had started later than he had, we had both been drinking together almost all afternoon. When he picked up his beer I looked again at the small white scar on the big knuckle on his right hand.

"Taking out that guy's tooth didn't leave much of a scar on your hand." I said.

"Doc Lovey pulled it out with pair of needle nose pliers. Good thing the Sheriff didn't see it. He never would have let me go. There you go again, don't change the subject. I got you L-T. You lied. You did." he said and he smiled broadly again.

I don't know which he enjoyed more, pinning me down, or remembering that fight in a bar long ago in Nashville.

"All right what part of what I said was a lie?" I asked.

"Well, you talked all about our mothers like you knew them personal. Not just me but them other two guys as well. But, but you didn't even know them other two guys before then. They was from Bravo Company, not Alpha Company. You never even seen them before, much less seen their mothers. You never even talked to them before. Did you?" he asked.

"Well, they had mothers too, and all mothers worry about their sons. That was the important part. You boil it down and that's all I really said. Besides I knew by then that the Sheriff was a real sucker for mother stories."

"But then you said that I was a great soldier." he said.

"So?" I replied.

"And, that I had never been in any trouble before." he said.

"O-K, I lied."

Three

This one is about jumping out of airplanes again. Being paratroopers, it is one of the things we did regularly at Fort Campbell, along with a lot of running and a lot of pushups. "*Paratroopers at play*" was what our company commander Captain Tom Gaffney would say about both the running and the pushups, and then he would double our dose, but he always did them right along with us.

We did the running in the morning in bright white tee shirts, purple running shorts with the big "*Pair of Dice*" logo sown on one leg, backpacks and spit shined, black, Corcoran jump boots. It is no wonder that some of the locals watching early in the morning thought that we were all crazy.

I cheated a bit because I filled my backpack with crumpled newspapers rather than the required twenty pounds of stuff. You could tell who was running with light back packs, they bounced on your back in a way the fully laden ones did not. Most of them bounced like that. Given what my pack was filled with, I elected to ignore the others as we ran.

What Goes Up, Must Come Down

"Had that to happen to several jumpers while station at Everux-Faulville AFB, France. The DZ was the grass run off at the East end of the runway. A 5 second green light. A WWII German Base full of C-130's. Jumps every Saturday for navigator training. Two jumpers. We were not allowed to use the risers as there was money bet on each drop on which jumper would be the closest to the "T" on the ground.

Got In better than 200 jumps in two years to include several drags down the runway. This was before they had cap release. I was one two E-4's to return back to Fort Campbell with master parachutist wings and headed to Benning to OCS."

Dee Dallas, Major, Ret. USA
former S-4 (Supply)
3/506th Abn. Inf.

It is not true. I don't care what they say, or who says it, the stories are just not true. This is what really happened that day.

As the XO, or executive officer, of Alpha Company, particularly before I also became a platoon leader, I missed some things, but I got to do some things too. Early on I was sent to Jumpmaster School at Ft. Campbell. After I passed Jumpmaster School, I was assigned to the rotation for qualification jumps at Ft. Campbell.

Since paratroopers who drew jump pay were required to jump at least once every 90 days or they went off of jump status, there was always a need for a qualification jump or two at the end of every month. These jumps allowed these troopers to continue to draw their jump pay if for some reason they had missed their unit jump for that quarter.

A qualification jump was always a "*Hollywood jump*", which is defined as one with no equipment and no tactical exercise after the jump. After you landed on the DZ you just got on a truck at the drop zone and it returned you to your unit.

Since most of the qualified jumpmasters were E-6 Staff Sergeants, or E-7 Platoon Sergeants and E-8 First Sergeants, they all had jobs to do. So, they were too important to spare even for such an essential, if not at all that demanding, assignment.

I on the other hand was a brand new, second lieutenant, and an XO, not even a platoon leader yet. That made me perfect for the job of qualification jump, jumpmaster. I guess it was assumed that nothing I had to do was as important as what almost any senior sergeant was doing. The assumption was probably right too.

In any event, I was assigned the first post wide qualification jump after Jumpmaster School. We were to take off from Ft. Campbell Army Airfield at 6:30 AM and the Drop Zone was in the far eastern portion of the Fort near Clarksville, Tennessee. Almost all of the jumpers were from Headquarters Company, 101st Airborne Division.

After drawing parachutes early that morning I went over to the tarmac at Ft. Campbell Army Airfield with a big, brand new, role of green duct tape. I walked up to the C-119, the old Flying Boxcar that was our designated jump aircraft already parked on the tarmac. The first thing a jumpmaster does at the airfield is check out the aircraft. As I recall it was flown by an Illinois, Air National Guard unit.

C-119, By USAF – Travis Air Force Base Public Affairs, Public Domain, file photo.

While there is an Air Force, or Air National Guard, sergeant responsible for the aircraft called the loadmaster, the paratroopers are the responsibility of the jumpmaster. The first thing you check on the aircraft as the jumpmaster is the doors of the aircraft. You do not want a sharp edge on a door to cut a static line.

That is what the roll of duct tape was for, to cover any sharp edges I found. The rules say that you both look at and feel all of the edges that the static line might hit when a trooper exits an aircraft. However, when I looked at the frame of the door we would jump out of, it was already covered with duct tape far beyond where any static line would hit. Lots and lots of duct tape, everywhere. In fact the duct tape on the edges was at least a half an inch or more thick in most places. The same thing was true of the door frame on the other side of the aircraft too.

Probably just to be doing something, I plastered on one more strip of duct tape on each door frame. After that I went back to the troops. I checked the troopers' parachutes, loaded up the aircraft and then, Army style, we sat there and waited.

Finally, a few minutes later the pilot started up the engines. I have never heard louder engines in my life. The C-119 is a piston driven, propeller plane of World War II vintage. I always thought it was a very cool plane, both because of its nickname, the "*Flying Boxcar*" and because of its unusual double tail. I was really looking forward to jumping out of it, and the sound of those powerful engines roaring really increased my confidence in the plane.

I just knew that when the pilot released the brakes that the plane was going to leap into the sky. Then, I noticed that the plane was already moving forward, just a little. The engines were still roaring and now the plane was shaking a little too. You could even hear the plane's airframe rattling above the noise of those engines, but you had to look real close to see the forward movement. The brakes were off.

Although everyone else was sitting down, as the jumpmaster, I was standing up in the back of the aircraft between the open side doors. I could move around if I wanted to. After a while, I walked over to a door and looked out. We were still moving slowly, a little faster than crawling speed I guessed, but we were less than a quarter of the way down the runway. Plenty of room I thought. This was a jet runway; it was really long. I was not worried yet. Not me.

I started worrying when we were almost half way down the runway and it still looked like I could have gotten out and walked faster than the plane was moving by then. It was at that moment that I realized that the plane and its engines were probably older than I was. They were probably a lot older. Not a comforting thought at all.

I looked at the loadmaster. He had an enormous amount of hair stuffed into his cap, a red pen protector full of ball point pens stuffed into his uniform pocket, and he was chewing on a toothpick. I got nothing reassuring from looking at him.

Finally, the plane began moving faster. I was afraid to look out the door again. I was afraid my head being outside the plane would increase wind resistance and slow the thing down.

No, I actually thought that, and then I thought:

"That's really stupid."

So, I looked out the door and immediately wished I hadn't. By then, the end of the runway was coming up fast. The engines were still screaming and the plane was still shaking and rattling, but it did not seem to be moving fast enough to fly yet.

At the end of the runway the pilot just sort of blipped the plane into the air at the last minute. We were still flying low, but when the pilot retracted the wheels out of the way of the tree tops in the next field that we were flying over, I could feel that we immediately picked up some speed. Fewer leaves blew through the open doors too. All good signs.

Slowly, we climbed to about 300 feet.

When we got there I shouted:

"Get ready!"

"Stand up!"

"Hook up!"

"Stand in the door!" All in one quick sentence.

Then I told the jumpers in each door that if the plane lost any altitude at all, we were jumping, drop zone or no drop zone, green light or no green light. I did not want to land in that thing. I had the distinct impression that the troopers standing in the doors thought that jumping rather than landing in that plane was a really good idea.

However, the pilot was good and the plane slowly climbed. I sat every body back down at about 500 feet and we waited. Ultimately, we reached a real jumping altitude of about 1,100 feet. Later, when the Red Light came on, I ran them through a complete series of jump commands, rather than the abbreviated set I had used before.

When the light turned green, we jumped.

It was a beautiful, clear, already very hot, sunny day, a perfect jump day. I even did one of the best PLFs (Parachute Landing Falls) of my short jumping career. I was still smiling and had just finished gathering up my chute when I saw the sergeant on the ground crew running over toward me. He was pointing up. I looked up and saw the plane disappearing in the distance, probably headed back to Illinois I thought.

   "No, Sir! Look! Look! Look up Sir!" the sergeant yelled again at me. He was still running toward me.

So, I looked again, this time to where he was pointing, and then I saw him, way up in the sky. He was probably already at least at about 2,000 feet already; he was still headed up, and he was picking up speed heading East as well.

When you jump in the Army, you jump into a DZ. A DZ, or Drop Zone is a cleared area, usually a large cleared area, usually surrounded by trees.
The DZ we had jumped into that day was fairly small, but then so is a C-119. I had only jumped about 12 or 13 parachutists that day so we did not need a big DZ.

The problem, as was later explained to me in excruciating detail even though I was not the one that had picked the DZ, was that when you jump, particularly early in the morning as we did, the air on the DZ is rapidly heated by the sun and rises. Colder air pours in from the surrounding forest and it is rapidly heated as well. On a large DZ this is rarely a problem, on a small one it can create quite an up draft. That was clearly what had happened.

This problem was compounded by it being a "*Hollywood jump.*" That is, a jump without equipment. The chutes were designed for troops and their equipment. Adding the equipment would have almost doubled the weight the chute was carrying. Or, put another way, not carrying the equipment cut the weight about in half.

I waved my jeep over and the sergeant and I climbed in:

"*Follow that paratrooper!*" I said to my driver and off we went bouncing across the DZ.

We tore across the DZ, then down a dirt road trying to keep the trooper in sight. The trooper seemed for a while to have leveled off, but then he started rising again. If I had had a radio, I would have called for a chopper. Since I had no radio; I had no chopper.

"Ignore the speed limits. Drive as fast as you feel comfortable, but keep him in sight." I told my driver.

We raced out a gate and turned left onto the highway still heading mostly East. We had to drive a lot further than the kid above had to fly to keep him in sight. He was really moving but my driver had a lot of confidence in his ability to drive that jeep. The sergeant on the other hand had a death grip on the back of my seat. His knuckles were bone white on the back of my seat.

As a young second lieutenant still new to the Army I did not know then how unstable Army jeeps were then, particularly at speed, but the sergeant did. Later our Recon Platoon Leader wrecked all of the recon platoon jeeps in one week, all five of them, one a day. We nicknamed him *"Crash"* because of it.

According to our battalion commander, Lt. Col. Geraci, *"Crash,"* yes Geraci called him that too, did not even have the courtesy to get hurt at least a little when he had crashed the jeeps. On the following Monday, Geraci revoked all the battalion lieutenants' military driver's licenses.

It was about the end of morning rush hour time when we got to downtown Clarksville. When we were stopped by the traffic I told the driver to drive on the sidewalk, but to keep that trooper in sight because he seemed to be coming down. So we bounced up and down crossing streets, going over the curbs, yelling at people, dodging people, dodging parked and moving cars and just stuff, but we kept the kid in sight.

Ultimately, we could see that the trooper was really coming down. He was going to land. Although he was not one of my troops, I was really proud of his training, because when he first landed on the edge of the roof of a three story building, he pushed off rather than try to land there.

If he had tried to land there, even a small gust of wind could have dragged him over the edge, but his chute would almost certainly not really be open. So, pushing off was the smart thing for him to do. After all he had been through, and he still had his wits about him. I was impressed.

We saw him land on the sidewalk next to the building. After his PLF, he jumped up, collapsed his chute and waited for us to drive up. He was so excited. He thought it was all *"fun."* He would not shut up on the drive back to base.

So, if you hear stories about some crazy second lieutenant standing up in a jeep waving a .45 caliber Colt pistol around yelling at people to get out of the way while the jeep raced down a sidewalk in downtown Clarksville chasing a lost paratrooper dangling from a parachute in the middle of morning rush hour, that part about the pistol waving is just not true. It is not true at all.

Four

We went over to Vietnam on an old USNS ship. USNS stands for "*United States Naval Ship*" and is used to identify a non-commissioned, generally unarmed, ship that is owned by the United States Navy, but is operated by the Military Sealift Command rather than by the US Navy. This also means that the crew of the vessel is primarily civilian, although there were a few US Navy personnel on board as well.

This story happened while we were on the way to Vietnam in that ship. It needed repairs so we stopped at the naval base in Subic Bay in the Philippines for three days while they did the repairs.

While not the most luxurious of accommodations, the food on the ship was very good. Unfortunately, while we were at sea some had a lot more trouble than others keeping their food down, particularly when we went through the tag end of a typhoon after we left the Philippines. All of that is in this story about a group of young Americans on their way to a war halfway around the world.

The Stop in Olongapo

"By the time you arrived L-T a group of us had already staggered back to the boat. There was a bunch of us from Alpha Co. We pushed 3 or 4 tables together it was covered with mixed drinks at one end of the table, on the other we had cases of beer stacked. The Shore Patrol came up to our table and the shit hit the fan. At one point I crawled under the table and just watched, it was the coolest fight I had ever seen. It looked like something out of an old cowboy movie, a real knock down dragged out fight. I exited the building with several others and we laughed and bragged all the way back to the boat. The next day was one of the worst hangovers I have ever experienced. The good news, all my buddies were hung over as well, some worse than I. What a great time. Thanks for reminding of one of my most memorable good times. LOL"

Ron G Ford, formerly Sergeant, 2nd Platoon
Company A, 3rd Battalion Airborne, 506th Infantry,
101st Airborne Division
October 3, 2016 at 2:34 pm

I knew things had not gone exactly as I had planned when I saw the white pick up truck make a wide right turn onto the pier. It was the one with the big wire cage in the back that the Shore Patrol used as a paddy wagon to haul the drunks off to the Brig. Even before it began to weave as it drove down the pier, despite being the perpetual optimist, I was certain that it was not a good sign. Not a good sign at all.

Of course, there had been hints of trouble before this. For example, lots of the men returning to the ship had been wearing different hats when they came back on board. I preferred to assume that they had traded for the Navy and Marine hats, and for the one Aussie hat that I saw as well. So, I did not ask any questions.

However, I still thought that it had been a really good plan, right up until I saw that white truck driving down the pier. That scared me. We were all on our way to Vietnam, on a troop ship that was docked in U. S. Naval Base at Subic Bay, the Philippines.

When we arrived at Subic Bay Naval Base we tied up in the middle of a long concrete pier inside the Naval base. The pier looked to me more like a big four lane, concrete highway jutting out into the water than a pier, but a pier is what it was.

The problems had all begun late that afternoon, when a sergeant had said that there was a major on the pier that wanted to talk to me. That was when things first began to look different as far as my plan went. I walked down the gang plank and met a Navy Lieutenant Commander standing there at the bottom. Since Army majors and Navy Lieutenant Commanders both wore a gold leaf as their rank insignia, I had already figured out that the Navy guy was who the sergeant was referring me to.

"Are you the Provost Marshall?" he asked without any preliminary.

"Yes. I'm Lt. Harrison. What can I do for you Commander?" I said as I saluted.

I knew that Navy Lieutenant Commanders loved to be called "*Commander*" just like Army Lieutenant Colonels liked to be called "*Colonel.*" A little light sucking-up to start never hurts I thought.

"You can come get your men out of my EM club." he said.

"What?" I replied.

"They have taken over one of the EM clubs on base and they won't leave. They have my bartenders and a couple of Shore Patrol in there with them." he said.

"Oh." I said and then I turned to the sergeant that had followed me down and said.

"Go get the Response Group please."

He said: *"Yes Sir"* and ran back up the gang plank.

In a moment he came back with a Sergeant First Class from the 503rd leading eight large sergeants carrying axe handles, four sergeants each from the 503rd and the 506th.

"Let's go." I said.

We walked quickly over to the EM Club and found what looked like about a platoon of Marines in formation along with another Lieutenant Commander on the street in front of the club's parking lot. There were also six Shore Patrol led by a Petty officer who looked very angry. His men were repeatedly slapping their black billy clubs, or batons, on their palms as they waited under the shade of a tree.

"Are you the Provost!" this second Lieutenant Commander practically shouted at me as he too ignored my salute.

"Yes Sir." I replied. *"I am the ship's Provost Marshall. What's going on?"*

"I'm about to break some heads. Your men have assaulted and kidnapped my men. We are going to take this club back right now." the second Lieutenant Commander said.

"Well, you're probably going to have a lot of hurt Marines and Shore Patrol if you try that." I said.

"We'll hurt some of your jerks too. You can bet on it." he replied.

I looked over at the door to the EM club. The whole area in front of the door was littered with beer cans, lots of beer cans. Some were still spewing beer in the hot sun, so it was pretty clear that they had been full, or nearly so when they were thrown. A couple of the Shore Patrol uniforms looked wet, but no blood I could see. It looked good to me. I thought things still looked pretty good, considering.

"Sergeant." I turned and said. The SFC snapped to attention behind me.

"Yes sir." he replied.

Then, I turned back to the Lieutenant Commander.

"I am the Provost Marshall of that ship. Those men are my responsibility, not yours. You are interfering with a United States Army troop

movement. *Get out of my way Commander or I will have you arrested."* I said.

The Lieutenant Commander looked at me like he could not believe what he had just heard. In a word, he was gobsmacked.

I thought it sounded pretty good. I had no idea if any of it was true, or if as Provost Marshall I actually had that kind of power. It did not seem likely that I did on a naval base, particularly on his naval base, but I thought that if I could get the men back on the ship, it just might be true.

Then, the sergeant behind me bellowed:

"Port arms." and eight axe handles came up with eight hands smartly slapping the wood.

The Lieutenant Commander stared at me a moment longer, looked at my sergeant, and then he stepped slowly back.

"You go right ahead Lieutenant." he said smiling, and then he nodded to the Shore Patrol group. Sort of a *"Now, watch this boys."* nod.

"Follow me." I said to the sergeant.

When we were about halfway across the parking lot and well in front of the Shore Patrol and the Marines. I turned and said:

"Sergeant, you come with me. The rest of you form a line. No matter what happens, they do not come forward of your line." I said to the the eight sergeants with axe handles and indicated the Marines and Shore Patrol behind.

42

As we walked toward the front door of the club the sergeant said *sotto voce* to me.

"I hope you know what you are doing Sir."

"So do I, sergeant. So do I." I said.

"They're going to kill us both Sir." the Sergeant said.

"They might." I said.

I was thinking of our guys, and the others from the ship probably all drunk as lords inside, and then there were all those Marines as well as the Shore Patrol. It did not look so good anymore, even to me.

We were still walking toward the door of the EM club when for some reason a scene from the then recent movie *Dr. Zhivago* that we had just seen on the ship flashed through my mind. In the movie the Russian army was falling apart during World War I. The Russians were deserting the front in droves. They were literally walking home from the front in their hundreds of thousands.

In this scene, a Russian officer climbs up on a barrel and harangues a group of the fleeing Russian soldiers trying to get them to go back and fight the Germans. He was doing pretty well, but then he lost his footing and fell into the barrel. With that, he lost all of his dignity as an officer. One of the men shot him, and then they continued to desert the front.

I was wearing flip flops because Dr. Andrew Lovy, our battalion surgeon, had operated on my ingrown toenails a few days before. I knew I did not look very dignified, flip flops on my feet and a big white bandage taped on both of my big toes. You can't blouse flip flops so my pants legs flapped as well. I had my butter bar on one collar, crossed rifles pinned on the other, and probably most important I had silver paratrooper wings on my chest, but that was about it for dignity. I could already see myself dying in that barrel.

However, we were lucky. When the door opened, it was an Alpha Company man.

"What are you doing here Lieutenant?" he asked.

"God damn it!" I said.

While I cussed a lot, I very rarely swore. He looked like I had just slapped him. He saluted. Looked for his hat. Found it; fumbled it; put it on his head. Saluted again, hitting himself in his eye the second time.

"Everybody out!" I shouted as I pushed him outside.

"Get out. Form a column of twos. Let's go. Do it! Right now! Don't embarrass me in front of these jarheads! Move it!" I shouted.

I just kept shouting; kept cussing; kept swearing; kept moving; kept looking for faces I recognized; kept making eye contact and kept pointing to the door. I looked over and the sergeant behind me was doing the same. Slowly at first, they left the bar and then formed up into a ragged column of twos in the parking lot.

"Call them to attention sergeant and move them out. Back to the ship." I said.

"Yes Sir." my sergeant replied.

As we marched past the Marines and Shore Patrol I snapped a salute at the two Lieutenant Commanders and then shuffled the rest of the way back to the ship on my flip flops and with my two sore big toes.

Except for yelling at the Lieutenant Commander I thought it had all gone surprisingly well at the club, but I did wonder what had happened to the two Shore Patrol and the bartenders that he had said were inside. At least our own troops, drunk or not, hadn't killed us when we ordered them out of the bar, but the jury was still out on what the Lieutenant Commander, the Shore Patrol and all those Marines would do next.

I found out later that the guys had initially taken away their nightsticks and then locked the two Shore Patrol in the walk in beer refrigerator for a while after the two Shore Patrol and some others had tried to close the place down. While in the refrigerator, which was full of beer, the two Shore Patrol had gotten just as drunk as my guys. The other Shore Patrol had been driven out of the bar the door by repeated, accurate, volleys of flying beer cans.

When my guys saw they were drunk, they released the two guys in the refrigerator, and then they all drank at the bar together until the two Shore Patrol had passed out. That's where they found the two Shore Patrol, passed out, under the bar.

The troopers had paid for all of the beer they drank, and for the beer the two Shore Patrol drank at the bar. They even paid for all the beer cans they threw at the Shore Patrol to drive them out and when they had tried to rush the place after the first two had disappeared inside. Really, they had not broken all that much, considering. All three bartenders were still behind the bar. They were fine. Well tipped even.

I guessed that getting drunk while on duty had reduced the effectiveness of the two Shore Patrol as witnesses against my guys. Anyway, no charges were ever filed as far I know. While I did not know that when I saw that white truck, that part ultimately worked out better than anybody could have anticipated.

Sometimes you just have to be lucky. It is the only thing that will work.

USNS Weigel, Navy photo, public domain

We were on the *USNS William Weigel*, an old troop carrier on her final voyage, top speed twenty one knots or about twenty four MPH, 622 feet long, 75 feet wide, the *USNS Weigel* had lumbered as she departed US Army Oakland California Terminal on 3 October 1967 loaded with elements of the 324th Signal Brigade, the 3rd Battalion (Abn) 506th Infantry, 101st Airborne Division, the 3rd Battalion (Abn) 503rd Infantry, initially assigned for training purposes to the 82d Airborne Division, reassigned to the 173rd Airborne Brigade (Separate) for fighting purposes in Vietnam, and the

201st Assault Helicopter Company from Ft. Bragg, NC, and a few more as well. All of us were headed to Vietnam as fast as the old ship, the *USNS Weigel* could get us there.

The *USNS Weigel* was originally supposed to stop at Okinawa, but engine trouble had us putting in for two days of repairs at the big US Navy base in Subic Bay, the Philippines instead.

We arrived one afternoon. We spent two full days there, and then left the next morning, early.

3-506th Paratroopers on board the USNS Gen. Weigel at Cam Ranh Bay (Oct. 1968)

The 3/506th at Cam Rain Bay, October 1967. Photo by Jerry Berry, 3/506 (Airborne) PIO

I was the Provost Marshall, or head cop, on the ship. As such, I was responsible for maintaining order on the ship, for posting man overboard guards when underway and for running the Brig, or jail on the ship. At sea that meant that I posted guards throughout the ship and maintained a duty roster of the Officer of the Guard and Sergeant of the Guard for each day. Since I was from the 3/506th, my deputy, a Sergeant First Class who also led the Response Group, was from the other airborne battalion on board, the 3/503rd.

A couple of days before we got there, I had been warned by the ship's Troop Commander, Major George E. Fisher, Jr., that we would dock in Subic Bay Naval Base to repair the ship's engine. He told me that there would be some form of liberty for all the men on board, and to prepare a plan. How bad could it be I had thought as I walked back to my office from our meeting?

Liberty in the Philippines. That sounded like a lot of fun to me. After three weeks on that old ship, I was looking forward to it.

So far being the ship's head cop had been fairly easy, except that I rarely got to sleep much at night since the Officers of the Guard routinely got lost at night checking on the various guard posts throughout the ship. Of course, getting lost was not unusual for second lieutenants. Unfortunately, since below decks on the ship everything looked the same, they got lost quite often.

While it was always disagreeable to be awakened from a sound sleep, sometimes where we found the lieutenants was so incredible that it almost made it worth it. In any event, I was required to know if they were lost somewhere in the ship, or if they had fallen overboard. So far nobody had actually fallen overboard, but I really worried about some of those second lieutenants, especially when they were walking around the ship at night, alone. At least they didn't have a map or a compass, or we might have never found them.

Each time they lost one, the Sergeant of the Guard was required to wake me up and tell me. Particularly at first it happened at least twice every night, sometimes more often. It actually would have been easier for me to just check the guard positions myself at night, but that was not the way the Army worked.

My Sergeant assistant from the 503rd was extraordinary.* He had been in the Army fifteen years, all of it as an airborne infantryman, but he also knew paperwork. Since we were actually in a shooting war at the time, paperwork was not something that Infantry OCS (Officer Candidate School) at Ft. Benning had spent much time on.

The one thing that I did know for certain was that was that as Provost Marshall I was personally responsible for the Brig, or the ship's jail. Screwing that up could put me in prison. Ft. Leavenworth Prison in Kansas to be exact.

The 503rd had waited for the boat ride to Vietnam to catch up on a lot of Article 15's (Army speak for non-judicial punishment) and summary courts martial, so the Brig was full most of the way across the Pacific. My sergeant from the 503rd was the one that noticed that the paper work of his own battalion was not correct.

We had made a deal the first day, I would deliver any bad news to his battalion commander and he did the same for mine. So, one day out from Oakland, I took eleven smiling miscreants back to the 503rd's battalion commander and told him that the paperwork needed to be redone because I was letting them go. He was not happy.

He informed me that he out ranked me. I immediately agreed that he was absolutely correct. However, I politely suggested that we could talk to Major Fisher, the troop commander on the ship, if he wished. He decided that he wished to redo the paper work instead. Smart man.

49

That, a little gambling and the disappearing second lieutenants were the biggest problems that we had faced so far. That all changed when we got to the Philippines.

There were a little over 2,800 soldiers on board. All of them were on their way to a combat zone. Almost 1,700 of these soldiers were in the two Airborne battalions of paratroopers that had both just completed a rigorous six month training regimen to prepare them for combat. For six months all of those paratroopers had done nothing except learn, and then practice over and over, various ways to maim, disable and/or kill someone else. However, they had not been allowed to actually put any of those deadly skills to use as yet.

When we arrived in Subic Bay, we had all been onboard the *USNS Weigel* for almost three very long, very boring weeks. As I thought more about the Philippines, the idea of turning all of those paratroopers loose anywhere but into a war zone seemed to me to be the absolute quickest form of career suicide that I had ever heard of. Particularly if you added alcohol to the mix, and of course alcohol would be a big part of that mix.

I went down into the ship to find my company commander, Tom Gaffney. Tom had been a Sergeant Major in the Green Berets and about to retire when he was offered the chance to retire out as a Captain if he would agree to stay in another year to help train an airborne rifle company and then take them to Vietnam.

While the war was heating up in early 1967, it was still fairly low key but building up steadily to what it would become in 1968. Tom had already been to Vietnam twice with the Green Berets. So, he said yes to the offer.

As far as I could tell, Tom Gaffney knew everything worth knowing about the Army.

What he told me was helpful I guess, but it did not allay my fears at all. The real place we were probably going to according to Tom Gaffney was Olongapo, a Philippine town just out side the gates of the Subic Bay, US Naval Base.

Olongapo, Tom said, would be our first introduction into the Third World.

According to Tom, Olongapo was only a sort of town in the Philippines. It was really only there because something had to be just outside the gates to the United States Navy's, huge Subic Bay, Naval Base. That something was Olongapo.

As near as I saw, in late 1967 Olongapo was composed mostly of bars and whorehouses. All of the whorehouses had their own bars and all of the bars had their own whorehouses, or at least they all had rooms upstairs and bar girls that you could rent along with a room by the hour, or for the night if you were ambitious and feeling flush.

As far as we could see, Olongapo was one long muddy street of mostly wooden buildings, with a money-changing kiosk right in the middle of the street just after you left the base. Then, the bars and whorehouses started on both sides of the street. It was hard for me to tell the two apart, but they insisted that there was a difference.

According to Tom, during the Korean War when he had been in the 187th Infantry (Abn.) Regiment (aka the Rakkasans), after a similar period of training at Ft. Campbell, Ky., they too had stopped in Olongapo on their way to the Korean War. It had led to a riot of epic proportions.

Tom smiled broadly when he told me about that riot. I knew that smile. While it was a happy smile, there was a lot more to it than that and it did nothing for my mood. I went back to my office not at all comforted by what I had learned from Tom.

We let the officers and senior NCOs go into of the town Olongapo, the rest of the enlisted men were restricted to the Subic Bay, Naval Base. Besides several enlisted and NCO clubs, the Naval Base also had a big PX, several chapels, and a base library. While the later two received some use as well, it was beer, lots of beer that was the goal of most of the men. They all succeeded in achieving their goals.

When they returned to the pier getting them back on board ship was more like herding stoned cattle than moving elite paratroopers around. Some needed to be assisted in walking. Some were missing parts of their uniform, or had made unauthorized additions from someone else's uniform. Some had minor abrasions that according to them, all came from falling down some stairs, located somewhere on the flat as a board base. Some seemed to be escorted back by, or were closely followed by, groups of Shore Patrol. However, as long as they were peaceful and kept moving, we ignored almost everything.

Both days I had twenty sergeants on the pier. There were ten from each airborne unit, and they worked in pairs. Most of the men from the ship were happy drunks, very happy, and almost all of them were also very, very drunk.

We let half the men off the ship the first full day in port and the other half the second day. Then we left the next morning early. The real trouble was all on the second day. First it was that EM Club, then there was that white pick up truck.

Shore Leave, Subic Bay

Photo by Jerry Berry, 3/506 (Airborne) PIO

As the white pick up truck drove along the pier, it picked up a little speed but it was still weaving erratically. I ran down the gangway as fast as my bandaged toes and flip flops would let me. About half way down the white truck passed the gangway I was on. I could see some men hanging on the roof of the wire cage behind the cab and there appeared to be some more men inside the cage as well. The ones on top were laughing and throwing beer cans as they went. The beer cans they threw appeared to be empty as they bounced along behind the truck.

It looked to me like the truck was heading straight for Subic Bay. I already knew that there were sharks in Subic Bay. Lots of sharks according to the Navy. We had been told that a naval rating chipping paint on the side of a ship in the harbor had lost a foot to one the week before we got there. On our first day in port several guys had decided to *"fall"* off the ship into the water. One of them had fallen into a remarkably good swan dive.

I never saw those USNS sailors work so fast to get a boat in the water to pick them up. They were dead serious about it. I began to believe the story about the shark and the sailor's former foot.

The guys that *"fell"* off the boat stayed in the brig the rest of our time in port. The threat of missing liberty had cured that problem, but I had no ideas at all about how to fix that weaving white truck.

Instead of flying off the pier, the truck ran into one of the big concrete and steel stanchions, or more correctly a *"bollard"* that the US Navy used to tie up their big ships to the pier. As soon as the white truck stopped, everybody piled out of it, and jumped off of the top of the cage in back. It looked a lot like one of those clown cars in a circus act that more and more people kept leaving.

They were all laughing and some fell as they ran toward the ship's rear gangway. There were two ways into the ship, two gangways, one in front where I had been and one at the rear of the ship. The last of them made the turn for that rear gangway just before I got there.

Since I did not know the condition of the truck or if anybody was still in it, I kept going to the truck. Inside the cage, there were four, almost naked, beer soaked, very angry men. They still had their boxer shorts, their tee shirts and their boots, but the rest of their uniforms and equipment were somebody's souvenirs.

Since the cage itself was locked, I was really glad that it had not been driven off the end of the pier. They would never have gotten out of that cage. Not much blood that I could see though the wire. I thought that was another good sign.

I went around to the cab and there piled on the seat were four equipment belts, a Master at Arms badge on a white lanyard, two handheld radios and four wallets. The keys to the truck and the cage were in the ignition. They had purposefully left everything that would have gotten the Shore Patrol guys in big trouble if they had lost them, and then stolen everything else.

My guys, I was actually proud of them.

The rest of the Shore Patrol's stuff was now souvenirs. I knew that the Shore Patrol arm bands were particularly prized as souvenirs. They were hard to get, those guys were tough.

I had just taken all this in and was letting the Shore Patrol guys out of the cage when I heard a siren and looked up to see a jeep and a grey four door sedan that were tearing down the pier toward me. Inside the sedan sitting shotgun was that second Lieutenant Commander that I had already met at the EM Club earlier that day. Even in the weird light on the pier I could see that his face was bright red.

However, he no longer wanted to talk to me. He wanted the Troop Commander on the ship and he wanted him right now. It seemed that the Admiral wanted to talk to him. That sounded fine to me.

After all, it could have been a whole lot worse—the Admiral could have wanted to talk to me.

In the real world, there are some really great things about being a Second Lieutenant; one of the absolute best is that you cannot be the troop commander of a ship load of young men, most of whom are paratroopers, docked in Subic Bay for two or three days. Being a *"Butter"* bar had saved me again.

After they left in the sedan, I waited on the pier for Major Fisher, picking up and throwing away empty beer cans to pass the time. There were a surprising number of them still on the pier.

The major was white faced when the sedan brought him back, followed by a whole truck load of Shore Patrol. Other than smartly returning my salute with the battalion's reply of *"Airborne!"* Major Fisher did not say much when he got back. He just went up the rear gangway, and then straight to his cabin.

The Shore Patrol from the truck on the other hand, sealed the ship, and the pier.

Except for running into the tag end of a Typhoon, the rest of the trip to Vietnam was uneventful, beautiful even, as soon as they rid the ship of the smell of all that upchuck. That stuff was slippery too.

You would not believe how much one man, even a little guy, can throw up until you have been on a troop ship with him riding on the tag end of a Pacific Ocean typhoon. To avoid all the upchuck, some guys spent most of their time on the bow getting doused by seawater as the old ship bulled its way through the biggest waves I had ever seen.

We arrived at the port of Qui Nhon in Vietnam in darkness. I could see a plane over the perimeter in the distance. Suddenly it spurted a stream of bright, red fire from its side. A little later came a sound much like that of a very long, very loud, possibly PBR induced, belch. Spooky, a C-47 gun ship, had given us its own version of, "*Welcome to Vietnam.*" I came to love those planes, but that is another story, for another time.

After disembarking the 503rd at Qui Nhon the next day on 23 October 1967 we continued down the coast of Vietnam to Cam Ranh Bay.

The *USNS Weigel* made only three stops on the coast of Vietnam with her final stop being at Vung Tau near Saigon. We got off at the second stop at Cam Ranh Bay. Then, we rode in a truck convoy to Phan Rang, home of the 1st Brigade, 101st Airborne Division, and our final stop on our way to the Vietnam War.

They probably should have brought us back from Viet Nam on a ship too. It would have been useful both psychologically and physically, but they would not have been able to let it stop in Olongapo — according to Major Fisher, we were forever barred from returning by the Admiral that ran the place. It was about the only thing that the Major ever told us about his meeting with the Admiral. He indicated though that the Admiral had been absolutely unmistakable on that point.

So now, when I think about Olongapo, I smile. I smile broadly, exactly like Tom Gaffney had smiled. Our short time there is one of my favorite memories from my service in the Army.

That's Capt. Tom Gaffney calling his own cadence on the right. Sgt. McDaniel has the Guidon flag in front. Lt. James Schlax on the right (WIA 2/19/68), and Sgt Carl Ratee on the left (KIA 2/19/68) leading 1st Platoon, Company A, 3rd Battalion (Airborne) 506th Infantry Regiment ashore from the pier at Cam Ranh Bay. Photo by Jerry Berry, 3/506 (Airborne) PIO

- Unfortunately after almost 50 years I cannot remember the sergeant's name. He was a good man. I hope he made it home. Like all good sergeants he kept his officer, me, mostly out of trouble.

Five

When we arrived in Vietnam we went to the 101st Airborne Division's base camp at Phan Rang on the coast of South Vietnam. While we were told that the base itself was very safe since it was protected by a South Korean airborne brigade, but we trained outside the wire in what was called P School for two weeks. Outside the wire was not safe.

The South Koreans boasted, correctly as far as I know, that not a single round was ever fired over the wire at the 101st Airborne Division's base while they had the duty of protecting it. They were tough.

However, when we first arrived, the main thing that we were really doing was simply adjusting our bodies to the incredible heat of Vietnam. We arrived in the hot dry season. They said that we drank about five gallons of water a day, per man, for the first week in country, but even so, you almost never had to pee. You sweated it all out. After two weeks or so your body adjusts, and then you drink about the same as you normally would on a hot day in the states.

While the troops stayed in Phan Rang, all of the junior officers like me got sent up North to where the First Brigade was operating. The sole purpose of our trip North was literally to get all of us brand new, very green lieutenants shot at for the first time so that did not happen when we were leading troops in the field.

There are many things that you never forget your first time doing. Being shot at in anger is one of those. For me it happened when I was out on a patrol up North with a rifle platoon from the 1st Brigade of the 101st Airborne Division. We were way up north, high in the mountains. I think it was my second day in the field. We were walking along beside a trail when all of a sudden shots rang out.

The bullets crack as they go by because they fly faster than the speed of sound. Sometimes you hear the crack of the bullets as they go by, and then the bang of the shot when they were fired. Sometimes when the shooter is closer to you, the bang of the shot is mixed in with the crack of the bullet as it goes by. Either way, it gets your complete attention every time.

However, because it was a sound that I had heard many times before I was certain that experience had made me ready for it. Wrong.

Really, I had thought that getting shot at would not be that big a deal. After all I had spent the entire day once in a target pit down range on record fire during Advanced Infantry Training at Ft. Ord California. The bullets had cracked over us all day then. The bullets had even flown fairly close over our heads as we stayed down the dug in, target bunkers putting up and taking down targets for others to shoot at. While we were safely ensconced down range in those bunkers, I was sure in the field that it would be much the same.

I was wrong. When you are walking beside a trail in the boonies, and they are actually shooting at you, it is entirely different. When that first bullet cracked on its way by my head, in complete violation of all my training, I just sat down. I happened to be in the open. So, there I was, just sitting on my ass, being shot at, in the open, still sitting. I did not shoot back. I did not move to cover. I just sat there, dumbfounded.

Why would anyone shoot at me? I was only a visiting lieutenant. Didn't they know that?

Later, I would learn that it is almost always the outsiders in a unit that draw the enemies' fire. For some reason the enemy always shoots at the new guy, or the guy that is about to leave because his tour is up. The guy about to go home. I think that it is because both new guys and short guys move out of rhythm with the rest of the platoon. Even the old hand who is short ("short" or about to go home because their one year tour is almost over) has become in a visible sense an outsider, and that attracts the eye, and then it attracts the bullets of the enemy.

The well trained rifle platoon that I was with that first day immediately squelched the VC that had fired at me. It turned out that he had been using an old, slow firing, Russian, Mosin–Nagant rifle. That is a five-shot, bolt-action, internal magazine fed, rifle first used in 1882 by the Imperial Russian Army. However, it is also still a very accurate, very powerful rifle, and it is often used in many parts of the world even today as an excellent sniper's rifle. There was nothing wrong with his equipment, he was just a bad shot.

it turned out that he was a real VC with an old rifle, black pajamas, Ho Chi Minh sandals and everything, a classic guerrilla, not an NVA. Nevertheless, he had almost ended my war story before it had even really started. It is not as unusual as it sounds since over the course of the entire war almost a thousand men were killed on their first day in country according to the records.

Even so, as the old saying goes, "*Don't shoot at the king and miss.*" Well a good corollary to that advice is,

> "*Don't shoot at bunch of veteran paratroopers of the 101st Airborne Division because they will kill you if you do.*"

So, it was the VC's story that ended that day rather than mine. That is how close it can be. That was how I got a good look at the weapon that had come very close to killing me.

The following is the story of our first combat assault as a unit in Vietnam, and of our first contact as a unit not only with the ever elusive Mr. Charles, aka the Viet Cong, but also with the physical reality of Vietnam itself. While we were extremely well trained as paratroopers, Vietnam and Mr. Charles still held a lot of surprises for us. It was a very good thing that only some of them were dangerous.

We started our one year tour up in the mountains, near Cambodia in the middle of Vietnam in II Corps. This one is Infantry humor.

The Attack Of The Peacocks

"What a good example of how things in a war zone can happen that are so funny after it is all over. Yet while it is going down; now that is a different story."

Ken Glass, US Army Retired
Vietnam Veteran
August 8, 2016 at 3:18 am

Phan Rang - A "Warlord" slick comes in with more Currahees at LZ Atlanta during Company A first combat assault (11 November 1967) during Operation ROSE (11-30 November 1967).

This is where we made our first combat assault the day before the action started. Photo by Jerry Berry, 3/506th PIO

It was Lt. Len Liebler's first contact with the enemy, and we watched the whole thing unfold. Len's 3rd Platoon was moving in a platoon column formation across a draw when he made contact. The rest of Alpha Company was still up on top of the mountain that Len had just walked down from. We were in a climax forest up in the mountains near Cambodia. It was too high for jungle and the light underbrush of a climax forest made movement easy.

Second Platoon, my platoon, was acting as Alpha Company CP (Command Post) security, and as a reaction force. Meanwhile, the other three platoons of Alpha Company did clover-leaf patrols out from the mountain top where we had spent the previous night. Len's platoon, first out, had headed due east, down the ridge line and then through the draw up the next ridge line until the shooting had started.

When Len's point man saw movement in front of him, he had immediately fired a long burst, an entire magazine on full automatic from his M-16 into the brush in front of him. The slack man immediately faded right and followed suit with another long burst of fire. Meanwhile the rest of 3rd platoon had rapidly moved up on line to engage the enemy. It looked like textbook perfect Infantry battle drill in a classic movement to contact situation.

Particularly up in the Cambodian highlands, Vietnam could be stunningly beautiful.
Photo by Jerry Berry, 3/506th PIO.

Even from where I was on top of the mountain, about a football field and a half away, I could see flashes of what looked like bent over, dark forms, running low and fast through the brush; perhaps as many as 5 or 10 of them, darting quickly, back and forth, across the front of Len's platoon which was by then already all up on line, firing at them. Watching Len's platoon flow smoothly from a platoon column formation into a platoon on line was strangely attractive, almost elegant, if you like loud, violent, very dangerous, but nonetheless beautifully done things.

I did not know it then, but it was really rare to actually see the enemy in a firefight. They were good at their job and the VC, like all good infantry, knew that what you can't see, you also can't shoot at. Seeing them moving, even just in flashes through the brush should have told me something.

Then, I heard Len on the radio asking Captain Tom Gaffney for gunship support for an assault. Like me, Gaffney had come over to look when all the firing started and he too was standing near me on the military crest of the hill looking down on the draw. His RTO, (Radio Telephone Operator) was right beside him, just as mine was standing near me. We could all hear Len against a background of gunfire blaring loudly from the radios as he talked and at the same time we still heard, a little less loudly, the firefight a ways down the hill in front of us.

Gaffney and I watched as the action progressed below us. Since we were in a climax forest at the top of the mountains, rather than the jungle we had crawled through to get to the mountain's base, we could see Len maneuver his platoon. Both of us were trying to figure out exactly what was going on. What had Len's platoon run into?

I turned to my platoon and yelled:

"Saddle up!" so that we would be ready to move if necessary.

When I looked back at Len's platoon in action, it appeared to me that there were even more bent over, dark forms running around in front of Len now. Had he found some of the the famous black pajama clad, hard core, VC guerrillas?

I remember actually feeling a little twinge of jealousy that Len had gotten into them first.   All the Alpha Company platoon leaders were very competitive, very aggressive.

However, Tom Gaffney and I were way to far away to be sure what was going on below us in the draw. Neither of us carried the Army's almost useless but nonetheless heavy, 6 power, field glasses. So we just stood there Tom and I, and stared.

In truth, we were both still trying to figure out what was going on below. What had Len gotten into?

And then, I saw Gaffney begin to smile. So, I turned back to look where he was looking, but I did not see anything to smile about. However, Gaffney had lived in these mountains for months at a time on his last tour in Vietnam as a Green Beret, so he had a lot of experience that we did not yet have.

This was Alpha Company's first search and destroy mission after our short orientation in country at Phan Rang. It was even our first set of clover-leaf patrols. Except for Gaffney and a few of the others, we were all still green, very, very green.

Gaffney told Len "*No*" on the gunships and ordered him to advance immediately. A few minutes later, an obviously deflated Len called in to report that he had successfully attacked a "*flock of peacocks*". Gaffney immediately corrected him and said:

> "*This is 6. A group of peacocks is called a cluster, and that is a good start for a word describing what just happened.*" Gaffney said evenly, but he was smiling broadly as he talked into his radio handset.

> "*How many did you kill? Over.*" Gaffney asked.

> "*This is 3-6. A lot, over.*" a now completely crestfallen Len replied.

> "*Good battle drill 3–6. Finish your patrol. Alpha-6, out.*" Gaffney said, still smiling.

Tom turned, took a sip of coffee from his steaming canteen cup and walked back to the top of the hill, his RTOs trailing behind him.

After hearing that, in spite of all the dead birds laying about I'll bet that Len was smiling too because Gaffney was very careful in giving praise. If he said the battle drill was good given his extensive combat experience as a Green Beret and earlier in the Korean War, there were few alive better able to judge it than Captain Tom Gaffney.

I found out later that a peacock can be over four feet long even without considering the length of the tail and it can weigh about fifteen pounds. They are really big, and more important they looked like even bigger birds. It is the males that are really colorful. The hens are mostly dark grey or brown. After seeing them running through the brush from a distance, particularly the darker hens, I was glad that it was Len that had encountered them first.

I would have attacked them too. No question. Of course, that did not stop us from harassing Len about it. Nothing could stop that.

And, it had been good battle drill too, probably not so good for the peacocks though.

Six

Artillery fire, close combat air support, and rapid medical evacuation, or Dust-Off, were often the only things that kept many of us alive during our one year tour of duty in Vietnam. While it is hard to believe now, we were in so many fire fights during our one year in country that I can no longer remember all of them.

You always think at the time the fire fight is going on that, "*I'll never forget this.*" However, over time you do forget. You forget a lot. Each time I go to a reunion of my unit, the 3/506th (Abn.) I learn about something that happened, and I usually remember some things that I had forgotten as well. Each time I returned home from a 3/506th reunion, I would add to, or try to correct these stories. Mostly I would add to them as I remembered more and more of what had happened during our tour.

At the time it is all going on though, it seems as though you will never forget it, because infantry combat is always such an intense, such a personal experience. It really should be impossible to forget something as memorable as being shot at without effect, but you do.

Even so, I remembered this particular incident. I remember it well. This one is not infantry humor.

"Fire Mission!"

Battle is such a strange place to be. Each time is absolutely unique and two guys, even two guys fighting right next to each other in a battle can still have totally different experiences. Battle is a strange place and an extremely dangerous one as well. While any infantry battle is also always intensely personal, it really is all about you, you and all those bullets cracking on their way by.

Leonard Cohen wrote the song "*Hallelujah*" many years ago. It took about 15 years before it got noticed, but now it is among the most covered songs ever. Like many others, it is one of my favorites too.

Even as well known as the song is though, a good friend asked me the other day, "*What is it about?*" Similar to me, he has heard the song many times; he had even read the lyrics; but still he said he really did not understand the song.

I say all this because like the song "*Hallelujah*", battle itself is fundamentally an emotional experience. It is not what words in the song say. The song is actually about how you feel when you hear it. In a similar way, battle is reason unbound and it cannot be fully understood or even appreciated by the rational part of our mind, but you can feel it.

No matter how long it last, battle is always experienced in a flash. It is raw emotion. You will get that emotion in full when that first bullet cracks on its way past your skull. However, battle is so much more than that first stark realization of merciless, individual, peril.

One night in the Cambodian Highlands we were climbing up a steep hill in thick jungle. It was brutal. Even so, as the point platoon, 2nd Platoon actually had it relatively easy compared to the others in Alpha Company. All we had to do was bust our way through thick jungle while climbing up a 60 to 75 degree slope.

However, as we did that we also broke what is called the surface tension of the ground underneath our boots and doing that released a lot of moisture. The ground itself was red clay, very slippery red clay even before it became wet. After a while we were all fighting for each upward step, and the guys behind us had to work even harder because each troop's step made it more and more slippery for the trooper behind as the boots got heavier with each step, as more and more mud attached itself to our boots.

As we pushed it, or cut the jungle out of our way with machetes, we also used the vegetation on the mountain to pull our way up. We grabbed it. We stood on it. There was nothing else to hold on to. Soon we had stripped it of its greenery, leaving green slime on the branches. Soon even the thorns were gone, leaving a red slime as well.

Then, the bark was gone too. It left you with nothing to grab, nothing to hold on to. Then, it pulled out of the ground entirely. Then, when you put your boot down, you could actually slid down lower on the slope than where you had started.

We were all carrying probably about at least a hundred pounds each when you include our individual weapons, the water in the multiple canteens we all carried, and all the ammo that was strapped around us. The M-60 machine gunners, the grenadiers and the RTOs (Radio Telephone Operators) were carrying even more than that. As we slipped and slid around on the slope that heavy pack on our backs shifted as well, unbalancing us each time it did, and usually it slipped at precisely the wrong time.

Then, the guy in front of you slipped and you had to stop him. You had to stop him and his pack from carrying both of you right back down the mountain slope. People who have not done this may forget that weapons have sharp edges, and triggers, and bullets in them, and that all our rucksacks have metal frames, until one or the other bangs into your shins driven hard by a 175 pound paratrooper still clawing at that slope to stay on that mountain, but losing.

With the sun being down and with the high elevation, it was probably about 70 degrees or so that night, but we were all sweating profusely going up that mountain.

Sweat gets in your eyes and it burns. It gets into the cuts on your hands and your arms, and it burns there too. Because of the mountain and your weapon, you can't even free up one hand to drink some water and anyway it takes two hands to unscrew the top to open a canteen and that was way beyond impossible on that mountain. If you let the mountain go, you fell off the mountain.

So, the saliva in your mouth dries, and it thickens until you can't even spit it out. You actually dream about the water in your canteens. The water that you got from a muddy ditch earlier that day. Six tablet water, brown water, but wet.

But still, you crawl up that damn mountain. You find that the more skin that you can put down on the mountain, the less you slide backwards. You find that if you jam the butt of your rifle behind the sliding boot of the rifleman in front of you fast enough, then he will stay there and will not wind up on top of you again.

You find that you like the taste of your sweat. You like the salt in it too.

You can't complain though. It is a tactical movement. So no talking is allowed.

You scream against the world in your mind. Your muscles scream against the mountain, against your weapon, and, most of all, against that heavy pack on your back. They scream against all of it, all in your mind. Your blood would scream too, at least the blood moving in your muscles would scream if it could talk. You know all that, and you literally claw your way up that damn mountain.

And then, we hit an elephant trail on the mountain.

> "Where does an elephant go in the jungle?" the joke begins.

> "Anywhere it wants." is the answer.

In this case the elephants wanted to go up the same mountain just like we did. Just where we did. When elephants decide to go up a mountain, the first two or three break a trail, and the following elephants follow and step exactly into the places that the preceding elephants have stepped, creating almost stairs, a little more than an elephant foot wide stairs all the way up the mountain. They had cut a three elephant lane wide highway of stairs up the mountain just for us.

According to Hal Dobie, my RTO, and as a born and bred third generation apple tree farmer from the middle of Washington State in the real world, he was our expert on all trees, broken and cut limbs, and plants of all description and type, the elephant trail had been made too recently to be boobytrapped or ambushed. Dobie was certain that it had been made that very night. So we could use it this time, but now we had to watch out for wild elephants too.

Then you realize that even though the steps left by the elephants are too short for your jungle boots, and the risers are way too long, that you love the wild elephants because now you can just climb the rest of the way to the top of that damn mountain standing up. You no longer have to wallow in the mud and the slime.

You still must pull up the man behind you, and push up the man in front of you, but that is so much better that you do not even mind the incredible piles of stinking manure here and there, and there, and the puddles of elephant urine, although you do try to avoid them both as much as possible. However, you can't avoid all of them. There are too many piles, too many puddles.

It is a small price. The elephants had obviously supped very well that afternoon. That at least was clear from the still steaming, huge piles of dung on that damn mountain.

Why do I say all of this, because that is what you did for 12 long hours right before the battle began. You are filthy. You are tired. You are sleepy because you spent most of the night before the battle crawling up that mountain. Then the bullets fly. That is when you must go to work, because you are Infantry.

Your hands are so dirty that if your rifle ever stops firing during the battle and you have to take the bolt out to clean it, touching that bolt with your filthy hands will only make it dirtier. You are not your standard Hollywood hero with a small smear of telegenic light brown dirt across your brow, or on your jaw. You are covered with it.

You stink. You are filthy beyond description. You are soaking wet in your own sweat, and you are so thirsty. Your uniform is torn. Your hands and forearms are bleeding from infected cuts from wait-a-minute vines too many to remember, much less count.

You are not wearing any underwear, either because you never put any on, or because the underwear that you did put on has entirely rotted away. The socks you put on a month ago, have also rotted away.

Then, early in the morning of the very next day, right before breakfast while you are still scraping caked dirt off of your hands with the razor sharp edge of your K-Bar fighting knife trying to get your fingers clean enough so you can eat, the Captain, Tom Gaffney gets called to the radio.

It is the Colonel. Breakfast is over before it even began and the company immediately moves off of the top of the hill we had just worked so hard the night before to climb. The Company must get to an LZ. Charlie Company is in trouble.

The movement to the LZ is as fast as you can make your tired men move. So you go down hill to an LZ. It is a seven ship LZ and the choppers will have an ACL (Allowable Combat Load) of six troopers each for each chopper.

When the crew chief approaches to tell you that, and to tell you to tell your men to roll down their sleeves before they get on the choppers because of the risk of fire, you can see him wrinkle his nose in disgust. He decides he does not want to talk to you at all. He holds up six fingers and goes back to his position as door gunner where the still rotating blades of his chopper blow your smell away.

So you fly to an LZ near Charlie Company, and when you arrive, there is another hill to climb because Charlie Company is on top of that hill, but at least it is day time. At least it is only a 40 degree or so slope on the ridge that you will walk up, and Charlie Company is only a few clicks, only a few kilometers, away.

Then you draw heavy fire from the front, up just above you on the ridge line. They are spread out, dug in, across that ridge right in front of you. There the enemy waits for you, just like they waited for Charlie Company the day before, but now they are set up between you and Charlie Company.

As you look up the ridge, you can see that they are well dug in. That their fields of fire are cut. That grenades, magazines, belts of machine gun ammo are probably all laid out and ready for battle. They knew we were coming. They knew where the closest LZ was to their mountain. They were ready for us. They were waiting for us, right here.

Battle is always a "*Come as you are.*" affair. No time to dress, or prepare, ready or not, battle starts now.

So the platoon automatically deploys on line, returns fire and waits for your order. The rest of the company is in back. They all seek cover. The curious watch, carefully; the rest will just sit and wait. They will only look up only when the noise stops.

This is to be the 2nd platoon's fight. This ridge is only wide enough for one platoon to deploy. The VC will not be allowed to leave though. It will be an immediate attack, hey diddle diddle, straight up the middle, fire and movement. *Currahee!*

How's your guts this morning? Feeling feisty? They have interlocking machine guns and a lot more than that just waiting for you on that ridge line.

However, Tom Gaffney has another idea. He calls me back to talk.

Instead of a straight fire and movement infantry assault, we will advance under cover of a rolling artillery barrage. This will be World War I stuff. The idea is that the strikes of the artillery shells will be in a moving box in front of the infantry.

The key for the infantry is to stay very close to the explosions, but not too close. If you do it just right, and if the artillery does it just right, you will be standing there among them when the enemy emerges from their holes in the ground after the thundering artillery barrage passes over. Then you can kill them.

Since a rolling artillery barrage was something that OCS failed to mention, Tom gives me about a sixty second class on how to do it as we hide behind a large rock. Meanwhile, Bob Richardson, our artillery FO (Forward Observer) was huddled on the radio talking to two 105mm batteries setting up the barrage. It is a complicated order for the artillery but like all calls for artillery it starts with the phrase:

"Fire mission. . ."

Since we had never done it before I naturally wondered if our artillery support had ever done it before as I listened to Tom describe exactly what 2nd platoon was about to do.

When I returned to the platoon I moved them into a double assault line across the top of the ridge and then we waited. As soon as the artillery started, pounding the VC positions on the ridge with fire and hot steel, we moved forward. Standing up, walking right behind the explosions as they too moved slowly up the ridge. I pushed it too close at first and one of the guys, I think it was Patterson points to some shrapnel landing behind our first line.

"Not good, L-T." He was pointing at the dust behind us thrown up from some shrapnel strikes.

So, I slowed it down a little.

However, according to Tom, it is better to risk some shrapnel rather than be caught standing there in the open, right in front of them. Far more preferable is to be standing there among them when the enemy comes out of their underground bunkers to fight. It is a balancing act in a place that is itself unbalanced.

It does not matter what you want to do that day, you must fight, or they will kill you. Worse, they will kill your friends, they will kill the man to your right, or the man on your left, or all three of you. They will kill you one at a time, or all together. So, fight you will.

It is time for your training to take over. It is time to react as fast as you can. No thought now. The time for thought is past. The rolling artillery barrage has worked.

We are among them.

Target acquisition.

Sight picture.

Fire!

Take cover.

Target acquisition.

Sight picture.

Fire!

Fire!

Again and again.

Stand.

Move.

Target acquisition.

Sight picture.

Fire!

Fire!

18, drop magazine.

Lock one 18 round magazine, load.

Move.

Target acquisition. . .

Until there are no more targets.

Quiet. It is so suddenly, so perfectly, quiet.

And then finally, you realize that this battle is over, and that you are still alive, and that the chorus sings, but with your sound shattered ears you cannot hear it wafting across the mountain top battlefield,

Hallelujah—Hallelujah—Hallelujah!

Author's Note

Leonard Cohen, author of *Hallelujah,* died recently but his songs and recordings still live. Look him and them up on You Tube. You'll be glad you did.

Seven

This story is a continuation of the description begun above of our first real battle in Vietnam. Most of the time contact, particularly with Hardcore VC, or Mainforce NVA units would be over in a matter of minutes. Mr. Charles knew that he had to get his licks in early and then get away fast, get far away if he wanted to live to fight another day.

Otherwise Mr. Charles risked massive American artillery, American helicopter gunships and, my personal favorite, air strikes. Lots and lots of air strikes. The VC/NVA were very experienced warriors, and they quickly learned that they could not fight our firepower. They had nothing to give back in response. So their most often used tactic was to hit us hard, and then run fast before we could reply.

This series of battles was the first time for us that Mr. Charles did not just fire us up, and then leave as rapidly as possible. He was dug in, prepared to endure what he had to endure, and then to fight.

These two relatively short stories about our first battle with Mr. Charles are a long way from the complete story of that particular battle, because this battle was by rights mostly Charlie Company's story, Charlie Company's fight, but, this is the rest of our part of that first battle, up in the clouds, in the highlands.

This is what we found waiting for us when we finally joined Charlie Company on the top of that mountain.

The Battle of the Knoll

"The landscape has certainly changed since you were here. A small road about 6km east of The Knoll now leads due-south from QL20 over the plateau and down the "escarpment" as it follows hydropower pipes off the plateau. N-NE of The Knoll a river was dammed for hydropower (and changed 3 of the notable waterfalls in the area: Thac Gougah, Pongour and Bao Dai)."

Steve Broering,

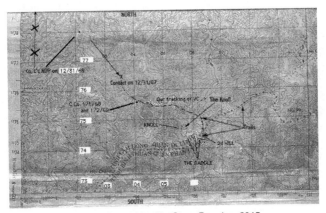

Map locations plotted by Steve Broering, 2015

The real heroes are all dead. They put it all on the line. They put everything they had, everything they could ever be, and then they were gone. Forever. The absolute anguish that we faced in Vietnam as a unit that had trained together in the states for six months before deployment was that this was happening all of the time to people we had trained with at Ft. Campbell, climbed with in the Great Smokey Mountains of Tennessee, and jumped with into the swamps of northern Georgia.

Operation Crocigator - The Currahees of the 3-506th make a mass jump into the swamps of Georgia during war game exercises. Operation Crocigator was conducted at Ft. Stewart, Georgia (10-15 July 1967).

Photo by Jerry Berry, 3/506th PIO

These men we knew like we know our own brothers. Often we knew their wives or their girl friends as well. Not just the men in our own companies, but particularly for the officers and NCOs of the 3/506th, the men in the other companies as well. We all worked together to train the 3/506th for combat in Vietnam.

We all wore the *"Pair of Dice"* patch, from World War II fame, on our fatigues at Ft. Campbell. While some of those at Ft.Campbell derided it as the mark of the *"Purple Heart Battalion"*. As one battalion, we wore it with pride. The patch identified us as members of a special battalion even when we did already know each other personally. Both proved useful in many bar fights in and around Ft. Campbell, and also later in combat in Vietnam.

Early in our tour, Captain Nick Nahas's Charlie Company fought the ferocious Battle at the Knoll. Lieutenant Ron Newton's platoon bore the brunt of the bloody fight. Captain Tom Gaffney's Alpha Company was called in to help the morning after that battle.

In the afternoon after we arrived my platoon moved over the knoll itself where the actual battle had taken place the day before to check out the area. We found numerous well-prepared, individual fighting positions and strong, mutually supporting, well fortified, well placed, fighting bunkers all over the knoll and on a nearby saddle between the knoll and another hill top.

Indian Country, by Jerry Berry, PIO. 3/506th

Some of the bunkers had been torn apart by artillery, or airstrikes, but most of them were still there. It was the partially destroyed bunkers that led us to the hidden weapons and equipment.

When we tore the rest of the bunkers apart, we found weapons and ammunition as well as gear hidden in the walls and even hidden in the overhead cover. Cover is called a roof in civilian terms, but it is called *"cover"* by the military because the military version would stop steel shrapnel shards from airbursts that would tear straight through a civilian roof.

However, even good cover will not stop a 750 pound, Hi-drag, Air Force bomb. It will not even slow it down. It was the big bombs that had exposed the hiding places.

Some of these prepared fighting positions on the knoll had been used against Charlie Company and some had obviously been empty during the battle. We tore them all apart.

It was not anger; it was purely practical. We were looking for more weapons, more ammo, and supplies of any type.

We found stuff hidden everywhere around the knoll, and particularly down in the valley behind the knoll. The tally of captured goods included AK-47s, other weapons, boxes of ammunition, piles of rockets for RPGs, boxes of medical instruments and medicine, even a 100 pound plus bag of penicillin vials lying under a bush. There were over 1,000 vials of the French made penicillin when they were counted later in the rear.

This is just a fraction of the kinds of weapons we captured as a result of Charlie Company's Battle of the Knoll, by Jerry Berry, PIO. 3/506th

They had left very quickly. They had left too quickly to take all of their stuff. Behind the knoll that Charlie Company had fought so brutally on, we found a huge base camp in a valley that was protected by those fighting positions on the knoll. In the valley itself, there were several large classrooms, a couple of very impressive, completely dug into the mountain side, medical operating theaters, a huge kitchen with running water in bamboo pipes and the most ingenious smoke and heat dispersal systems for the stoves running up the side of the mountain.

For the VC, the battle on the knoll had allowed their personnel behind them in the valley the time to escape, but a lot of their equipment and supplies stayed behind and were lost. What we could not destroy on site, we helicoptered out. That huge base camp was why the NVA had fought so ferociously to stop Charlie Company and us on the knoll. We found so much equipment and weapons the NVA had left in the base camp that two generals flew in to look at it all.

When you come upon the site of an infantry battle, like the one Charlie Company fought on the knoll, if you have the experience, you can actually read it just like you could read a story in a book. However, this story was written first in the blood of the men that fought there.

Recent picture of the Knoll and the saddle, circa 2015. While there is a lot of agriculture there now, back then this was climax forest, not jungle; the elevation was too high for jungle. Photo by Steve Broering

Walk this scene with me, over there in between two sizable but still very shot-up trees growing close together are two large piles of expended M-60 machine gun ammunition, shiny brass 7.62 mm shell casings in one pile and black, now disconnected, metallic links in the other, near that a twisted pile of bloody, originally OD green bandages, now black because of the still wet, clotting, blood, nearby next to another badly shot-up tree with multiple bullet slashes and ragged holes stands a clump of empty M-16 magazines, shiny brass 5.56 mm shell cases and then a large jumble of expended, metallic-brown, M-79, 40 mm, grenade shell casings.

Recent picture of a NVA/VC fighting position found on the Knoll, circa 2015. See the trail below. Steve also found some shrapnel nearby. Photo by Steve Broering

There was a little blood and more sap still dripping from a low gash on another tree, and over there lay a discarded steel helmet with a bullet hole through it. The bullet had exited cleanly out the other side of the helmet. Lying nearby was the blood encrusted helmet liner. There were several empty OD green, plastic canteens lying around, their caps open. Empty, gunmetal grey, M-16 magazines and bright brass, 5.56 mm shell cases were scattered in singles and clumps everywhere.

Battle had happened here. You could see that. Anyone could see that.

All of these signs pointed to hard, close, combat. They point to the infantry at work, only 8% of the armed forces, but they suffer 85% of the casualties.

Perhaps there was great courage here, at this place of battle. That, you are too late to see.

Perhaps the dead soldier that fought here, right here behind this shot-up tree, where all of his blood is still pooled, and the empty, bright brass, 5.56 mm shell cases are piled high, and also scattered deserves the Medal of Honor, but he and everyone that saw his deeds are dead.

No medals. No bugle calls. The real heroes are all dead.

First Memorial Service

Phan Rang - 1st Brigade Memorial Service following Operation KLAMATH FALLS (1 December 1967 - 8 January 1968)

Airborne! RIP by Jerry Berry, PIO, 3/506th (Airborne) Infantry Regiment

Eight

The animals were in our war zone too. There were a lot of them there, even considering that it was mostly jungle, there were an incredible number of living things, really. However, the Army almost entirely forgot to mention that to us. These animals became a big part of our war experiences, from the wild and also the tame elephants, to the tigers, to the leaches that attached themselves to you every time you were in or near the water, to the bugs that crawled in your boots if you took them off at night and the bright yellow pit vipers that could climb bamboo. They were all part of the full Vietnam War experience.

Strangely, the poisonous snakes were actually much less of a problem than the tigers, and particularly the falling trees. The tigers could be fierce, and there were stories of them, true as far as I know, killing and dragging away some luckless soul on outpost duty. But tigers were rare. The falling trees on the other hand were every where. Sometimes they had been damaged by bombs or artillery, or both, but they also were often just old and they fell with no warning.

Every thing out in the boonies was wild, and that was the real problem. The constant random artillery fire and bombing strikes probably did not help either. There were a lot of wild animals, all over Vietnam, driven crazy by the even crazier humans fighting a war.

It was not a tiger, or a falling tree this time, but it was scary.

A Dangerous Tossing Game, Only Played At Night

"It was an every night occurrence at the Rockpile. Lasted until around 03:00; then after being lulled into complacency the rocks began to go BOOM! Apes gone; VC now playing the game!"

Ray Miskell
Vietnam Veteran

The highlands. That is Captain Tom Gaffney walking toward the camera. Photo by Jerry Berry, 3/506th PIO

Second Platoon was circled up for the night in a defensive position high on top of a jungle clad mountain as near to Cambodia as we ever got, and I was sound asleep when the man on radio watch shook my shoulder. It was early in our one-year tour of duty in Vietnam, not long after the Battle of the Knoll but well before my Mother got me another machine-gun.

"Sir, its 3rd squad." My RTO, (Radio Telephone Operator) Hal Dobie said as he handed me the black plastic, radio handset.

"There is something moving in front of us. Over." whispered the man from 3rd squad over the radio.

"What is it? Over." I said very quietly, but not whispering since I had been taught in OCS (Officer Candidate School) that whispers actually travel further than just talking very quietly at night.

"I don't know. Over." he replied.

"Do you have a target? Over." I asked.

"No. I can't see anything at all. I just hear it. Over." he replied

"Well, when you do see it, shoot it. 2-6, out." (2-6 is my radio call sign. It means I am the, 2nd Platoon, platoon leader.) I said and gave the radio handset back to the man on watch.

Then I rolled over, back into my poncho liner, and tried to go back to sleep. I think I had just about made it when the man on radio watch shook my shoulder once more.

"Sir, it's 3rd squad again." he said as he handed me the radio handset.

"This is 2-6, over." I said into the handset.

"They are throwing rocks at us. Over." he said.

"So, throw them back. Over." I replied.

"We already did. But, they are better at throwing them than we are and they throw them really hard. One of them just put a dent in my steel pot. Over." he said.

"Can you see them?" I said.

"No." he replied.

"All right, cook off a hand grenade and toss that at them, but make sure you don't hit a tree when you throw it." I ordered.

"Roger, out."

Throwing a hand grenade in the jungle, in the dark, is extremely dangerous because you might hit a tree and then the hand grenade could bounce back and worse, in the darkness you might not be able to find the hand grenade in the underbrush to throw it again before it goes off. The Army, the thrower, and any others near by, would all consider that a to be very bad result.

At the time and perhaps still, the American M-26 hand grenade we used had a 4.5 second fuse. There is always a dynamic tension in choosing exactly the right amount of time for a hand grenade fuse so that it allows the thrower sufficient time to get rid of an armed hand grenade, but it does not allow the receiver sufficient time to throw the hand grenade back before it goes off.

When it explodes, the M-26 hand grenade punches out about 1,000 stainless steel fragments to a distance of about 10 meters, which is considered the casualty-producing radius for the hand grenade. The lethal radius for 50% of those casualties is about 5 meters, or 16.5 feet. However, the danger area around such a hand grenade blast is 25 meters on soft ground, and out to about 300 meters on hard ground. A soldier in good condition, standing up, can throw a hand grenade about 20-25 meters, or about half that distance accurately, all of which is well within the danger area of the shrapnel blown outwards by the blast from by the hand grenade's plastic explosive core.

Using a hand grenade effectively at a short range requires "*cooking off*" some of that 4.5 second fuse time because otherwise the recipient has too much time left to throw it back.

When you "*cook off*" a hand grenade, first you pull the pin. After you pull the pin, you let the spoon go, letting the spoon go arms the hand grenade, and starts the 4.5 second delay counting down. At very close range, the Army considered it safer to "*cook off*" up to 3 seconds of the fuse time rather than to give that time to your enemy to throw it back.

The use of the word "*safer*" rather than "*safe*" was done on purpose. As a philosopher would say, when it is a question of being more or less safe, it is not really a question of safety at all.

There is nothing safe about a hand grenade, much less about cooking one off, particularly at night, particularly in the jungle where there are trees in the way in every direction you could even think about throwing one. Hand grenades are just dangerous things, period.

So, I had ordered someone, who would be working in the dark, to "cook off" a hand grenade by counting slowly to 3 after he let off the spoon. He would then throw it, with only about 1.5 seconds or so left, before it explodes. Then, immediately after throwing the hand grenade, if he is trained correctly, and if he remembers it in time, he will quickly drop to the ground, or better yet, get behind something really thick before the hand grenade goes off.

Phan Rang - Company A on search and destoy operation during Operation ROSE (11-30 November 1967).

Photo by Jerry Berry, 3/506th PIO

Assuming that the hand grenade fuse was made properly, cooking off a hand grenade before throwing it is considered safer than the alternative for well-trained, iron-nerved troops. On the other hand, consider that because of the inherent danger of cooking off a hand grenade, it is never even practiced in training with live hand grenades.

I hoped that it was one of my experienced, well-trained, iron-nerved, troops throwing the cooked off, hand grenade, rather than an F-N-G (F= standard Army descriptive adjective for nearly everything beginning with the letter "F", N= new, G= guy), but it was the 3rd squad leader's job to choose the hand grenade thrower, not mine.

In recognition of all this I did not roll back into my poncho liner, I stayed flat on the ground; the radio handset glued to my ear. Hand grenades are fearsome things when they go bang in the night, and in the daytime too for that matter.

The hand grenade went boom. There was some thrashing around in the bushes in front of 3rd Squad that was so loud that I could even hear it back in the platoon CP, then it was quiet for the rest of the night. I went back to sleep, my time on radio watch did not start for over an hour.

In the morning, we figured it out. We were high up in the mountains, in the jungle, hunting guerrillas, but it appeared that we had set up for the night in the home of a band of gorillas or of some other primate with a strong throwing arm, but not guerrillas, definitely not guerrillas. They had tried to drive us out of their home by throwing rocks at us. We had replied first by throwing back the rocks, albeit completely ineffectually, and then by cooking off and throwing a single hand grenade, very effective.

There was some blood, and some bits of matted black fur near where the hand grenade had exploded, but I was glad that there were no bodies, nor even any blood trails, to be found anywhere.

I wondered as we looked around, if gorillas that get caught up in a war they have no part of, can nonetheless be awarded their own version of a Purple Heart, just like us. They should, because when someone said that war is hard on people, and all other living things—they were right.

Afterword

A reader of my blog complained that there are in fact no "gorillas" in South East Asia. I looked it up and he seems to be correct. However, after doing some more research I learned that there were multiple reports, of which I was not aware of when I wrote *A Dangerous Tossing Game, Played at Night,* of large primates, black in color, that liked to throw rocks at US troops and at others.

As I found out from several readers some large primate prowled the highlands we were in and also further North near the DMZ (Demilitarized Zone). These primates delighted in throwing rocks at troops and others that had invaded their territory. As another reader pointed out and my research confirmed, these rock tossing primates are often called *"rock apes"* for the obvious reason.

Also, in recent years they have discovered two new primates in South East Asia, and there has been at least one Vietnamese government official expedition trying to find a "rock ape" or two.

I also learned that while there were numerous *"guerrillas"* in South Vietnam no one has ever seen a real gorilla in either North or South Vietnam.

We met lots of *"rock apes"*, tigers, elephants, snakes, peacocks and many other animals, great and small, in the wild. Often with deadly results for the animals. However, other than snakes, the Army mentioned none of them in our training. I never found out why they left that, seemingly obvious, certainly important, part of our training out. But they did.

Since we never actually saw who was throwing the rocks at us we can't contribute much to the science of the thing, but the world is a fascinating place in which to live—and fight.

Nine

Soon after the events described in the *Dangerous Tossing Game, Only Played At Night*, we were pulled out of the field and sent to back Phan Rang. We were officially marshaling to get ready for our combat bast. It was to be a real combat jump to be made even closer to Cambodia than we had been. We would be the blocking force for a major attack by the rest of the First Brigade of the 101st Airborne Division.

However, right before we left the highlands for Phan Rang this happened. There was just enough time left for us in the field for the Army to prove that it was still the Army. Sure, it was all my fault, but still.

You would think that it would be different, but even in Vietnam the Army was still the United States Army. Now and then that reality would intrude on the war that we were fighting in Vietnam. This is a story about one such intrusion.

There were others as well, but they will remain our secret.

Numbers Can Be Deceptive

"I thought this to be hilarious. Your commanders handled it well. The script of this is so funny that it should be made into a movie. A movie of these events would be hysterical especial if it spawned off the ramifications of your actions e.g. a marine having to parachute with no training, the 70 yo Lt. etc. Thank you for giving an uplifting day. 2/501/101st Airborne '68-'70. Didn't make it thru primary helicopter."

Greg Kaepp
September 12, 2016 at 6:14 pm

When I originally enlisted in the Army it was for Warrant Officer Flight School at Ft. Rucker, Alabama. While I had to successfully complete the flight school to actually become a warrant officer, I was guaranteed on enlisting that was where I would be sent. The only question remaining the recruiter explained when I enlisted was whether I would pass the flight physical. If I did that, it was on to Ft. Rucker right after AIT (Advanced Individual Training) he said. That all sounded good to me.

So, I filled out all of the enlistment forms. There were two complete sets, one for entry into the Army and another set for entry into the Warrant Officer Flight Program. There was only one question on all the forms that I did not know the answer to, my social security number. However, the forms showed how many numbers there were in a social security number, so I just filled in the blanks and then turned the forms in.

As everybody knows who has ever been in the armed forces, even before basic training, it all starts with taking a bunch of tests. It turned out I did very well on the officer aptitude test, so they offered me the chance of going to OCS (Officer Candidate School) instead of Warrant Officer Flight School.

I had a long discussion with the second lieutenant who was recruiting men for OCS about this. Ultimately, according to him, the Army promised that if I flunked out of OCS that I would immediately be sent to flight school at Ft. Rucker. With that assurance, I signed up for Infantry OCS at Ft. Benning, Ga. Again I filled out a whole bunch of new forms, then I was on the way to Benning's school for boys. Right before commissioning we filled out two more sets of forms since in effect all of us were leaving the Army as enlisted men, and then immediately rejoining the Army as newly minted, commissioned officers.

I passed OCS and after Jump School was assigned to the 3/506 (Abn) Infantry Regiment with the 101st Airborne Division at Ft. Campbell, Ky. The Commanding Officer of the 3/506th was an old war-horse on his third war named John P. Geraci.

Our battalion trained for six, long hard months in the states and then we deployed to Vietnam as a unit. Like everybody else in the unit I felt that we were very lucky. We had Lt. Col. John P. Geraci, later inducted into the Ranger Hall of Fame, as the battalion commander. We had Tom Gaffney, working on his second war and like Geraci this would be his third tour in Vietnam, as our company commander. And, we had Master Sergeant Theron V. "Bull" Gergen, also inducted into the Ranger Hall of Fame, as the company's First Sergeant. All three of them were tough, knowledgable, demanding warriors who took no prisoners.

In fact, Geraci relieved, Army speak for fired, one company commander and Gaffney relieved a platoon leader during training in the states. They both believed completely in the old adage that, sweat in training saved blood on the battlefield. We sweated a lot even before we got to Vietnam because for them, even really good excuses were never a sufficient reason for a failure to perform.

After a couple months in Vietnam we were on a resupply out in the field when I was told to come over to the single ship LZ (Landing Zone) in the center of the Alpha Company perimeter where I found Geraci and Gaffney waiting for me, not talking, looking very stern.

They sat there for a minute, both of them just looking at me. Then Gaffney passed me an inch thick sheaf of papers. You read Army documents from back to front so I turned immediately to the last page, then I had to turn forward four pages to where the first document in the stack began.

It was a memo from a full bird Colonel in St. Louis, directed by name to my commanding officer, Lt. Col. John P. Geraci, USA, Commanding Officer, 3rd Battalion, 506th Infantry (Abn.) Regiment.

Me; James Albert Bunn, (KIA) my platoon sergeant; John Geraci, CO 3/506th Abn Inf; Tom Gaffney CO Company A 3/506th Abn Inf; Bob Mairs S-3, 3/506th Abn Inf. This was an earlier meeting. Photo by Jerry Berry 3/506th PIO

The memo did not begin well:

"This officer, and I use the term loosely. . ."

And, it went down hill fast from there. I soon figured out that not only had I used different Social Security numbers each time I had filled out a set of forms, I had also often varied the numbers within each set of forms.

In total I had filled out at least six sets of forms: first set, Army enlistment, second set a Warrant Officer flight candidate, third set Officer Candidate, fourth set ending service as an enlisted man, fifth set beginning service as a commissioned officer and a finally, a shorter set for Jump School. The Colonel did not say how many different Social Security numbers I had used because I gathered he was still not sure of the exact number.

The Army had recently changed from keeping track of its soldiers by their service number to keeping track of us by our Social Security numbers instead.

Apparently as long as the Army had kept track of things by service number, my little fictions had caused no problems. However, when the Army switched to Social Security numbers there were no end to the problems I had caused.

All of the numbers I had used turned out to be real Social Security numbers for somebody and many of them were, or had been, in the Army. At least one of them was in the Marines too, but the Colonel seemed not to be as worried about him.

Among other things, there was a large, brand new, computer on an Army base near St. Louis, Mo., that had suddenly spewed out all sorts of numbers and forms. According to the Colonel, at great cost of time and money, the computer had been shut down completely as each number was traced—back to me.

Among other problems, there was that Marine. He was drawing jump pay, but had never been to jump school and on being assigned to a Marine airborne position had objected strenuously even though he had been getting more money, probably particularly when they told him he had to exit an aircraft in flight.

The Colonel had also spent some time looking for a by then nonexistent 78-year-old second lieutenant who, according to the paper work, had been commissioned twice.

The Colonel's memo went on and on. I finally stopped reading and started to go through the documents on top of the original memo. The first was from another Colonel, also Adjutant General Corps, who pointed out in some detail that wars are not just won on the battlefield, but also by keeping careful, accurate records. He only went on for two pages talking mostly about me, and he was also very definite.

Then, the documents travelled up through all of the various Army and Joint Commands to CONUS, or Continental Army United States from whence it went CINCPAC (Commander in Chief Pacific Area Command) then to USARPAC (United States Army Pacific) and on to MACV (Military Assistance Command Vietnam). It actually went a lot of other places as well, and each commander, or his designee, had added their endorsement page to the memo. By the time it got to me it was about an inch thick.

It was hot on the LZ, but that was not the reason for all the sweat pouring out of my body. I was stunned, speechless.

I glanced up—Geraci and Gaffney were still sitting there, still looking right at me, absolutely stone-faced.

Then, Geraci laughed, not just a "*Ha, ha, ha. . .*" but real belly laughs, and then Tom Gaffney joined him. There were tears in their eyes when they finally stopped laughing.

A week later the battles of Tet '68 started. No one ever mentioned that memo again, and strangely, it never made it into my 201 File. (the 201 File is the permanent file the Army keeps on every soldier and officer)

Ten

As I already mentioned, because of a breach of security, our combat blast that we had trained so hard for was cancelled. So, on January 17th, 1968 we were sent instead to Phan Thiet, a small town on the coast of Vietnam to form a special task force for II Corps in the central part of Vietnam. As Task Force 3/506th we had several units attached in direct support including our own assault helicopter company, the 192nd Assault Helicopter Company.

Our job there was to be the final reaction force for most of II Corps. We also defended Phan Thiet which was the capital of Bình Thuận Province. Phan Thiet was a small fishing town at the time on the coast of the South China Sea about in the middle of South Vietnam.

No matter where you are, when you go to war, it consumes your time, your energy and sometimes even your life. While you leave your family at home, the war can often be almost as hard on them, if in a completely different way. Since you are gone and busy, you may never learn what they went through while you were off fighting a war. I did.

I heard this story mostly from my Mother and my grandmother after I returned from Vietnam. In a strange way that I did not realize at all when I was in Vietnam, my Mother was serving there in Vietnam right along beside me. She's tough—you'll see, she's really tough.

This is by far my favorite story. I think you'll know why when you read it.

My Mother's Machine-gun

"All true as I remember my mother relating it. Sad to say, she would not ask Senator Russell to send me a machine-gun. Ninth grade could have been so much better!"

Ned Libby, Col. USA Ret.
And my cousin, who had also heard the story, from his mother my aunt.
July 16, 2014 at 2:24 am

In October of 1967 my unit, the fabled 506th Airborne Infantry Regiment of World War II, Band of Brothers fame, deployed to Vietnam as part of the 101st Airborne Division. Although we did not know it then, we would be there for the bloodiest year of that long conflict.

After a short orientation at Phan Rang, we were sent to the field, Search and Destroy the Army called it; but to us we were chasing Charlie as the saying went even though we rarely caught up with him at first. Since we were resupplied either every three, four or even five days in the field, and since I did not want my Mother to become accustomed to getting a letter from me on some regular basis, I purposefully wrote to her spasmodically, rather than regularly.

A few months later, I was sitting on an LZ in the field near Phan Thiet on the coast and more or less the center of Vietnam waiting for a resupply when I realized that I owed my Mother a letter. It had been two re-supplies already, over eight days, since I had last written. However, I could not think of anything to say to her.

As usual, I had started the letter with the date in the upper right hand corner followed by approximately where I was in Vietnam. So, I wrote *"January 25, 1968"*, followed by *"Phan Thiet, RVN"*, but that was as far as I

107

could get. Then, I looked down at the last page of a *Stars & Stripes* newspaper in my lap and it had a small article about a strike at the Colt Patent Firearms Company plant in Connecticut that made the M-60 machine-guns we used. Each platoon usually carried three of them but since one of mine was in for repair, I was out in the field with only two machine-guns.

So, I started the letter, "*Here I am in Vietnam short one machine-gun for my platoon and these Bozos at Colt are sitting safe at home and are out on strike while we are fighting a war. . .*" That finally got me started, and then I went on with the letter, talking about how quiet it was where we were, how hot the temperature was, how beautiful the South China Sea was, how safe the Phan Thiet area was, then some more about the missing machine-gun and so forth.

Then, I sealed it; ran it to the helicopter, and thought no more about it.

When my Mother arrived home from her job at Georgetown University on February 3, 1968, she was already worried and wanted to watch the evening news. The battles of Tet '68 had started and they led the news.

Therefore, she was particularly happy to see a letter from me in the day's mail. She got herself a glass of wine, turned on the television to the CBS evening news, and sat down to read my letter.

She opened my letter only moments before Walter Cronkite's face appeared on the screen; she just had time to read the date, and location when Cronkite's famous voice intoned his lead story:

"Today in Phan Thiet, Vietnam, there was savage fighting as the Viet Cong tried to seize the normally sleepy provincial capital. Units of the

108

101st Airborne Division met the enemy head on in a series of exceptionally violent battles that started early in the morning and continued all day. There were heavy casualties on both sides. . ."

My Mother sat there stunned. She read the top of my letter again; she read the name of town on the screen; she read the top of my letter again; she read the name of town on the screen. She started crying. Then, mercifully the news program broke for a commercial. The news from Vietnam actually got worse from there. She continued to cry, and to sip her wine.

For those of you that do not remember, CBS's Walter Cronkite was a god, an oracle of truth at the time, and unfortunately he was not at all upbeat about the chances of even the legendary 101st Airborne Division to hold on to the town of Phan Thiet under such a ferocious assault by a well armed, well supplied and numerically superior enemy.

It was about the only time Phan Thiet made the national news, but we made it big time that night. According to Cronkite the fighting was severe everywhere, up and down the coast of Vietnam, so there was no possibility of reinforcements for the embattled paratroopers of the 101st Airborne Division in Phan Thiet. This dire prediction was his close off line for the extended news program.

Except getting up for more wine during commercial breaks, my Mother watched it all. Then, she sat there in her living room staring at the now blank TV screen. She cried for a while, then she finished reading my letter and the rest of her bottle of wine, her dinner forgotten. Her son was in trouble, and he needed a machine gun. She was sure of that.

A little after midnight my Mother called her mother in Savannah, Georgia. A Depression era baby, it was a testament to her worry that my Mother did not once think of the cost of the long distance call. She had opened a new bottle of wine as well.

They talked for a while. They both cried together for a while. They talked about machine-guns repeatedly, but not very knowledgeably. However, they knew all about war. Both had lived through World War II and the Korean War by then. Finally, around two in the morning, her mother, my grandmother said:

"Let's call Dickie."

It turned out that *"Dickie"* was Senator Richard B. Russell, Jr., the senior senator from the State of Georgia and probably the most powerful Chairman of the Senate Armed Services Committee ever. However, many years before he had been a young boy in my grandmother's, then Miss Varina Bacon's class for two years at the Seventh District Agricultural and Mechanical School in Powder Springs, Cobb County, Georgia. In addition, Senator Russell's mother, Ina Dillard Russell, was a teacher and was my grandmother's best friend.

That was probably why my grandmother had Senator Russell's home phone number, which she talked an AT&T operator into making a conference call to at about 3:00 AM. The two women just cried on the phone again together as they waited for the call to be put through to Senator Russell.

With Senator Russell on the line now, the three of them discussed machine-guns, and why Lieutenant Harrison's platoon, did not have enough of them. My grandmother wanted to know exactly what Senator *"Dickie"* Russell was going to do about this problem of national importance, how had he let it happen in the first place and could he also see to it that the strikers were put in jail, or better yet, shot.

After midnight, both my grandmother and particularly my Mother could be of a seriously violent inclination. My Mother was the one that suggested shooting the strikers.

My father had always said that United States District Court Judges, United States Senators and any truly pissed off American mother could cause more trouble than anything else in the world. Here we had two angry, very scared American mothers and a powerful but sleep deprived United States Senator. Things were sure to be interesting in the morning.

Although the majority of our training was for combat patrols in the jungle, the majority of the fighting we actually did during Tet '68 was street fighting in the cities and towns of Vietnam. We used trucks for a while because the VC had shot up so many of our helicopters that we were saving the ones we had left for Dust Off.

Meanwhile, the battles in and around Phan Thiet continued. Luckily, my missing machine-gun had been repaired and returned before the start of Tet '68 because we had been busy. Finding Charlie was no longer the problem.

A day or so after the telephone call to Senator Russell my platoon was embroiled in some of the fiercest house to house fighting of the war in downtown Phan Thiet, RVN, when my RTO (Radio Telephone Operator) Hal Dobie of Yakima, Washington, handed me the radio hand set saying there was a man that said he was a Colonel on the radio asking for "*Lieutenant John Harrison*" in the clear. This violated so many Army rules and regulations that he had not answered the transmission.

We were actually being shot at when this picture was taken. I am left middle left, in front of my RTO, Hal Dobie of Yakima, Washington. That is "Bull" Gergen, a full blooded Cherokee Indian member of the Ranger Hall of Fame and our First Sergeant, coming up on the right. It was his second war, third tour. James Philyaw third from right. I am sort of bent over looking over a hedgerow. We are on our way back into Phan Thiet. Photo by Jerry Berry, 3/506th PIO

I truly did not know what to do. After the third time I heard him identify himself as Colonel something or other, I have forgotten his name, and again asked for "*Lieutenant John Harrison*" I just said "*Yes.*" rather than saying, "*This is Alpha 2-6*", meaning, Alpha Company 2nd platoon leader, as I usually would have identified myself.

The Colonel then said he had a machine-gun for me and where could he put his helicopter down so he could deliver it to me. I said I was pretty busy at the moment—after all a lot of people were shooting at us.

Then, he reminded me that he was a Colonel, that I was only a 2nd Lieutenant and he demanded in the most forceful manner a landing zone, immediately.

Since he was so insistent, I said that the area in front of my platoon was wide open, plenty of room to land a helicopter, but then I had to warn him that he would be under heavy fire, both machine-guns and rockets as he landed. His choice. I think the pilot talked some sense into the demanding Colonel and he decided to leave the machine-gun back at our base camp, LZ Betty.

When we finally got back to LZ Betty a couple of days later, the Company armorer was still cleaning that machine-gun. The Colonel had tried to deliver an M-60 machine gun, to an active firefight, encased in a wooden box, enveloped in thick plastic shrink wrap, and full of thick Cosmoline, but with no ammunition.

It took our armorer, Carl Rattee, three days and a tub of gasoline to get the machine gun ready to fire. But when he was done, it was beautiful.

Strangely, unlike every other weapon in the battalion this particular machine-gun was assigned directly to me, to Second Lieutenant John Harrison. It was my very own machine-gun, from my Mom. I liked it and when the Army made me give it back when I left Vietnam, I thought about calling her, but then, I thought it might make her angry. . .

Ten

While it is really hard for some to understand, there are actually a lot of laws, rules and regulations specifying exactly how you can, and cannot fight a war. They were enforced after World War II at the Nuremberg Trials and at several other places. After these trials many officers and enlisted men were hung for war crimes. It was made very clear to everybody that *"I was just following orders."* was not going to fly as a good defense in a war crimes trial.

War or not, orders or not, under the law of war every individual, officer and enlisted, remains personally responsible for their own actions. They did mention that to us in OCS, but they neglected to tell us how it worked. Exactly how do you refuse even an illegal order from a man carrying the same kind of rifle that you carry?

Like the lack of classes on the animals native to Vietnam other than poisonous snakes, the Army's failure to spend much times on these laws, regulations and rules of land warfare before we went to war has always been utterly inexplicable to me. However, I had seen the movie *Judgement at Nuremberg* when I was growing up and it had made a profound impression on me. Getting hung by the neck, until dead, really did not appeal to me at all.

So one day, Tom Gaffney and I had this little discussion. . .

Hunting One of the World's Smallest Deer
in a War Zone

"I remember TET well. B company was lifted out of the field in the middle of a mission because of the intelligence received from higher ups. The enemy violated Tet, and Christmas of 67. My Buddy Tom Croff was wounded as was others, but after 2 beers (Christmas), and turkey, we manned our perimeters well and fought off a probe. Blood trails were found in the morning. Airborne."

Frank Gilbert
Bravo Company, 3rd Battalion (ABN.) 506th Infantry
November 3, 2014 at 4:46 am

If you read the history books, they will tell you that the famous North Vietnamese General Vo Nyguen Giap scored a major tactical "*surprise*" with his '68 Tet Offensive. You will also see phrases like "*large scale*", "*well planned*" and "*well coordinated*", attacks. And, to a limited extent, these descriptions of the '68 Tet Offensive are correct when viewed from our side, except for the surprise part. That is just totally wrong.

However, there is another side even of the true part of the '68 Tet Offensive story, and it began for the 2nd Platoon of Alpha Company with one of the world's smallest deer, the Muntjac deer. Long after I left Vietnam I learned that an adult Muntjac deer stands approximately 45cm, about 18 inches, at the shoulder and have an average weight range of between 10 – 16kg, or about 22 to 35 pounds. When running, they seem to lean forward.

During the summer months, May till October, a Muntjac's coat is a red-brown color often with very pale, sometimes white hair under the chin, throat, and tail.

Muntjac bucks have small, un-branched antlers, which slope to the rear and end in a pointed tip. They also have long canine teeth, which look like small tusks projecting downward from the upper jaw.

All of this was true of the single Muntjac deer that we saw for just a moment on a bluff overlooking the South China Sea and located southeast of LZ Betty. The real question though is, what was the 2nd Platoon doing there, and why was it hunting deer rather than Charlie in the middle of a war zone? That is the interesting part of the story.

As had been agreed every year of the Vietnam War prior this, at the end of January 1968 there would again be a Tet cease-fire. Tet, the Vietnamese Lunar New Year, is easily the most important celebration of Vietnamese culture. It combines the elements of our holidays of Thanksgiving, New Years Day, Father's Day, Mother's Day and even some of the aspects of the Memorial Day all into one really big family centered, but also very religious, three day celebration.

Merging so many ideas, the Tet holiday has several names as well. It is called poetically, the Feast of the First Morning of the First Day and since the Vietnamese consider Tet to be the first day of spring, the festival is also often called more prosaically, simply the Spring Festival. Traditionally Tet takes place from the first day of the first month of the Vietnamese calendar until at least the third day thereafter.

Much like our Thanksgiving and Christmas, many Vietnamese prepare for Tet by cooking special holiday foods. Since it is a "*Spring*" festival they also celebrate by thoroughly cleaning their homes. There are many other customs practiced during Tet, such as visiting a special person's house on

116

the first day of the new year, ancestor worship, wishing special New Year's greetings, giving "*lucky*" money to children and elderly people, or even opening a new shop.

Again, like our Thanksgiving holiday, Tet is the occasion for mass pilgrimages home and for large family reunions. Like us at Thanksgiving, during Tet, Vietnamese often travel long distances to visit their relatives, or they all agree to meet at their families' shrines during the holiday. Once together, they try to forget about the troubles of the past year and focus on hope for a better new year.

This holiday is and was universally revered in Vietnam, even in the aggressively secular, Communist North. That was the reason for the yearly truce agreements.

Tet '68, and the Tet truce were set to start on January 30, 1968. On January 29, 1968, the C-O of Alpha company, Captain Tom Gaffney called me aside to tell me that he wanted me to take 2nd Platoon on a patrol in the morning the next day outside the wire of LZ Betty our base camp near Phan Thiet, RVN, on the coast of the South China Sea.

However, a combat patrol on January 30, 1968 would be a clear violation of the Tet cease fire agreement.

Tom and I shared what can only be described as a strange relationship. There was never any question that he was the boss, the Commanding Officer with the final authority. However, there was also no question, that if time allowed, I could question, or suggest, or discuss, and even disagree with almost anything, and I often did. In recognition of this curious dynamic SFC John H. Gfeller, Platoon Sergeant, Weapons Platoon, (KIA, 2/19/68) had nick-named us: "*god*" and "*god, junior*" because no one else was allowed by Tom into this little club.

Given that Tom was ordering what appeared to me to be a clear war crime, this was one of those times where we had a heated, an extended, heated discussion. Finally, we agreed that the 2nd Platoon would go "*deer hunting*" south of LZ Betty to try to get a deer for an Alpha Company, Tet barbecue later in the day. What ever we saw, we saw. Whatever happened, happened. It seemed to me that it might even be legal.

In light of this, it is at least passing strange to report that the only time that I ever saw a deer during the entire time I was in Vietnam was when we were deer hunting that one morning south of LZ Betty. Mid-morning walking near the bluff over the South China Sea we kicked up a Muntjac deer in the brush and it took off in front of a hail of gunfire from the entire left side of the platoon.

The Muntjac deer is a small, very fast, mobile in three directions, hard to hit, target. It runs forward; it jinks suddenly sideways, and it leaps up and down constantly. Running between the clumps of brush and thickets of bayberry bushes along the bluff made it even harder to hit.

Right after we shot at the deer, my RTO, Hal Dobie, passed me the radio handset and said "*6*", meaning that Tom Gaffney, the C-O was on the horn. Since the first thing that always happened anytime an Alpha Company platoon shot at something was that Tom would immediately call to ask what was going on, I thought that was what Tom's call was about. Although I did wonder how he had heard our firing from LZ Betty, which was probably over a mile or more away by then.

"This is 2-6, go ahead." I said into the radio handset. *"2-6"* was my call sign meaning that I was the 2nd Platoon, platoon leader.

"This is 6. There has been a change. You are hot. Go ahead." Tom said. *"6"* was part of Gaffney's call sign *"Alpha 6"* meaning the Alpha Company, commanding officer.

"2-6. What? Go." I said.

"I say again, you are hot. Go." Tom replied.

I got ready to rehash all we had said before, but Tom broke in before I could even start.

"This is Alpha 6. This is an open net. I say again, you are hot. Do you copy? Go ahead." Tom said.

I literally took it down from my ear and looked at the black plastic radio handset as though it could tell me what was going on. I understood what he was saying; Tom again wanted me to run a full tactical combat patrol in the middle of the cease-fire. We had talked about that, but something had changed. I could hear that in his voice. He was excited, but it was more than that too.

One of the other many things that they do not have time to teach in OCS (Officer Candidate School) is that most of what you actually do in a combat unit is ultimately based on trust. You understand that in combat men are killed, but you trust your superior officers not to waste your life. As strange as it may sound, you accept that you may be killed, but that your life will not be wasted. It will mean something. You understand that at home, in the real world, you live by certain moral rules, but in a combat zone, you do what a

119

superior tells you to do, and you trust that he is right. You understand that people will shoot at you; that they will try to kill you, but you trust in your training and your buddies to bring you home.

None of this, all of this, flashed through my mind. I put the radio hand set back to my ear.

"Wilco." I said. *"Wilco"* is a radio *"pro-word"* or radio procedure word meaning; "*I will comply.*"

Just as Tom had re-identified himself as my company commander for emphasis, I chose to use the radio pro-word reply that emphasized full compliance. However, just as I knew by his tone over the radio that something was going on, he knew by my tone that I was not happy.

"Return to base, hot. This is 6 out." Tom said.

So, we turned around. As we turned, I told the point man to put his M-16 on "*rock and roll*", full automatic. We were fully tactical again. The deer would have to wait. I doubt that it minded.

When we got back, Tom told me about the attack on LZ Betty that intelligence was sure was coming later that day, or early the next morning at the latest. He said several bases and towns had already been hit hard. He also told me that intelligence had secretly warned of the attacks even earlier. That warning had been the real reason for sending 2nd Platoon "*deer hunting*".

The only thing about the '68 Tet Offensive that was a surprise, was that a combat commander with the well earned, and seriously good reputation of General Giap would try such a mishmash of violent, but under supported, widely separated attacks which defied almost every rule of war. However, we did not know then that General Giap had actually been opposed to the whole idea of a '68 Tet offensive and was only in command of the '68 Tet Offensive because the general that had planed the offensive originally had died suddenly before the offensive was launched.

So, no matter what you heard, the '68 Tet Offensive was not a surprise at all, and, by the way, General Giap was right, they lost. We won that battle. It is still a mystery to me that no one in America noticed since it was a really big battle, a really big victory—for us.

Oh, and that deer, that deer got clean away.

Elevan

This is the first part of our story of what happened on 2/2/68 near Phan Thiet. February 2, 1968 was by far the bloodiest day in our year in combat for the Second Platoon, Company A, 3/506th Airborne infantry, 101st Airborne Division.

In effect this was the story that Walter Cronkite had told my Mother and the rest of America about. It was hard, brutal, combat, and we won.

The Day Smith Died

"Thanks for posting that event. It was very intense. The part about the F-4's was really a memory jogger. There was a night that we were really glad to see them coming."

Otis Elkin
Vietnam Veteran
March 10, 2015 at 2:46 am

I saved PFC John Smith's* life three days before he was killed. In 1968, I was the platoon leader of the Second Platoon, A Company, 3d Battalion of the 506th Infantry (Airborne), 101st Airborne Division. Smith was one of my men.

On the last day of January 1968 we were based at LZ Betty around an airfield just outside of Phan Thiet, which is a small city in the middle, and on the coast of the South China Sea of what was then the Republic of South Vietnam (RVN). Since we had been told to expect an attack in force against our perimeter around the airfield that night, we were aggressively patrolling the wire around our well fortified base that afternoon to clear the area in front of our defenses.

Some of the land in front of the airfield was chopped up into small fields with tall, thick, hedgerows separating them almost like the ones that I had read about in Normandy after D Day in France during World War II. Our hedgerows were six or more feet tall, three or four feet thick at the base and were often massive, rock hard, earthen berms topped by thick, tough, green, twisted and snarled but very prickly vegetation. When you went through one hedgerow and into another field you were cut off from the rest

123

of the platoon behind you, and from their support. You could not even see them.

Because the hedgerow terrain was so tight, I was walking right behind the point man so that I would be up front, where the action started, when it started and would not have to move up through fire to find out what was going on.

Smith was my point man. Therefore, I was his slack man as well as his platoon leader. The slack man's job is to wait until the point man has fired a full magazine at the enemy and then the slack man fires at the enemy as the point man reloads. He literally takes up the slack.

After the slack man has fired a full magazine, the first squad, under the covering fire of the point man and then the slack man was supposed to have moved up on line. At that moment, as the platoon leader, I would have a decision to make, either to attack immediately, or to maneuver the two trailing squads right or left. On this day, it was all run-n-gun, so we usually just attacked immediately; killed or captured the VC we had found and then kept right on moving.

We had just climbed up through a hedgerow and into a new field. Smith, Hal Dobie, of Yakima, Washington, my RTO (Radio Telephone Operator) and me were the only ones in that field so far. This field was narrower than the others, so our left and right flanks were in the adjacent also hedgerow lined fields on our left and right. While we could not see our flankers, we kept in constant voice contact with them as we moved forward. The rest of 2nd platoon and A Company were coming along in platoon column formations behind us.

It had been a running gun battle all day; we were moving fast and had been rolling up, killing or capturing irreplaceable VC cadre in those hedgerows. It was Tet, the first day of the Tet Offensive, 1968. So far, the day had been a turkey shoot. These guys, they turned out to be the VC Province Chief, his assistant, a VC tax collector, a senior VC intelligence officer and several other VC had all been just no match for our combat hardened, veteran paratroopers, the famous Currahees of the 101st Airborne Division.

Whatever else may be said about Tet '68, the local force VC around Phan Thiet never recovered from that battle. We were never again surprised near Phan Thiet. As 1968 moved on we more often than not surprised the Main Force NVA battalions and even the Hardcore VC units as they moved around Binh Thuan Province. Tet '68 was an utter military and political disaster for the VC in Vietnam, its other political effects at home in the US to the contrary notwithstanding.

We were a separate battalion, the 3rd of the 506th, of a separate brigade, the 1st Brigade, of the 101st Airborne Division. The word "*separate*" by our battalion name means that we fought independently from any other American unit. During Tet 1968, since everyone else in country was busy too, we were very much on our own in Phan Thiet, RVN.

That was fine with us. "*Currahee*", a Cherokee Indian word and the 506th's motto means,"*Stands Alone*". The Currahees had earned our nickname at Bastogne in World War II, now we would earn it again in Vietnam. Standing alone was what we did.

Although it is not generally known, Phan Thiet had once been the home of Ho Chi Minh. It was where he had worked as a teacher right before World War II. Phan Thiet was also a place that we later heard that Vo Nyguen Giap, the North Vietnam Defense Minister, had personally promised Ho Chi

Minh that he would take from the Americans in his first wave of attacks. In 1968, during Tet '68, Phan Thiet was, riveting.

Phan Thiet from the air. Most of the round white dots you see were caused by airstrikes of bombs. Artillery does not make a big enough hole except for the 8 inch cannons which throw a 200 pound shell. Photo by Jerry Berry, 3/506th PIO.

In contrast to what I have sometimes read about some other areas of Vietnam, our intelligence in Phan Thiet about planned VC operations was often very good. During and before Tet '68, contrary to all reports that we were surprised, the intelligence was right on target. We knew when they were coming. We knew where they were coming. And, we knew both in time to prepare. It is impossible to do better than that as an intelligence operative.

The VC were planning to hit our perimeter around our airfield, named LZ Betty, and they had placed a large part of the entire VC cadre of Binh Thuan Province around the LZ Betty perimeter in the hedgerows to act as guides for the sappers, and the Hardcore VC and Main Force NVA units that were to make the actual assault on our base. All day we had been killing, or capturing those guides, mostly killing them.

Suddenly, when we were about halfway across the narrow field, a man surged out of the hedgerow in front of us. He was firing a pistol at us, a little Russian Tokerev pistol I noted automatically. I yelled at Smith to shoot him, but Smith just looked on at the man as he ran toward him, shooting that pistol at Smith all the way. Smith still just stared at the man as I shouted at him again to shoot him. Even then, Smith did not return fire.

The man was running, shooting toward all three of us. He had started running toward us from about fifty feet away. By now he was only about thirty or so feet away, and he was still firing that pistol at us.

Things can happen incredibly fast in combat, but this all happened in slow motion for me. That man, like a lucky NFL quarterback avoiding a sack, seemed to have had all the time in the world to shoot his pistol at us. Since Smith would not shoot him, I started shooting him. My RTO, Hal Dobie was behind me and could not get a clear shot, but I could, and I did.

Like a trained infantryman, I counted the rounds out in my mind as I fired them. Starting a little below his waist and ending in his head, I shot him exactly sixteen times. I could see little puffs of dust as each 5.56mm bullet from my rifle drove home into his body. Even on his face, I could see the little dust puffs thrown up by each bullet's impact.

It was not like director Sam Peckinpaugh's classic movie, *The Wild Bunch*, at all. It is not blood splattering that you see in real life when you shot someone. It is dust. A little puff of dust blew up as each bullet smashed its way into the man's body. I was surprised to see that even on his face a little puff of dust would fly up at a bullet's impact.

The blood, often in a pink haze, comes out the back, but only if the bullet punches its way all the way through the man's body which the lightweight

M-16 bullets rarely did. However, even if the little 5.56mm, M16 bullet punches its way through, if you are the one doing the shooting, you can't see that pink haze coming out the back. The rest of the body blocks your view.

But still he fired at us, my bullets slamming into him and all, but still he fired that pistol. Now he was firing at us from less than fifteen feet away. He was still running toward us. He was still shooting.

I did not have time to wonder how many rounds his little gun had held. I was worried I was going to run out of bullets for my own rifle. My magazine had held only eighteen rounds when I started shooting at the man with the pistol. I was sure I was going to have to beat him on the head with my M-16 after I fired the last bullet into this man that would not lie down and die. He was dead. I had shot him so many times, including several times in his head.

He had to be dead, but he was still shooting at me. I was still shooting at him. I was hitting him. I could see each of my bullets hit him. He was missing. At least me, he was missing. I was pretty sure he was missing me as I fired back.

So, I aimed carefully and squeezed the trigger as fast as I could, still carefully counting each time my rifle fired a bullet. A trained infantryman is never surprised when he fires the last round in a magazine. He counts the bullets out, drops the magazine immediately after the last one fires and then reloads. Even though I was a 2nd Lieutenant, I was trying very hard to act like a trained infantryman.

Finally, Spec 4 Francis Edwards came through the hedgerow behind us and put the better part of thirty rounds from his M-60 machine gun into the man. I did not know then that Edwards' assistant gunner, Ed Blanco, had practically thrown him through the hedgerow when he heard our firing in front of him. Blanco had tried to follow but he fell, tripped by those gnarly bushes. By the time Blanco got there, it was all over.

Drawn by the firing, others, including Sergeant Ron Ford, firing over the side hedgerows, had put a few rounds into the man as well. One bullet actually went down the barrel of his pistol. After it was over, we found that he still had one bullet left in his magazine, so that accidental bullet down the barrel of his pistol was probably what ended his shooting rather than all the bullets in his body.

When the M-60 machine gun bullets had slammed into the VC's body he stopped, and finally, fell backwards. After he fell, I took literally two steps forward still aiming my M-16 rifle at his head; we were that close by then. I had two bullets left. I looked down at him through the sights on my rifle. He was dead. Carefully I moved around his body and kicked his head a little. Finally, he was dead. I was sure. Then, I looked down at me. He had missed. He had completely missed.

After that I changed magazines on my M-16, chewed out Smith for not firing and we moved into the next, thankfully wider, hedge row encircled field as I brought the Captain, Tom Gaffney, up to date on the radio. That was only the middle of a very busy day for us.

Smith was still on point. Usually I rotated point men and the point squad to the rear of the platoon after each contact, but Smith had not fired so in a sense he had not been in this contact. However, Smith had never failed to fire before and it never happened again. He was one of my best point men and he and his squad did rotate to the back of the platoon after we found and killed the next VC guide.

The VC did not attack our base camp that night. Other than a few rockets and a spectacularly successful mortar attack they never mounted a full scale infantry attack on our base camp while we were there, and although they tried several times, they never took Phan Thiet while the Americans were in country. Neither Ho Chi Minh, nor Vo Nyguen Giap ever said if they were disappointed by their failure, but I hope they were.

Three days later, on another sweep during Tet, Smith at the head of a fire team walked into a house next to where we were stopping for a moment to check it out. Unfortunately, there were several VC in that house waiting for them. While the rest of the fire team escaped the house in the hail of bullets that followed them out of the house, Smith was shot and fell on his back on the raised front porch of a blue painted Big House (See arial photo below) built of concrete blocks just outside of Phan Thiet proper.

That firing was the signal for all of the other VC and NVA in the area to open up on us, and there was an entire Mainforce battalion of them. While we had avoided the ambush they had set up for us on the Cart Road they had expected us to walk down, there were an awful lot of them dug in along the Cart Road and all around the huge dry rice paddy in front of us. It was early in the day, before lunch, and Smith lay there on that porch and bled all day while the Second Platoon fought fiercely and ever more violently, to get to him.

We yelled to Smith to roll off the porch so that he would be easier to get to. Sergeant Ron Ford and Spec 4 Michael Trant did most of the yelling but Smith would not or could not roll. We tried everything we could think of to find a way to reach him.

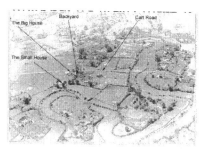

The VC had lined the Cart Road (above) with bunkers and expected us to move down that road, right to left on the above aerial photo. However, we moved along the tree line below and sort of parallel to the cart road leading to the Small House, which turned out to be behind both VC ambush sites. The area to the left of the Big House and the Small House was a huge dry rice paddy field. The VC had numerous bunkers ringing that field as well as their fighting positions on the Cart Road. The ring of bunkers around the open rice paddies was a second ambush set up to ambush a relief force coming in by helicopter to help a unit trapped by the first ambush on the Cart Road. However, we were behind rather than in front of all of their bunkers. The round white circles in the picture are bomb craters.
Photo by Jerry Berry, 3/506th PIO.

We attempted to blow a hole in the side of the Big House so that we could get in there, kill the VC in the house and then drag him inside. I shot a case of LAWs (a Light Anti-tank Weapon also useful against bunkers, a 66 mm rocket in a disposable fiberglass firing tube) into that house and I requested satchel charges. The LAWs punched nice, but unfortunately small, round holes. However, they did spray the inside of the Big House with a lot of shrapnel.

Even if I had been able to blow a big enough hole in the concrete block wall, there was still all of that barbed wire in the way. There were three barbed wire fences running between the houses, each fence was a little more than hip high with three strands of wire, and no gates.

So, we tried to attack the Big House from its rear. My Platoon Sergeant James Bunn took Sergeant Stacy Raynor's squad there as I called in air strikes, helicopter gun ships, 4.2 mortars and 105mm artillery in front and on both sides of the Small House we were in.

At first, we were being fired on from 360°. The 1st and 3rd platoons took care of the NVA in our rear, while helicopter gun ships call sign *"Tiger Shark"* from the 192nd Assault Helicopter Company, Air Force F4 Phantom jets and 105 mm artillery from LZ Betty pounded the NVA units in our front, and on both sides, of us.

Maj. James Pratz
FAC Pilot
March 68

Air Force Major James Pratz, call sign "Jack Sprat", standing in front of his light observation plane. A veteran fighter pilot, Major Pratz was our FAC, or Forward Air Controller during Tet '68. Photo by Jerry Berry, PIO 3/506th, taken at LZ Betty.

It was those incredible Phantom jets that won the firepower contest for us. The FAC (Forward Air Controller), call sign *"Jack Sprat"* sent the Phantoms roaring in every time I asked. He seemed to have an unlimited supply that day. The F4 Phantom was the best fighter bomber in the world at the time, and in recognition of its record of downing large numbers of Soviet-built MiGs over North Vietnam, it was also known as the "*World's Leading Distributor of MiG Parts*".

A great aircraft flown by great people, I called it, savior, friend and guardian on the field of battle. There are no words sufficient to describe what I felt about what "Jack Sprat" and the United States Air Force F4 Phantom close combat air support pilots did for us on that bloody day

The Second Platoon lost more men that day than during any other single day of the war, but not all at once. John Smith was hit at the very beginning of the battle, several minutes later George Schultz was hit, shot in the chest, as he returned fire from the front yard of the Small House that we were in.

Still later my Platoon Sergeant, James Bunn, was killed at the back door of the Big House, almost but not quite inside. While Jim Bunn did get a hand grenade, and fired an M-16 magazine into the back of the Big House, he was shot dead from a supporting spider hole.

Even later in the day, three more men were wounded taking Schultz back to the company CP (Command Post) to be medivaced. Several more of my men were also wounded as we fought during that long day of battle.

Late in the day a second Airborne rifle company, Captain William Landgraff's Company B, 3/ 506th, came up to help. One of their platoons, led by Lt. Jim Kissinger, actually one of Captain Nick Nahas's Charlie Company platoons, but operating with Bravo Company that day, joined us at the point of the spear, on the firing line. We had trained together in the states, now we fought together in Vietnam; and together we attacked the Big House again and again.

It was the only time in the war that no matter what I did, we could not achieve fire superiority sufficient to maneuver. Even with the two rifle platoons firing together, that meant six M-60 machine guns on the firing line as well as all of the M-16s and M-79s we had firing together it was still not enough. Even crueler, although we had pounded them with airstrike after airstrike all day by multiple flights of two fighter-bombers each, usually F4 Phantoms, plus hours of 105mm artillery fire, 4.2 mortar fire and repeated helicopter gunship attacks as well, the enemy's return fire never slackened no matter how many we killed, no matter how much we fired at them.

There were just too many of them in spite of everything still shooting at us, still trying to get closer and closer to us to avoid all of the air strikes and artillery that I was raining down on them through out the day. Finally, late in the day, as the sun was going down, we were ordered to leave.

When I got back to the company perimeter, our artillery FO (Forward Observer), Lt. Robert Richardson and I located the NVA positions for an artillery and heavy mortar barrage. We foolishly climbed up on a mound of dirt in the twilight to get a better look at where the shells would land. However, we forgot that being on the dirt mound gave the enemy a better look at us as well. We both dropped precipitously to the ground when a machine-gun opened up us, but Lt. Richardson had gotten a good enough look and when I called for it much later that night, he dropped the massive 105 mm strike, battery six—four quadrants—fire for effect, in the right place.

Later that night after we had set up the artillery strike, Sergeant Ron Ford and I led a small, all volunteer night patrol, some called it a suicide patrol, surreptitiously back to the Big House to recover our men. When the call went out for volunteers, the night patrol was immediately over subscribed.

Among many others, the entire third platoon volunteered. Since the idea was secrecy, I whittled it down to a few more than a dozen.

About three hundred men, all elite, all veteran paratroopers, fighting all day had not been able to penetrate the enemy position, but now we going to try it again, at night, this time with a little more than my dozen plus, patrol. We drew ammunition and shortly after midnight we snuck quietly out of the company perimeter single file heading back to the Big House.

Almost at the Big House, our night patrol picked up the body of another fallen paratrooper. It was First Sergeant Phillip Chassion who had just replaced "Bull" Gergen, a full blooded Cherokee, as our Company First Sergeant. First Sergeant Chassion had been shot and killed trying to get to his friend, Jim Bunn.

One of the night patrol, Sergeant Ray Mayfield knew where First Sergeant Chassion had fallen. Ray later received the Silver Star for leading a three man group out from our patrol that recovered First Sergeant Chassion's body.

Unfortunately, we also picked up the attention of the NVA when we found that first body. From that point until we rejoined Alpha Company hours later we were under almost constant rifle fire and intermittent mortar fire from the enemy.

So the NVA were alerted and ready by the time we got to the Big House where Bunn and Smith were. Chris Adams was one of the team of three paratroopers that went up to that porch where Smith still laid. Even though they heard several NVA talking in the Big House, Chris and the two others were able to get Smith off of the porch and return to the patrol before the shooting started. However, Smith was dead.

After we recovered Smith from the Big House the NVA counter-attacked, but we fought them off. Then we attacked, this time we drove them out of the house to recover our last man. In the dark, we fought our way into the Big House and recovered the body of Sergeant Bunn. Now, all we had to do was get away from the NVA, and get back to Alpha Company.

Suddenly, the NVA fired machine guns, rockets and mortars at us, but strangely they missed us entirely in the darkness. They literally fired the wrong way. Their mortar shells exploded uselessly in the rice paddy right next to us, and their rifle and machine-gun fire, bullets arcing, green tracers flaring, cracked over still another nearby rice paddy. We laid there with our friends and listened to the "*thump*" as their mortars fired, waited as their shells arced overhead and hoped they continued to land in the adjacent field rather than on us. When they finally stopped we moved out.

They were not as adept in the dark as they had been during the day. On the other hand, we owned the night. That night we went where we wanted, when we wanted, but only as violently as necessary. We eliminated everyone we had to eliminate to recover our men. All of the rest of the night on the way back we dodged their bullets as the pursuing NVA tried to stop us, tried to bring us to a battle we could not win.

Our night patrol carried all three of our dead comrades out under the almost constant enemy fire. Because of the small size of the patrol we tried to avoid rather than fight the enemy if we could. We put our friends down only when we absolutely had to fight our way clear. The rest of the time we stayed low and quiet, moving fast. Everybody but me was helping carry a body. I was on point; rifle in one hand, compass in the other. There was no slack man.

Phillip Chassion was our new company First Sergeant. This was literally the first time he had been to the field with us, but it was a long way from his first time in the field. Here he is in 1966 briefing a long range patrol he would lead. Photo by Robert C. Lafoon, U. S. Army, PIO.

On the way back to Alpha Company we used the terrain to hide from the enemy, moving as quietly as possible from shadow to shadow, ditch to ditch, hiding, but as a result tacking right and left like a sailboat in a heavy head wind trying to get to port. The wind for us was the enemy bullets whizzing by. It took a lot longer going back.

At one point on the way back I became completely disoriented. I not only did not know where A Company's position was, I did not even know where we were anymore. At first being lost did not make any difference—no matter where we were, we had to get away from the NVA that were too close on our trail at that point.

The darkness, moving fast and staying low had helped staying hidden from them, but it also meant I could not see any topographic features to tell me where we were. We were lost, completely lost in Indian Country.

Finally, after we gained a little distance from our pursuers, I called Tom Gaffney and asked him to shoot three tracers straight up in the air. As long as I could find A Company, it really did not matter where we were.

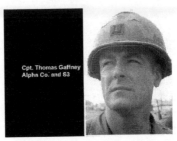

Cpt. Thomas Gaffney
Alpha Co. and S3

Photo by Jerry Berry, 3/506th PIO.

Tom did not object nor ask why even though it placed all of the rest of Alpha Company at risk by telling every NVA in the area exactly where they were. In a moment, three spaced shots rang out. When we saw the tracers against the dark sky, I took a compass heading on them and we moved out again.

Finally, we had to do what is probably the most dangerous job of the Infantry. We had to rejoin a unit, at night, that has been in a brutal firefight all day. That is exactly what had killed Confederate General Thomas "*Stonewall*" Jackson in the Civil War after his classic victory at the battle of Chancellorsville.

What scared you is that you know as you are walking in that there is always someone that does not get the word. There is always somebody that does not know you are coming in, and you know that particular somebody is there, right there in front of you; he is watching the darkness; he has a loaded automatic weapon in his hands; although tired, he is relentlessly looking for movement, ready and waiting to fire after a long, hard, violent day.

No warnings. No pass word. Just bullets await.

Even if you are not religious, you pray; you stand very tall because you do not want to look like you are sneaking around; and you walk very slowly.
While before we left the FO and I had set up a powerful strike of preplanned artillery and heavy mortar fire on the NVA just as we were leaving the Big House to try to shake their pursuit.

Even so several of the NVA had stayed right on our trail, shooting at us, trying to call their mortar fire on us, all the way back to the Alpha Company perimeter. If one of them fired on us, or on the perimeter as we were coming in we would be smack in the middle, standing up in the open, no place to hide, right in the middle of a fire fight.

We prayed harder; stood straighter and walked even slower.

That final walk in was the most scared that I had been all night. A few more than a dozen paratroopers had left the perimeter earlier that night. We had been shot at for hours by people really good at shooting people, but in spite of that we recovered our friends, and we had all, almost, made it back.

But, this one time everybody did get the word:

"Friendlies coming in. Do not fire."

Smith had been a tall, thin, African-American man who had lived his short life courageously. He was interested most in photography and women. Although remarkably thin, he was enormously strong. Since he did not like

139

to hurt anyone, he did not. He had smiled a lot and always did more than his share when there was work to be done.

No one complained when Ron Ford and Paul Clement carried him out that night through the almost constant rifle, machine gun and mortar fire to send his body home to his family. He had been fun to be around. I do not know to this day if Smith even had a chance to shoot when he was inside the Big House. I hope he got off a shot, but I do not know if he did.

My Platoon Sergeant Jim Bunn was heavier, harder to carry out. He had been a professional soldier who could not stand the thought that young men would die in Vietnam when he could have been there to help them. So, after returning from his first tour in Vietnam, he had volunteered to go right back to Vietnam, with a young, inexperienced lieutenant to train when he could have stayed in the States for at least another two years. Jim Bunn too had been fun to be around as well, and to learn from. He got off his shot and then some more before he was killed.

Photo by Jerry Berry, 3/506th PIO.

Jim Bunn had also liked Smith a lot. Jim had talked to Smith after Smith had failed to fire that one time in the hedgerows. Not to chew him out, but to find out why, and to ensure it did not happen again. It is a testament to how good Jim Bunn was as a platoon sergeant that it did not happen again, and that on the very next contact, Smith took care of business. Smith was one of the 500,000 or so reasons why Jim Bunn was back in Vietnam again.

Jim Bunn was white; Smith was black. About a third of the guys that helped carry them out were black. Jim Bunn and Smith were from the second platoon, my platoon; the other Airborne KIA, First Sergeant Phillip Chassion, we also carried out was not from our platoon but he was from Alpha Company. I do not know about atheists, but there were no racists in our foxholes. They were all our men, all Currahees of the 101st Airborne Division, the famous 506th Band Of Brothers. We brought them all home.

The Airborne recovers its dead.

John Melgaard was our platoon medic that day. He had gone with Bunn and Raynor's squad when they had tried to rescue Smith from the rear of the house. He was there when Bunn was killed trying to get into the back of the house while Smith was laying on the front porch dying. On the way to the back door of the Big House, John had pushed David Stiles to safety into a small hut when Stiles had been temporally disoriented by being shot in his helmet.

Later in the day, John and three others had carried George Schultz back to the Alpha Company CP to be medivaced. Everybody that went with John helping carry Schultz back to the Company CP were wounded while they were on the way back to the CP. However, later that night, even after all of this, John Melgaard still volunteered to go on the night patrol to help recover our men.

Each time John Melgaard had risked his life, just in case one of the men was still alive, just in case so that he would be there with his aid bag to help them, if they still lived. John Melgaard also, earned the Silver Star that long day and night.

That is David Stiles with the bullet hole in his helmet that he received accompanying SFC Bunn in his attempt to get into the back of the house where Smith was. Sergeant Ron Ford, the assistant patrol leader of the night patrol, is on the right smiling. Photo and caption by Jerry Berry, 3/506th PIO.

Over forty years later, a month ago now, while I was watching the movie *Gettysburg* on television I thought again about what a man that VC with the Tokarev pistol must have been. He had been the Viet Cong Province Chief, a political officer, not a military man at all, but truly courageous nonetheless.

He, in Vietnam, and Colonel Josiah Chamberlain, at Gettysburg, had each obeyed that most difficult and dangerous, but distinguished tradition of the Infantry, the Spirit of the Bayonet. When they were almost out of ammunition, when they were outnumbered and heavily out gunned, when there was nothing else to do, they had both attacked with everything they had. This is the true Sprit of the Bayonet.

They both put it all on the line for one final try. It cannot be done foolishly and still be within the spirit of the bayonet. There must be at least a chance of success; otherwise, it is just another suicide run.

The exhaustion of the rebels after a day of attacking and being up hill gave Chamberlain and his badly battered Maine regiment their chance of success at the battle of Gettysburg. The thick hedgerows, and the narrow fields by splitting my platoon into parts that could not directly support each other, gave the VC and his Tokorev pistol his chance.

Chamberlain's wild, down hill, bayonet charge succeeded; the VC's violent attack across the hedgerow enclosed dry rice paddy did not, but neither had hesitated. Chamberlain's heroic, cold-steel, bayonet assault broke the back of Confederate General Robert E. Lee's last attempt to take Little Round Top on the first day at the Gettysburg battle. It set the stage for the blood red high water mark of the Confederacy with Pickett's charge up to Cemetery Ridge the next day.

The VC Province Chief, I never knew his name, had died courageously and well, but even almost fifty years later he is still running, still fighting and still shooting that pistol every day, every night, in my mind. So too are PFC John Smith, Spec 4 George Schultz, First Sergeant Phillip Chassion and my Platoon Sergeant, SFC James Albert Bunn, and all those other brave, dead, infantrymen—black and white, red and yellow, who fought so long ago.

Author's notes:

The Day Smith Died is my factual history of what happened on February 2, 1968 near Phan Thiet, RVN. *"Cone of Violence", which appears* next, another of my stories, is more of a personal, emotional account of the same day.

* Not his real name. All of the other names are their real names.

Twelve

Several readers asked me about the genesis of the two stories, *The Day Smith Died* and *"Cone of Violence"*. *The Day Smith Died* was written first many years ago, probably right after I saw the mini-series *"Gettysburg"* on television for the first time. Watching it, I was struck by the similarities in courage of the Union Colonel Joshua Chamberlain, Medal of Honor, and the VC Province Chief I had run into near Phan Thiet, RVN. So, I wrote *The Day Smith Died* soon after.

While I have never regretted shooting the Province Chief that day, I have almost always regretted the necessity that required me to shoot him. It was probably the death of Jim Bunn, watching John Smith die, and the killing of the Province Chief that drove me from the Army—I have always hated killing people.

Nonetheless, I refight that day, February 2, 1968, every day in my mind's eye, sometimes several times a day. At one point when I was doing that, just sitting in front of my computer, I started writing, and *"Cone of Violence"* was what came out. It came out all at once, complete.

That was several years after I wrote *The Day Smith Died*. To me: one is a history, what happened that day, and the other is raw emotion, what was felt when my friends, and a brave enemy, were killed.

"*Cone of Violence*"

"I was Sgt. Bunn's radio operator. I took over when Campbell was killed in a night ambush that went afoul. I was separated from Sgt. Bunn with medic John Melgaard when my helmet was shot off my head. Melgaard kicked me in the ass and brought me back to reality. Possibly saving my life. Worst day of my life (2/2/68)."

Dave Stiles
Alpha Company, 2nd Platoon
3rd Battalion (ABN.) 506th Infantry
June 25, 2014 at 5:55 pm

One of my men, PFC John Smith*, was lying on the porch of a house next to us; he was bleeding out. There was so much blood that it was running bright red down the stairs from the porch he was laying on. I could see that blood clearly. I could look at him lying on his back, but I did not want to look at his blood, all that bright red blood.

A view like that is one of the reasons that the average life span of an infantry platoon leader in combat is supposed to be measured in seconds, not minutes, seconds. It was about 8:00 AM, February 2, 1968 near Phan Thiet, Republic of Vietnam and I had hours of heavy combat ahead for me that day.

I had already called in air strikes. I had called in artillery. I had called in 4.2 inch heavy mortar fire. I had called in helicopter gun ships. I had called all of them in at the same time; they never taught me how to do that in Officer Candidate School, but I did it, and I called them in separately too. I made it up as I went. I wanted Smith to live, so I created Hell and decorated it all around him with high explosives, burning napalm and hot steel; I put the NVA (North Vietnamese Army) right in the middle of it, but the bastards lived through it.

The caption reads: Phan Thiet: Paratroopers from Lt. Harrison's 2nd Plt. wait on the LZ for the remainder of their troops to arrive aboard "Polecat" Slicks from the 192nd AHC.The paratroopers shortly after leaving their LZ would engaged a large enemy force guarding the headquarters of the 482nd MF VC Battalion in the "Disneyland" area near Phan Thiet City (Feb. 2, 1968) Photo by Jerry Berry, 3/506th PIO

Still, they shot at us. I tried to kill them. I tried everything I knew. And, then I tried them all, again, and again. I created the "*pain that passes understanding*", and I gave it to the NVA without stinting.

I had called in air strikes so close to where we were that when the bombs exploded we bounced off the ground. Literally, my whole body bounced into the air with the explosions. Each time I bounced high enough that it hurt when I landed. I was bleeding in my eyes. I tasted red blood in my mouth, particularly in the back. My ears were bleeding. By the end of the day, there was crusting brown blood on both my ear lobes, and running down my neck.

Blood was oozing out of my nose and down my cheeks, and I asked for more air strikes. And, then I called the air strikes even closer, because I

147

wanted to kill those sons of bitches that were shooting at my men; keeping me from getting to Smith. I tried to kill them in so many different ways. The bastards would not die. They kept shooting. We kept shooting, and I kept calling in air strikes, gun ships and artillery. All day we fought.

I ordered my platoon sergeant, my friend, SFC James Albert Bunn, to take a squad and see if he could get in the back door of Smith's house. About an hour later the squad leader, Stacy Raynor, came back and told me that Bunn had thrown a hand grenade in, but had then been killed trying to follow it in the back door.

Smith, my soldier, my responsibility, was still dying 75 or so feet away from me, and I could not help him. He was still bleeding and I could not stop it. I could see his blood still running down the stairs. It was still red too. All I had to do was look out a window and I could watch Smith bleed. I could watch him die. I watched him for hours that day.

That is napalm stuck to the poles of the big house. That is blood running down the stairs. We were closer to the napalm than the big house was.

The porch where Smith lay, dying as we watched. Those were his canteens. That is his blood on the stairs. This photo was taken in the morning of the next day, February 3, 1968. Photo by Jerry Berry, 3/506th PIO

If I had given the order, 2nd Platoon, Company A, 3rd Battalion, 506th Airborne Infantry would have gotten up and attacked. I knew it and they knew it. But, then we would die too. As long as we held the house we were in, the NVA could not attack us. We were too strong, and more important, in too strong a position.

However, so were they. All of those houses were made of concrete blocks. As long as we stayed where we were I could use the Air Force and artillery to inflict damage on them, and they could do almost nothing in reply. But, if we left that house and the yard behind it, if we were out in the open attacking the other house, the one Smith was on the porch of, then their much greater numbers would begin to work for them.

Until then our far greater firepower, mostly courtesy of the United States Air Force, was working for us. If we attacked in the open, the NVA would probably kill us all, and Smith would probably die anyway. That I knew that this was true did not make it any easier not to attack. I wanted to give that order. Attacking was what we did best. But it would have been a stupid order, the kind I had trained very hard to avoid. I kept looking for another answer, an answer that would allow me to save Smith instead of watching him die.

I tried everything until I had nothing left to do. I had shot everything at the enemy that I knew how to shoot. I had been creative—I had walked artillery up from one direction, gun ships up from another, and jet bombers streaking in from yet another direction, all at the same time. I made it up as we fought.

We blew those bastards up creatively. We gave them a concentrated lesson in the American, war-fighting, combined-arms, doctrine of the vigorous application of massive amounts of high explosives and the accurate, continuous, exploitation of raw firepower dominance to solve a difficult tactical dilemma. It almost worked too.

During that day while we were orchestrating this lesson for the NVA somebody came up onto the Charlie-Charlie radio net. I told them to get off the net. I told them to stick what ever they were talking about up their ass, and I got really gross, and I got really angry. That was the only time that day I lost my temper.

"*Charlie-Charlie*" is the Command and Control radio net. It is air support; it is artillery; it is dust off; it is everything. To a unit in contact with the enemy, it is life itself.

In combat, the unit leader in contact with the enemy controls the Charlie-Charlie net. That was me and I had absolutely no intention of letting anybody else screw-up what I was doing. If there was to be a screw-up that day—I would be that screw-up. I was determined. I was a second lieutenant. That is the lowest officer rank in the army, but I demanded all that tradition gave me.

The Charlie-Charlie net was mine. I was in contact with the enemy. I would fight my platoon. Win, lose or draw—I would fight my platoon my way that day, no one else, me. And, I did. By God, we fought that day, all day we fought from about seven in the morning to almost nine at night and then later, in the dark of night, we went back and did it again.

I never heard a word about it. It's not often a twenty year old 2nd Lieutenant even gets to chew out a really senior officer, much less gets away with it as well.   Tom Gaffney, my company commander certainly never said a word about it to me—he had taught me the rules. He stayed off the Charlie-Charlie net that day if I was busy. He knew I probably needed it more right then. But, he too was a commander of a unit in contact with the enemy, so he had as much right to the net as I did, plus he was higher in rank. But, he was Tom, and he knew his business, and he knew mine, so he knew when to stay off the net. Now someone else did too. That was good.

The United States Air Force is my best friend. I believe that with my entire heart and soul. I love them in a way that is absolutely not understandable to those that have not been there. If they have not been in my position; that position had begun early that morning receiving heavy automatic weapons fire from 360°, and rocket and mortar fire from both the east and west, and with my knowledge and my training; they cannot understand my emotion, my reverence, when I say "*Air Force.*" All day my friend and I chipped away, blasted away, burned away the enemy—my friend, the United States Air Force and me, we did it.

When I told the FAC (Forward Air Controller) that the NVA were shooting at his fighter-bombers with machine guns when they came in for bomb and gun runs, he said, thank you for the information, but that he would not tell his pilots. He said it pissed them off, and that being angry made them less accurate, and that he was moving their bomb and napalm strikes in so close to me that he did not want them to be less accurate.

We knew each other. We had trained together in the states before we went to Viet Nam. We drank together several times. We got drunk together once. He was my United States Air Force Forward Air Controller in Viet Nam. I told him where I wanted the bombs. He lined up the planes and delivered the goods on target.

He called what we were doing: "*Danger close, U. S.*" meaning to everyone according to my friend the FAC, if it was not clear enough already that:

"We are dropping all of this very dangerous crap very close to the United States Army, and by the way these are the paras of the 101st Airborne Division that I trained with, and that I know personally! And, you had better know what you are doing or we are going to have a serious problem! You understand me?"

His voice actually got louder with every word and he was shouting to begin with. At least that was the general idea of what I heard him say to one flight leader on his other radio before the fighter pilot began his runs.

One flight, he waved off after only one pass and he would never let them close to us with ordnance again. They were not good enough to support his paras. Others he sent in even when they only had 20 mm cannon left to use, they had already used everything else but because they were good and on that day, he knew that more than anything else, I needed good. I needed all the really good, really close, combat air support, I could get. I had a target rich environment. So he sent the good ones back again and again until they were empty.

He knew I needed ordnance, lots of ordnance on target. I needed—boom on target—BOOM! The United States Air Force delivered lots of BOOM and bang, bang, bang, and quite a few whooshes, that day. *"Whoosh"* is what I think napalm sounds like when it flares off.

I don't know how he did it. I don't know what it cost him. But that day, I had flights of Phantoms, almost all United States Air Force Phantoms, but some times also US Navy Phantoms as well, F-4 Phantoms, the absolute best fighter-bomber in the world at the time.

All day there were United States Air Force F4 Phantom jets, overhead, often stacked up in multiple flights of two planes each, just waiting for a target that absolutely, positively had to be destroyed immediately. And, I had those targets, and we destroyed them one after the other. Soon we were being shot at only from 180°. Even that got better as the day wore on, but Smith's blood still reached the third of three steps. Some strikes were close, one was literally right next-door, blow off our roof close, exciting, and some were across the large rice paddy in front of the house we were in, visually arresting.

All day we worked on evening the odds by removing enemy from the battlefield. It had started as one American Airborne rifle platoon, mine, as the point of the spear against about a battalion of Hard-core VC and Main Force NVA regulars, mostly from the 482nd Mainforce Viet Cong Battalion. It was extremely dangerous, nerve-wracking, close-in work and it went on all day long.

The NVA had expected us to walk into their ambush. If I had done that, and lived; Tom Gaffney, the C-O, (Commanding Officer) would have killed me. No, we had maneuvered behind their ambush so they had to expose themselves in order to shoot at us.

When they did that, we shot them; we killed them. It is what the Infantry at work does. When they stayed in their bunkers we blew them up, or we burned them out with napalm, and sometimes we did both just to make absolutely sure they were, and remained, dead—stone dead. It is what the Air Force does for the Infantry when you ask nicely; but, there were so damn many of them.

Even so, they did not have a chance as long as we had good flying weather. Strike after strike I called in, and the Air Force delivered, on target. Or, near, near was good too. When you are playing this game with 750 pound high explosive bombs—coming close counts. It counted with napalm too.

But not with gun runs. Those had to be on target. Even the superb twenty-millimeter canon Gatling gun on a Phantom jet fighter cannot kill what it does not hit. But for the rest, coming close counted, being on target was better, but coming close was good too.

After returning from Viet Nam I talked to friends who had been with the Big Red One (1st Infantry Division), and the 1st Air Cavalry Division and they talked of sometimes waiting for air support, sometimes for hours. I never waited.

More often than not, and particularly during Tet '68, my United States Air Force was already overhead, waiting to rain death and destruction on anyone I asked, any where, any time, all day, everyday. I am Airborne. I pull risers, and I pulled KP before OCS. Apparently I also had pull with the United States Air Force. Huah!

The Phantoms were dropping very accurate 750 pound, hi-drag, high explosive bombs mainly, sometimes they had 500 pound "*slick*" bombs, dropped in pairs, or napalm droppable in singles and in pairs, and all that day I remember hearing a calm voice on the radio asking me, what I wanted, where I needed it, to kill those sons of bitches that were trying to kill me and my men. Where exactly did I want violence, death and destruction delivered this time?

The NVA were shooting at us. That is how we found out where they were hiding. They would shoot at us. Helpful little bastards.

How close could we take it this time? Particularly as it ran later in that day, that was the over-riding question. However, that day I could take it very close indeed. The NVA called it *"hugging the enemy."* They tried to get so close to us that we would not risk a bomb missing them and hitting us.

They did not know my United States Air Force, or me. That day I called 750 pound bombs in so close the pilots delivering them often were in danger of planting their fighter planes along with their bombs.

"Danger close—U. S." The fighter pilots could see my colored smoke that marked my platoon's position. They knew that their bombs could skip. They knew even if it went in true, it might not hit exactly where it was aimed. The fighter pilots could see what their 35 foot + bomb crater would encompass on the ground.

Seeing this, they elected to risk themselves and their aircraft rather than drop one on us even by accident. *"Danger close—U. S."* that day meant danger for the United States Air Force and for the NVA, but not for those of us Airborne Infantry on the ground. We had friends in high places.

There would be no *"friendly fire"* casualties from these pilots. They would fly their very expensive planes straight into the dirt first. Some of the high drag bombs they dropped for me that day did not have even enough time in the air to arm before they hit. They flew them in that close. They flew them in that careful. They flew their runs in low and slow, and they were being shot at all the time.

I think they knew it even though the FAC did not tell them. Something about the constant patter of bullets on their armor plating and the bullet holes in their wings, through their self sealing fuel tanks, probably gave it away, but still they came—low, slow, steady and accurate.

155

And, you wonder why I love them?

Finally, it was late afternoon. I had tried everything I knew. I had bombed them beautifully, repeatedly and beautifully.

A beautiful bomb is one that destroys, completely obliterates, turns to dust and smoke a concrete block house that is about 35 feet away from where you are. A beautiful strike means that the bomb crater's edge is still about 20-25 feet away. Beautiful is where the bomb strike is so close, so precise that it only blew the roof off of the house we were in while it destroyed the target house next door, and maybe even just a little bit of the front porch of our house, as well as that disappeared roof. Beautiful is when your nose bleeds from the concussion. When your ears bleed from the concussion. When you taste blood in your mouth from the burst capillaries in your tongue caused by the concussion; but you have none of those pesky pieces of red-hot metal in your body. Beautiful is when the pink haze you see is from the burst veins in your eyes from concussion, not from your own blood spraying on the ground in bright red arterial splendor. Beautiful is when it works.

And, then you tell them to do it again. Just like that. Maybe this time, a little closer please, but do it just like that.

"Do it again, just like that."

"One more time, please."

"Next house please."

"Beautiful."

156

"Thanks."

It is close when napalm flares off in the front yard of the house we were in instead of inside the house next door—but it was only about 10 or 20 feet short of where I had wanted it, and it was delivered at about 400 miles an hour. The FAC would not allow me any more napalm for a while that day— he had finally realized that I had a lot more confidence in his pilots than he did.

That napalm strike in my front yard had really scared him. It was so hot. It was beautiful. Most of it was in the other yard where some of the bunkers were.

I was satisfied. It had been beautiful, a little warm, but really beautiful. Man that crap can burn.

And, you wonder why I loved them?

Finally, I could not think of any thing else to do. So, I took off my pack and everything else until all I had on me was my clothes, M-16 rifle, ammunition, cigarettes and water, two canteens. It would be stupid to order my platoon to attack. They would be killed for no purpose. So I couldn't do that. But, I could go get Smith myself. I could probably do that I thought. I had to try. All day we had bombed, blasted, burned and shot the enemy. All day, and all I really wanted was to get Smith back.

It was the only thing that I could think of that I had not yet tried. Just go get him myself. I looked it over again. I had to run out the front door of the house I was in and across the front yard. In the front yard of my house there was a pile of hay and then a small tree to the right, and then a gate in the fence around the front yard a little further still. The napalm had burned

157

off most of the grass in the yard, but the pile of hay was still there. It was probably three or four feet or so high and about five or six feet around. It would shelter me as I ran?

Of course, it hadn't helped Schultz. He was lying beside me in the house with a sucking chest wound, periodically I would tell him to breathe, to just shut-up and breathe. The medic, John Melgaard told him the same thing. I don't know why wounded men want to talk sometimes, but some do. Schultz had been returning fire from the front yard when they shot him in the chest.

Smith was really tall, but he was a skinny kid and did not weigh much over a couple of hundred pounds. Christ he didn't even weigh as much as Schultz had, I thought. I could pick Smith up, carry him and run back. At least that was the plan.

If I was going to go, now was the time, the house to our left that had been full of NVA was completely gone. The United States Air Force had disappeared it along with part of our roof. The houses and bunkers across the large rice paddy in front of my house were gone too. Beautiful, well placed, craters had replaced them.

Of course, there were still an unknown number of NVA in the house that Smith was on the porch of, but I did not need to go inside that house. It was not a visit. I just wanted to get Smith off the porch.

There were still bunkers in the tree line to the right, 200 yards or so past the house that Smith was on the porch of, but not as many as before and they did not like shooting at me as much as they had at first, earlier in the day. It seems that I didn't play fair. Every time they shot at my platoon I called my big brother, the United States Air Force. If I could identify a target, my brothers in sky blue made it go away. Beautiful is great. Fair play is over rated.

I ran out the door, across the porch, past the pile of hay, to the gate. I had forgotten about needing to open the gate. I went through the gate. I really do not remember how. Maybe I just jumped it. I don't know. Although there were a lot flying around, no bullet hit me. That was good, and I was out of the front yard into the rice paddy. That was better than Schultz had done and Schultz was a good man. All in all, I was about forty or fifty feet closer to Smith, and I was not wounded yet. My plan was working.

I laid down behind the rice paddy dike on the other side of the gate. I had to go out the front door of our house, then through the front gate because there were three barbed wire fences between our house and the house next door that Smith was in. Unless I went out our front door, down to the gate, then down the rice paddy dike, back in another gate to the house next door, up the steps, pick up Smith and return, I would have to deal with all of that barbed wire. I did not think I could make it to Smith and back if I had to deal with the barbed wire too.

It really was a simple problem, except for the barbed wire, the machine-gun fire, rockets, mortars, rifle fire, and so forth. Going out of the gate did make it a little longer than a direct run to Smith's porch. There was that trade-off for no barbed wire— it was longer to go to get to Smith, but that way there were gates in the wire.

So, I got down and low crawled with the paddy dike on my right. It was pretty straightforward. The dike was almost as high as my helmet and I would be behind it from one gate to the other. Most of the NVA, and all of the NVA that were the closest to me, were on the other side of that dike. The dike looked like it could stop bullets. Until I got to the gate in front of

Smith's house the dike would protect me. Then, run up to the porch; grab him and run back. That was my whole plan.

The first surprise was when the paddy dike made a sharp right angle turn. I hadn't been able to see the turn from my house because of the pile of hay and the tree. But, looking at it, I would only be exposed for about five feet, then it turned back to the left again. So, I just made that turn right with it. I hugged that dike. It is surprising how flexible the human body can be when it has a really good reason.

I wrapped tight around that turn low crawling, and I must have been a little more than halfway around the turn, when the machine-gun opened fire on me. He had me right in his sights and because of that turn I had no protection at all. He was in a second floor window above Smith. My guys could not even see him. They shot at him of course, but their bullets thudded on a concrete wall.

Unfortunately, there was nothing at all between that machine-gun and me except my fatigue shirt. All of the others who had been shooting at me from the tree line beyond Smith's house hadn't worried me much, for them I was a small target beside or even a little behind the dike and my guys could and were shooting at them. They didn't worry me—but that machine-gun worried me plenty. I was right in the middle of his beaten zone, the cone of violence. Not good. Not beautiful at all.

A machine-gun is very different from a rifle. If a machine-gun operated the same as a rifle, the bullets would all go in pretty much the same hole. While you would be sure that your target was dead, it would only be the one dead target and that is not useful with so many bullets going out the barrel. So a machine-gun is designed to produce what is called a "cone of violence."

The cone of violence is most apparent between 500 and 1000 yards. This is the optimum range for a machine-gun like the one that was shooting at me. There will be a large oval made by the machine-gun bullets as they strike the ground, and within that oval, called the beaten zone, bullets will strike; again and again, bullets will strike.

I was in that cone of violence. I was right in the middle of that oval, the beaten zone, where all the bullets strike. All around me, I could feel bullets striking. Bullets tugged at my clothes, my equipment. At my waist, and lower, I could feel something warm, and wet. A bullet struck my rifle and my left hand was suddenly numb, and then it hurt, a lot. I could feel something striking between my legs. The warm, wet feeling was spreading, lower. Not a good sign at all.

I laid there. He shot at me. I laid there. He kept shooting at me. I did not move; not even a twitch. It seemed to go on for a long time.

When he stopped shooting, I went backwards. Up till then I did not know that you could low crawl backwards, and low crawl tight around a corner backwards—but you can. At least I can. Apparently you do not need training to do it, only motivation.

I did not stop low crawling backward until I was back to the pile of hay. But that is a guess because I really do not remember anymore than what I have told you between making the turn around the dike, laying in the machine-gun's cone of violence, and then returning to that big pile of hay inside the gate.

I laid back against the pile of hay. I remember that. It was soft, comfortable. I remember the sun above; it was hot that day. I remember the exquisite powder blue of the cloudless tropical sky, but not much about how I got back to the pile of hay. That little fact escaped me then, and now.

The flash suppressor and other less essential parts had been shot off of my rifle. I would need a new rifle. One of my two canteens had bullet holes in it, and it was empty. I would need a new canteen. I took a long lukewarm drink from my other canteen and lit a cigarette, an unfiltered *Pall Mall*.

Dying from cancer did not worry me. As a rifle platoon leader I knew there was no way I was going to live long enough to catch cancer. I took my helmet off, set it beside me and took a deep drag on the cigarette, feeling the raw smoke filling my lungs.

There were bullet holes in my pants, my shirt, my rifle, one canteen and canteen cover, but not one in me that I could see. The warm water from one canteen had run down my left side and then between my legs but that was it.

However, I had already been wounded often enough by then to know that many times in combat you are so hyped that you do not realize that you have been wounded; so I looked for blood, or piss or something else the body leaks when it has holes. Bullets going through always make a body leak something. I looked for holes and blood, and for smoke coming out in places it should not. I waited for the pain, but physical pain never came. He had missed me. Wow, did he have a bad day!

As I lay on the side of the pile of hay, Michael Trant called out to me to tell me that Smith was not moving any more. I said: "*OK*." And, I took another drag on that wonderful cigarette. Just for that moment, I withdrew from the war. Just for that moment, I went away. I was just smoking a cigarette, looking at that wonderful blue sky. I was not at war with anyone. But, I was still absolutely enraged.

It was right at dusk, after this vicious daylong battle when I returned to the Company headquarters that Captain Tom Gaffney had set up next to a hedgerow about a mile and a half away from the two houses I had been fighting in, or next to, all day.

My friend and Platoon Sergeant James Bunn had been killed earlier that day trying to get in the back of Smith's house, as had several others, along with Smith. We had also suffered a lot of wounded, including Schultz, the men who brought him back, and me. I sat down and began to tell Tom what had happened, when I reached the part where I had tried to low-crawl, using the rice paddy dike as partial cover, to the porch where Smith was lying, bleeding and dying; and had been driven back by machine gun fire my RTO (Radio Telephone Operator), Hal Dobie, who had seen it from the small house, said:

> "He did sir. He was right in the middle of the fucken beaten zone. There were bullets hitting all over him. I thought he was dea. . ."

But, Tom interrupted him, and very quietly, almost gently said to Hal:

> "Let the Lieutenant make his report. He has a right to make his own report."

Few people ever saw the gentle side of Tom Gaffney—but he had one. At the end of my report, I told Tom that as soon as we were set up for the night, I was going back for the men that we had left behind when we were ordered to withdraw. I did not ask. I did not suggest. I told him what I was going to do.

Those that know Tom might have expected him to be angry at this brashness by one holding the lowest officer rank in the entire United States Army. However, Tom's reply was:

"I'll ask the other two platoons for volunteers. Take as many as you need with you."

Those were A Company men out there, and Tom wanted them all back just as much as I did. One of us had to go back for them, and since two of the three were my men it should be me that brought them back. Tom would not order me to do it, nor even suggest it to me, but he had taught me. And, it needed doing, we both knew it.

So, I went back again for Smith later that night. I had a new rifle, it had just a little of someone else's blood on it but it worked, a new canteen and some help. Sergeant Ron Ford was the assistant patrol leader.

Later, when I tried to put him and the others in the night patrol in for a decoration after the day long battle, followed by the night patrol back to that battlefield, the brass in the rear said that we had already used up our allotment of decorations for the month and to try again another time.

Right, all used up on the second day of the month.

Before the night patrol left, Company A had holed up for the night in a defensive position with Bravo company from the 3rd Battalion, and some of them also volunteered to go on that night patrol as well. I bet some of the Air Force guys would have gone too, but they had done enough that day. Now it was time for the Infantry to go to work, to do what we did better than anybody; night work, in close, always bloody. In a very real way I was looking forward to it. Beautiful is fine, but we were ready to close with, and destroy the enemy.

We had to fight our way into that fucking house. Again they mortared us and they rocketed us; and they just kept shooting at us on the way getting into the house and all the way back. But it was dark, and the Infantry can use the dark. We can work in the dark. We were back in a target rich environment again; but we owned the dark.

There were only a few more than a dozen men in the patrol, all 101st Airborne Division paras—the best in the world. They were all I needed and we went where 300, two Airborne rifle companies, could not go in daylight. We went in; we found our men, all of our men; we took them back; we brought them home. Nobody stopped us. Nobody.

We brought Smith and Bunn and one other home that night. I walked second going, and point coming back because everyone else was helping carry a body on the way back. We had to fight our way through snipers and mortar fire most of the way back, and part of the way there. We only put them down to fight.

I was back in the war. I knew the rules of combat but I also knew that sometimes, for some things, only luck will work, nothing else. For example, nothing is supposed to be able to survive in a machine-gun's cone of violence—nothing. I knew that. It is one of the most reliable rules of combat. If you have a target in the beaten zone, even a six to twelve round burst will kill him—every time.

The Army had taught me that rule but it also said that a good machine gunner always does it twice, two bursts to be certain. Now, I had seen the first rule fail. Personally, I thought it really good timing for the Army to be wrong.

It seems that I am now living proof that even an overly long first burst will not always make up for the total lack of a second burst from a machine-gun. Or, it was luck. My guess is; it was just not my day to die.

That was how my February 2nd, 1968 was. How was yours? My friends, Platoon Sergeant James Albert Bunn, and PFC John Smith, spent an infantry soldier's day at work—their last. Specialist George Schultz died a month later. The doctors had re-inflated Schultz's collapsed lung and fixed the damage the AK-47 bullet had caused when it tore through his chest, but he caught an infection in the hospital in Japan, and it killed him.

Smith was nineteen, Schultz was eighteen and Jim Bunn was thirty-two. They were my friends, and my responsibility. I think about them every day, but I will not see them again in this world.

Airborne!

* Smith is not his real name. All of the rest of the names are real.

Thirteen

The battle of February 2, 1968, near Phan Thiet, made a profound effect on everyone that was there that day. Four Currahees died there that day—Guy Franklin,19, of Pasco, Washington, SFC James Albert Bunn, 32, of Miami, Florida, MSg Phillip R. Chassion, 34, of Fritchburg, Massachusetts and PFC John Smith. Several more had been wounded, some severely.

As noted before, George Schultz later died from his wounds in a hospital in Japan. He was the only man that we got out alive, that later died. That was how good the medics and the doctors were. That was how dedicated the Dust-Off pilots and crews were to coming in, regardless of ground fire to pick up our wounded. They knew how important speed was.

We had pulled back into a 360° perimeter that night. Right in the middle of that perimeter when we woke up were the bodies of three of our friends waiting to be extracted. They were tightly wrapped in dark green ponchos laying next to the company CP in the center of the perimeter.

I had been lightly wounded on 2/2/68, either a bullet or a piece of shrapnel had clipped my left ear. It stopped bleeding after a while on its own. Early on 2/3/68 as we moved back up to the blue house I got hit again. This time it was on the thigh of my left leg by a piece of M-79 shrapnel that I think bounced off after it hit me.

This time I had our medic, John Melgaard, bandage it. There was a big bruise, and a little hole not much blood. I could still walk pretty much all right.

Only a little later, again during a house entry, I was again hit by M-79 shrapnel, this time in my left arm. That one went in deep, and it is still there today.

We were not playing games as we moved back to the blue house that next morning. We had an interpreter with us. When we got to a house on the way, he would call out in Vietnamese for anybody inside to come put with their hands in the air. If some body came out fine, we would send them back to the Company CP.

If nobody came out we entered each house hard. We called it going in like John Wayne. Most times that meant an M-79 round or two fired inside the house as the entry team approached the door. Accidentally hitting a bar in a window with an M-79 round, rather than blowing up inside a house was what had put that piece of shrapnel into my arm. I don't know where the one that hit my leg came from.

Some of the guys got on the M-79 gunner about hitting me, but I told them to lay off. After all I had ordered him to fire the round. I knew he was new as a grenadier. If it was anybody's fault that I got hit, it was clearly mine.

The M-79 rounds sent in first would often be followed by a hand grenade or two, followed closely by a high/low entry team. One guy goes high, spraying the room with his M-16 on full auto, while another guy rolls in low and actually enters first as the high-guy fires. At the same the rest of the squad surrounds the house covering all of the windows and doors.

It is actually really neat to watch professional, veteran, Infantry work, covering each other, covering the potential enemy, constantly moving.
In a way it's lot like a ballet—a very violent ballet with guns, and bullets, and explosions, all very, very close. When you are fighting at seven feet,

somebody is going to die every time. There is no margin for error when you are fighting house to house.

After the second M-79 shrapnel hit I think Melgaard called Gaffney and asked him to order me from the field for medical treatment. The one in my left arm was in pretty deep and it was bleeding through Melgaard's bandage running down my arm. My left arm also did not work too good after a while as it stiffened up and that continued for a couple days after being hit. The pain both restricted and slowed my arm's movement down. Since I am left handed that was kind of important too, particularly if I wanted to shoot.

My real weapons though were the radio, and my whistle. That is what makes a platoon leader dangerous. Shooting, which was all that I couldn't do very well for a while, was always secondary. Gaffney agreed with me, so I stayed in the field until the evening of the third of February.

This one is the beginning of the story of that following day, 2/3/68 when we began to realize all that had happened during that long, awful, violent day, the day before. This was right before we went back to the blue house for the third time.

The Morning After, The Night Before

"I knew Sgt. Chassion quite well. His death turned me off from the idea of re-enlisting. He was a real career soldier...very much like my Dad. His death and a few others instilled some deep seated anger issues. That made the war personal."

"I get the full weight of the Bunn chocolate...a piece that connected you to his life. Thanks for sharing"

"It helps to know that these men are not forgotten... as long as we live."

Al Thompson, Combat Medic
Company A, 3/506th Abn. Inf. 101st Airborne
March 20, 2016 at 9:40 pm

Have you ever felt like you just don't care anymore? I have. I felt exactly like that on February 3, 1968. That was the day after I had watched Smith die.

The last time I had eaten anything had been at least 24 hours before. That was also the last time that I drank anything except lukewarm water from a plastic canteen.

It was dawn again. I had had maybe an hour of sleep after getting back late the night before. Now, it was already dawn again. Yet another hot, clear, sunny, day near the coast of the South China Sea in beautiful, but violent, South Vietnam near Phan Thiet.

I was tired, but most of all that morning, I did not want to go over the Company CP. There were three bodies at the CP, all neatly lined up in a row, each wrapped tightly in a dark O-D green poncho now.

We had brought them in the night before, or more accurately earlier that same morning. I did not want to see them again. Not that way, I did not want to look at them. I wanted to remember them how they had been; how they had been before, not the way they were now.

So, I rubbed the sleep out of my bloodshot eyes and started to make some real Army cocoa the way my Platoon Sergeant, Jim Bunn had taught me. Take one canteen cup about three quarters full of water, put it on a homemade, little stove over a heat tab, add two packs of cocoa, four packs of powdered coffee, three packs of powdered creme and two sugars.

Actually, Jim usually used at least three or sometimes even four sugars, but that made it way too sweet for me.

Before I added the first of the packets to the water, I took the white plastic spoon out of the pen slot in my fatigue shirt so I could stir them into the water that I had already started heating up in my canteen cup with the heat tab. As I did that, I looked around the perimeter for the first time that morning.

Our Company Commander that day was Tom Gaffney. His first war had been in Korea. There he had endured human wave attacks by both the North Koreans and the Chinese. You don't forget that. So, when Tom Gaffney picked a night defensive position it always, and I mean it always, had good visibility in every direction. If you wanted visibility, you could not do better than where we were set up right then. We were arranged around the inside of a dry rice paddy, in the middle of a huge field of dry rice paddies. We had great fields of fire and good visibility in every direction. It was a true, a perfect Tom Gaffney night defensive position.

Alpha Company had the southern half of the perimeter and Bill Landgraff's Bravo Company had the northern half. However, I had no doubt that Tom Gaffney had picked the site all by himself. It had his ideas of how to fight a war written all over it.

Captain Landgraff's company had come in late in the afternoon the day before to reinforce us, and then had stayed with us later in the night defensive position. We had trained together in the states, so we knew that they were good too, but Tom Gaffney had picked our position. In my military mind, there was no doubt of that at all.

The dinks started shooting at us right about then, just about when I had finished looking around the perimeter was when first bullets flew. It was probably some of the same guys that had followed us back from the Blue House the night before. While it was automatic fire, it was probably all just AK-47s, not real machine-guns so they had to stop now and then to reload. There were at least two of them, and probably three, firing from somewhere in a tree line several hundred yards to our north.

The guys from Bravo Company returned fire immediately. The guys from Alpha Company jumped over the rice paddy dike we were behind on the southern half of the perimeter to put it between them and the incoming bullets from the north. Alpha Company did not return fire since we would have been shooting directly over Bravo Company.

People who have never been shot at do not know what it means to be shot at, to have an excellent weapon in your hands, plenty of ammunition, but to elect not to return that fire because firing back might endanger your friends. That is real discipline. These paras were all pros. Both Bravo and Alpha companies, 3/506, 101st Airborne Division, aka, the Bastard Battalion. All of us flat knew our business of war by then.

Everybody on the south side of the perimeter had jumped over the paddy dike, all except me. I stayed inside the original perimeter beside my little tin stove that was still heating my Jim Bunn cocoa. I did lay down, and I did put my helmet on.

I figured that Bravo Company could fight this battle for me. I was done fighting for a while. I had had enough of war right then. I was tired. I was thirsty for that cocoa and I had used my last heat tablet to heat it. I was not going to let it go to waste just to sit safe on the other side of that dike and watch my Jim Bunn cocoa sit on my stove and grow cold. Being a little safer was not worth more than that cocoa was to me right then. I had thought that I didn't care anymore, but I found I did care. I cared about that cocoa.

Besides, at first most of the bullets weren't coming that close.

From the other side of the dike, I think it was John Melgaard, my medic, that asked me if I was hit. I told him "*No*", I was fine. I was just waiting there for my cocoa to heat up. No need for anybody to worry about me. I was fine, perfect.

There were little puffs of dust springing up all over the middle of the perimeter. Each one was a bullet strike. However, the VC were just pretty much spraying their weapons when they fired, not aiming them like we would have. At first, it looked like they were trying to hit the three bodies wrapped in ponchos in the center. At least that was where most of their bullets were going.

The only things left inside the perimeter were Bravo Company, spread out, but staying covered, close behind their dike on the north side as they returned fire, the three bodies wrapped up tight in ponchos laying out in the open in the center of the perimeter. And then there was me, laying down, sort of on the south side, waiting for my cocoa to finish heating.

Even with all of the return fire that Bravo Company was putting out, the VC were still firing back steadily from that tree line to the north. When the VC finished firing up the three ponchos I could see that they were now trying for me. It was getting to be, time to go.

Just for a minute though, laying there, I actually felt a little sorry for the VC or NVA or whoever it was that was shooting at us. They did not know Tom Gaffney like I did, but I knew that they would, and soon.

After they had started firing, it only took about a minute or so until my Jim Bunn cocoa was finished heating. When it was, I grabbed it and my rifle and joined my platoon on the other side of the dike. That was the safer side of the southern rice paddy dike of our perimeter. I looked up, back over the dike, carefully sipped my hot cocoa, and waited for the Tom Gaffney show to begin.

I did not have long to wait, right after I looked back over the dike, came the first artillery explosions along that tree line to the north. Tom had registered the artillery on the tree line the night before while we were gone on a night patrol to retrieve the three bodies of our friends. Tom almost always registered artillery before going to sleep. For him, it was sort of like; wait till dusk turned out most of the light, drop a few artillery smoke shells to

174

register the guns, wait as the rest of the light turns out and then sleep well. Sleep like a baby even.

So there were no ranging shots to acquire their target that morning; it started as airbursts, probably at least a battery six of airbursts. A battery six means that each cannon in the battery is fired as fast as possible six times in a row.

There are six cannons in a battery. Each 105 mm shell weighs almost 20 pounds and is stuffed full of cyclonite (RDX), T-N-T, or 50-50 T-N-T mixed with Amatol, with the explosive comprising about one half the weight of the shell. That means about 720 pounds of high explosives and steel shards of shrapnel were raining down on the VC, creating Hell on earth in that tree line.

Good morning Vietnam!

It started sort of like the biggest 4th of July celebration ever, but then it got even more serious as our Forward Observer, Bob Richardson, walked those artillery strikes up and down that tree line, airbursts mixed now with ground bursts.

Thunderous noise, billowing smoke and red fire, schooling the VC on the awesome power and accuracy of American artillery. Bob played that tree line with artillery strikes like Ringo Starr played the drums for the Beatles— he played it hard and he played it well.

Steel rain—how do you like it now?

By the time Bob Richardson had walked the artillery up and down the tree line a couple of times, gunships arrived from the 192nd Assault Helicopter

Company at LZ Betty. *Tiger Shark Lead* was on the horn asking Tom for targeting information. They were on station, ready to come in hot when the artillery was done tearing the place up.

As I laid there, watching the fireworks show and sipping my cocoa, I thought that it was a shame that Jim Bunn couldn't see it too. It was truly a remarkable performance by our Artillery Forward Observer, Bob Richardson. Stunningly beautiful really, as well as massively violent. Soon we would even have the rockets red glare from the two Tiger Shark gunships joining in as well.

Like me and Tom Gaffney, Jim Bunn loved American artillery. We all loved gunships too. Gunship pilots are almost as crazy as Dustoff pilots, and with all that ordnance on board, they are much more fun to watch. Bunn and his two buddies, Phillip Chassion and John Smith had the best seats in the house, but the ponchos they were wrapped in blocked their view—forever.

SFC James Albert Bunn, Photo by Jerry Berry, 3/506th PIO.

Fourteen

The Battle of Tet '68 came in multiple waves. In between the waves, we searched for Charlie, and sometimes found him among the ruins of Phan Thiet, and sometimes we found him in the surrounding area. One day we took back five towns well North of Phan Thiet. We were poised on the outskirts of the sixth town getting ready to go in when we were pulled back to our base camp at LZ Betty situated on a bluff overlooking the South China Sea near Phan Thiet.

Tom Gaffney said they were pulling us out because they could not find the topographic maps for the area we were in. That meant that without maps we could not call in artillery fire support for help. Artillery was our first trump card in the fight with Charlie, air support was the second. A lack of maps made both unlikely.

As we waiting to leave together on the last ship, of the last chopper lift out, I said to Tom:

"Well, we took back six towns today."

Tom in his usual dry, way replied.

"No John, we took back five towns, and only visited the sixth."

As usual, he was correct, and precise.

The second wave of Tet '68 hit us hard on February 18, 1968 and continued for a little more than a week thereafter. It was was much bigger, much more violent in Phan Thiet and its environs than just about anywhere else in South Vietnam. General Vo N. Giap wanted Phan Thiet because apparently Ho Chi Minh wanted Phan Thiet. Other than Ho Chi Minh had once lived there we never did learn why they wanted Phan Thiet so badly, but they did.

For whatever reason, things just kept happening in and around Phan Thiet on a regular basis that year. As the story notes, we even named part of the area around Phan Thiet "*Disneyland*" because it seemed that Charlie came there to play "*Infantry At War*" with us regularly.

This one is Infantry humor about that time. If you are Infantry, you will nod and laugh as you read it. If you are not Infantry, you will probably forever wonder where the humor is in this story.

It's there. If you look for it.

On Staying Alive by Being Inept

"I was a medic assigned to the aid station at the base camp at Phan Thiet. Dust off would bring us the casualties so we could stabilize them for transport on to a field hospital or mash unit. I got there about a month after the ammo dump was hit with incoming fire and exploded. My worst memories of Phan Thiet was of carrying body bags to Graves Registration. Even as an immature 18 year old soldier who thought he was bullet proof, I had this solemn feeling of finality and knew that someone would soon be grief stricken by this loss. I have long denied that I was affected by PTSD, I saw way too many that suffered so much more than I ever would. A fellow Vietnam Nam vet and I were sharing stories recently, he is 100% disabled. As our conversation ended, he asked me, "how many body bags does an 18 year old have to carry to get PTSD" ? Now I began to understand why we did not all come home."

Thomas Ewell
3rd Battalion (ABN) 506th Infantry

It happened in 1968, the bloodiest year of a long, bloody war. Alpha Company had just been resupplied with ammunition after yet another firefight. It was still Tet '68. We were moving across a wide expanse of rice paddies dotted with small groups of mud and wattle houses with thatched roofs in the Disneyland area near Phan Thiet, RVN, aka the place where the Infantry plays. That day, Disneyland had a lesson in humility waiting for me.

179

It was late morning that day, but it was already brutally hot. As usual, the 2nd Platoon had the point for Alpha Company.

Just after the point left a group of huts, a hand grenade exploded behind me, and a fountain of water shot up into the sky. Someone had dropped a hand grenade down a well next to the rice paddy. It created a cooling shower if you were standing on the side where some of the water came down. You also got rid of a hand grenade.

2nd Plat. A Co. on search and destroy operation

These guys were pros. Left handed rifleman standing to the right of the door. M-60 centered, ready to sweep the room. That is a squad leader to the right, Sgt. Harvey Mathis. Everybody ready all the time. Photo by Jerry Berry, 3/506th PIO.

The next thing that happened was that my RTO (Radio Telephone Operator) Hal Dobie handed me the PRC-25, radio handset and said simply:

"6"

Meaning that Alpha 6, or the Company Commander of Alpha Company, Tom Gaffney was on the horn and wanted to talk to me.

"This is 2-6. Go ahead." I said.

Meaning this is the 2nd Platoon, Platoon Leader. We had recently switched from using *"Over"* to using *"Go ahead"* and then *"Go"* as radio pro words probably because we thought it sounded cooler.

"This is 6, what do you have? Go." asked Gaffney.

"2-6. Nothing. Just one of the guys getting rid of an excess hand grenade from the resupply. I'll stop it. Go." I replied.

But for having to answer the radio, I already would have been doing exactly that.

"No. We felt something back here in the ground when the hand grenade went off. There may be a tunnel. Check it out. Go." Gaffney said.

"Roger. Out."

I went back to the well, just a four foot or so wide hole in the ground lined with rock and looked down it. When I asked for a hand grenade I had several offers. The M-26 hand grenade that we used weighed exactly a pound each and was rarely used except in very close combat. This meant, once you were issued one, you would be carrying it for a while. We had just been resupplied and they sent out too many hand grenades so a lot of guys wanted to get shed of the extra weight.

181

That little hand grenade weighed the same as half a canteen of water. As hot as it was, we needed the water; the grenades, not so much right then. Troops in the field are very practical about the weight they carry. If it is useful, it almost does not matter how much it weighs. If it is not useful, it does not matter how little it weighs.

Hand grenades are also just plain dangerous to be around. One company commander, and all of that company's medics had been wounded a month or so before when the pin on a hand grenade, which had been badly rusted from months in the field, sheared off and the grenade exploded in the company CP (Command Post) during a medics meeting.

Disasters like that were happening so often that a new order came down from division soon after requiring that all hand grenades be carried inside a canteen cover rather than on the webbing.

I took one of the many offered hand grenades; pulled the pin; let the spoon fly, and dropped it down the well as I stepped a little way back from the edge. In four point five seconds exactly, the grenade went off; a tower of water emerged from the well and then most of it splashed back down into the well.

I went over and looked down the well. Just to the left of where I was standing and about seven or eight feet down I could now see the top of a round hole in the side of the well's wall. It was about three feet in diameter and looked a lot like a tunnel to me. I asked for another hand grenade and again received several offers. I took one, pulled the pin, popped the spoon and tried to toss it into the round hole in the side of the well but it missed the hole entirely. It bounced off and landed in the water below.

Four point five seconds later, it went bang, large water plume. Then, I walked over to the side of the well and looked down again.

This time I saw an entire circle in the side of the well and it looked even more like a tunnel entrance. I took another grenade and leaned out over the well. I wanted to stay on my feet because I wanted to be able to move back from the edge quickly. After all, a grenade was going to explode. I wanted to be no where near that. This time I was even more careful with my toss, but the grenade hit something metal sounding inside the hole, bounced out and blew up in the water in the bottom of the well just like the first three hand grenades.

Since they now knew where the water going to splash, more of my guys managed to get wet from the spray each time I dropped a hand grenade. While they maintained the perimeter around the well, some rotated in each time for the spray.

This time I lay down on the side of the top of the well to try to look into the hole. I planned to try to lean down, toss in the grenade, and then just roll away from the well. I had even already pulled the pin from the hand grenade.

Then, for the first time I saw the bent, grey, metal fins in the hole. Like everyone, I had heard the old expression: *"My heart stopped."* Now I experienced that feeling as well. However, I would have described it as more like someone dropping a solid concrete block right on my chest from about ten or twelve feet above me. I kept a death grip on that hand grenade's spoon.

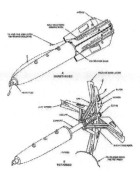

Now that the repeated water plumes had washed out the entrance to the tunnel, I could see the bent back fins, clearly. I could see the fins of what looked very much like the fins on a 750 pound, High Drag, United States Air Force, bomb. Clutching that hand grenade tightly, I rolled away from the edge of the well.

"Get back!" I yelled and kept right on rolling away from the edge of that well as fast as I could roll.

With a High Drag bomb, when the plane releases the bomb, the fins pop out. The fins do three things: they stabilize the bomb in flight; they slow the bomb down so the aircraft can get clear of the blast; and, they will only arm the bomb if the aircraft has enough time to get clear of the blast.

Since the bomb is more stable in flight because of the fins, it is more accurate. It can be dropped from the plane closer to the target because the fins delay the bomb's strike. The pilot can drop it more confidently because it will not go off unless he has time to get away from the blast. The disadvantage is, if the pilot drops it too close, it leaves the bomb there

184

unexploded giving the enemy a lot of free high explosive for their own improvised explosive devices.

When I was twenty or so feet away from the well I sat up and carefully put the pin back in the hand grenade. I took my time and cautiously bent the pin ends back to secure the pin in its hole.

I was really proud that my hands were not shaking—surprised me too. I think they did not know how scared I was.

Probably only my own natural ineptness as a tosser of hand grenades had saved my life and the lives of most of my men. An Air Force 750 pound bomb blast produces a crater of about 35 feet in width. Most of my platoon had been standing within a 35-foot wide circle around that well and of course shrapnel keeps going for a long way well beyond that.

If one of the hand grenades had stayed in that tunnel; if it had rolled down, past those bent fins, closer to the explosive in the bomb; if it had set off the bomb, we would have all literally become an emulsified mess of blood, flesh and small bits of shattered bone.

They spent about a week in OCS (Officer Candidate School) showing us the many ways to set off explosives. One of the best and most often used ways to set off an explosive is called sympathetic detonation. You just set off an explosion as close to another explosive as you can, and the first explosive blowing up will set off the second one as well.

In a way, that is what a blasting cap does. You slide the cap into the explosive, or sometimes you place it beside the explosive and when the cap explodes, it also sets off the main explosive. When engineers rig multiple explosives to blow, they use sympathetic detonation to set them off, usually with Det-Cord, sort of a thick rope made entirely of high explosive.

One example of sympathetic detonation that I had seen recently was watching the engineers throw a hand grenade into a lot different explosives they had piled in a hollow tree, because they were out of C-4 plastic explosive, to blow that tree out of the way to create an LZ (Landing Zone). The effect was the same as placing the blasting cap into the explosive you wanted to set off. Being in a confined space, like in that hollow tree, or in a tunnel, made it even more likely for one explosive blast to set off another nearby explosive through sympathetic detonation.

It had been just dumb luck that I had missed the tunnel entirely with the first hand grenade that I threw at it, and that the second hand grenade had bounced off of the high drag fins that gave the bomb its accuracy and stability rather than going down the tunnel. I do not know if a one-pound hand grenade is enough to set off a 750 pound bomb, but in the right place, in the close quarters of a tight tunnel, it might be.

If other bombs had been dropped nearby, almost a certainty since this bomb had not exploded and the fighter pilot surely would have tried again, then the explosives in this 750 pound bomb had probably become unstable as well.

If that was true, then even a firecracker exploding nearby might set it off.

When we walked on, leaving the bomb to our engineers, I tried to give the hand grenade back to its owner, but no one would admit that it was theirs and I could not remember who gave me that one. I did not want to carry that hand grenade either. I kept wondering about all the bending of the pin? It was heavy too.

186

Soon after that, we heard the bomb go off. Naturally, the engineers had set it off by sympathetic detonation.

I had kept that grenade, but when we passed the next well, I pulled the pin and tossed it in.

Fifteen

This was just another day searching for Charlie. However, this time we were successful, very successful. A little prior, proper, truly professional, planning produced some very real results.

This turned out to be the last battle that was planned and fought by most of the original officers who had trained the 3/506th in the states and then brought it to Vietnam and to war. After we got back from Vietnam we acquired the nickname of "*boat people*" because most of the originals in the battalion, except for a small advance party, had all arrived in Vietnam by ship. These were the officers and men who had trained together specifically for this war, but then we were broken up after a little more than five months in country.

This premature change in leadership exemplified one of the major mistakes of the way the Vietnam War was actually fought on the ground, the constant, useless, rotation of combat leaders. When we had been in country less than five months of a one year tour of duty, the battalion commander, the battalion executive office and the S-3 or planning officer were all transferred to other units. Soon they were followed by the company commanders and then by the few remaining, unwounded and still alive, platoon leaders. Why?

The real reason, the only reason was that there were other officers, who solely to advance their personal careers needed some time in a combat position. They wanted those combat leadership positions to advance their careers. That was it. There was no other reason.

Combat effectiveness was sacrificed for ticket punching by the very officers who should have known better and who should have been the first ones that objected to the process. It should have been a scandal, a really big scandal but while some did speak out against this stupid system, it did not change.

Contrast this with World War II where the first leader of the 506th, who ultimately became a Lieutenant General, (three stars) was Robert Frederick Sink (April 3, 1905 – December 13, 1965). Then Colonel Sink, who commanded the 506th Infantry (Airborne) Regiment throughout World War II, was a career Army officer, but he turned down two promotions offered to him during the war in order to remain with the 506th.

Or, compare Richard Winters, who rose to fame commanding Easy Company, the famous original *Band of Brothers* from the Second Battalion of the 506th. Promoted to major, Dick Winters assumed command of the 2nd Battalion of the 506th during the war because Col. Sink and others in the 101st Airborne Division had resolutely refused green replacement officers, preferring instead to promote from within, thus rewarding the demonstrated competence of the original officers and keeping their hard earned, combat experience within the unit.

On the other hand during the Vietnam War the Army preferred to constantly role the dice with new, completely inexperienced, officers and NCOs shuffling in and out of leadership positions even in units engaged in active combat at the time of the change. Regardless of the combat situation, these new officers usually served only about for four months before they too were rotated as well. In general, that meant as soon as they had learned, or almost learned what they were doing, they were rotated out of their position and replaced by a new, green, officer.

There is no question, that this stupid system caused unnecessary casualties throughout the Vietnam War. There is also no question that the Army knew that, but elected to continue it.

However, before Geraci, Mairs and Gaffney left, there was this. . .

The Day The World Was on Line,
and
Tom and I Got Into Another Argument

"Good stuff! Consistently good stuff! My ass tightens up with suspense, then you want to take your eyeball out and I'm laughing."

Dennis McQuistion
Vietnam Veteran
November 6, 2016 at 7:33 pm

It was going to be big, really big, they said, but you never really know. You learn that early on in the military. Until it actually happens, you just never know.

While I have said that I was part of the 3rd Battalion, 506th Infantry (ABN), 101st Airborne Division, that does not tell the whole story of who we were. Our battalion of the 506th was actually the base unit for a much larger task force, our separate Airborne battalion, attached artillery, the 192nd Assault Helicopter Company and several other units, whose job generally was as the last reaction force for the entire II Corps in the middle of South Vietnam. First we were called, *Task Force 3/506th*, later the name was changed to *Task Force South*.

Our mission also included the protection of our base camp at LZ Betty, located near Phan Thiet, and of Phan Thiet city itself. Phan Thiet was both the province capitol, and the former home of Ho Chi Minh. During Tet '68 in particular, some called Phan Thiet "target central" because of the Ho Chi

Minh connection, and because of its central location on the map of Vietnam.

After several battles, we had first bloodily blunted and then crushed the VC/NVA attacks on and around Phan Thiet during Tet '68. While we had driven the attacking VC/NVA Mainforce battalions out of the town, there were still some large and small pockets of the enemy left all over the place in and around Phan Thiet.

Some VC/NVA were probably separated from their units by the intense fighting but some were intentional stay behinds trying to cause what havoc they could as they withdrew. We needed to get rid of them all.

Infantry urban renewal. This is Bravo Company, 3/506th (Abn) Infantry working its way through downtown Phan Thiet during Tet '68. This was destruction on a massive scale not seen since World War II. There is nothing worse for the Infantry than house to house fighting against a committed enemy. Unfortunately, we did a lot of it. Photo by Jerry Berry, 3/506th PIO.

Lt. Col. John P. Geraci, the battalion and Task Force 3/506th commander, was intent on eliminating these enemy pockets, all of them. So, he and Major Robert Mairs, the S-3 or planning officer on his staff, came up with the idea of a huge sweep along a rail line near Phan Thiet as one part of their plan to accomplish their goal.

The raised, rail line would anchor one flank of the line. To make sure it stayed anchored Bob Mairs put a quad .50 caliber machine gun, that's four .50 caliber Browning machine guns firing together, protected by steel, armor plates, and mounted on the back of a 2 1/2 ton truck, up on the train tracks driving backward so that the four, 50 cals had a clear field of fire. Each of the four, M-2, HB (heavy barrel) air-cooled, machine guns had a cyclical rate of fire of 450-575 rounds per minute. So, that's 1,800 to 2,300, .50 caliber rounds a minute tearing down range, and that truck carried a lot of ammunition.

Like all John Browning designed weapons, the M2, or "*Ma Deuce*" heavy machine gun is among the most reliable weapons in the Army's inventory. Trees don't stop those bullets, building walls do not deflect them. They tear their way through most anything including people. Wonderful stuff for the Infantry.

Note the rail line, the black line with slashes originating at the Ca Ty River above and then running first North, then North-West. Map photo by Jerry Berry, 3/506th PIO.

Then, next to the quad .50, came Alpha Company, the base company for the entire line. The line itself consisted of A, B and C companies of the 3/506th (Abn.) Infantry, and interspersed between the three American rifle companies were two large Mike Force Companies of Montagnard mercenaries, one was led by the Australian SAS (Special Air Service) and the other by American Green Berets. Finally, there was almost an entire battalion of ARVN mechanized infantry along with their tracked Armored Personnel Carriers (APCs) right behind them to anchor the right flank of the long line. Many of the ARVN, APCs were carrying .50 cal machine guns of their own.

In the middle of the line we had our two Dusters. Dusters are essentially twin 40 mm machine guns mounted on a World War II tank chassis. They could fire explosive rounds, a lot of explosive rounds very quickly. More great stuff for the big show.

There were Gunships and Dustoff choppers already in the air overhead and joining them even further above was a flight of F4 Phantom jets on station just waiting for that target that had to be destroyed immediately. We were all locked and loaded, and about as ready for anything as it was possible to be.

I called it *"the world on line"* and when it was set up that is exactly what it looked like.   There was a heavy, skirmish line of troops and armored vehicles that stretched as far as the eye could see.

Lt. Col. Geraci was overhead in his command and control helicopter in overall charge of everything. Tom Gaffney was the ground battalion commander of the 3/506th and I was running Alpha Company was the way it was set up. In fact Tom still ran the company, but I had 2nd Platoon as the base unit for the entire line.

There were thousands of troops on line that day.

That is Australian SAS on the left. The SAS always wore soft caps, never helmets. Note the Australian pack as well. Photo and caption above, by Jerry Berry, 3/506th PIO.

Since we had never done it before, it took a while to put the line together starting at first light, but then we began to move forward slowly. You have to be very careful in this kind of operation, the line was really long and if it bent at all, you could have friendlies firing on friendlies in a heart beat. It was part of my job to make sure that did not happen.

There was different terrain all along the line, and some parts of the line would be checking villages and hamlets as we moved along while the rest of the line might be in the middle of a huge rice paddy. So, I had to take all of that into account as I set the speed of the advance.

The line was just barely set up and moving when we drew the first fire. The Australian SAS team leader, a crusty, long service, Warrant Officer, came walking down the line through the fire to talk to me. He was short so he was standing up on the rice paddy dike as he pointed with his Australian, L1A1

Self-Loading Rifle, or as we knew it, the FN-FAL, 7.62 mm, assault rifle. His rifle was almost as big as he was.

"I say John. I think the bastards are over there. In that tree line, there. What do you think?" he said and pointed with his rifle.

I was sensibly laying down behind the thick rice paddy dike that he was standing on. He was actually standing right then on his tip toes on that dike to see where the fire was coming from. He pointed again with his rifle.

"Damn! That one was close. That fellow over there can shoot, don't you think?" he said looking down at me and smiling as another bullet cracked close on its way by.

I thought for a moment about just taking my right eye ball out of its socket and holding it up to look over the dike to where he pointed. When I have told people about that, they think I am kidding. I was not kidding. If it had been possible to do, and not too painful, I really think I would have taken it out.

There were a lot of bullets flying around. That fellow the Aussie was talking about could shoot and worse, he was getting our range. Even so, I stood up on the paddy dike next to the Aussie and looked to where he was pointing.

"I agree." I said to him as several more bullets cracked close to us as they too went by.

A very small part of the trees he was pointing at had moved a little when we were fired at. There was no wind. The old Warrant Officer, that meant he was probably in his late 30's early 40's, but that made him an old man to us. Even so, he still had a really good eye.

You can tell the really close ones because you only hear the bullets when they crack behind your head. Sometimes they would buzz too as they went by. You don't hear the ones that hit you at all.

The last two bullets had cracked way behind my head on their way by me. He was coming close, real close. It seemed that the two of us, standing together, was a better, certainly a much bigger, and therefore a much more attractive target than my little Australian friend. On the other hand, he was smiling again.

I reached down and my RTO Hal Dobie immediately slapped the black plastic radio hand set into my hand.

"Alpha 6, this is Alpha 2-6. Over." I said calling the C-O, Tom Gaffney, on the radio.

"This is 6. What the fuck are you doing standing on that dike? Go ahead." Tom replied.

"2-6, Not my idea. We have a sniper in that tree line, about 280°, 350-400 meters. We can't seem to shut him down. I think he is up in those trees. Go." I said.

"6, I'll take care of it. Get down! Arty is on the way. 6- out." Tom said.

A minute or so later that tree line exploded with air bursts of artillery. Tom loved artillery. He used it like medics gave out Darvon pain pills after a parachute jump. He and our FO (Artillery Forward Observer) Lt. Bob

Richardson were really good with it too. The sniper fire stopped with the first artillery explosions.

The artillery blasts had arrived violently and then had quit just as suddenly as they had started. When it stopped, we began moving forward again. Not much later, I again called Gaffney on the radio.

"Alpha 6, this is Alpha 2-6. Over."

"This is 6. Go ahead." Tom replied.

I was struggling a little with how I was going to say this. I had just seen a little copse of banana trees in front of us and a little to the right. It was my experience that every time that I saw banana trees, I got shot at.

On the other hand telling Tom that I wanted to stop the advance of a line of about 1,800-2,100 heavily armed men just because I had seen a banana tree, or three, did not seem like a workable idea, but that was really what I wanted, and why I really wanted it. Thus, my struggle to phrase it in a way that was not completely ridiculous.

However, it was not a superstition at all. It was a cold, hard fact. Every time I saw banana trees, every single time I saw even one banana tree, we got shot at, usually with machine guns, often accompanied by a few rockets or mortar shells as well. As a result, I thought it best to be well prepared when in the presence of banana trees.

Maybe we could use some more of that wonderful American artillery as a bullet prophylactic? I thought a little more of that artillery fire would be a great idea. Of course, I always thought that artillery, or air strikes, or better yet both at the same time, were a great idea.

198

Unfortunately, Tom knew that.

I was absolutely not afraid of banana trees. Really, they did not scare me. I was afraid of bullets though. I looked down the line and it did not look quite as straight as it could be. I keyed my radio handset again.

"Uh, this is 2-6, the line is getting kind-a wobbly, we need to stop and straighten it up before we go much further forward or we are going to have problems. Go ahead." I said.

*"6. Keep moving 2-6. I'll tell Mal Hombre (*Lt. Col. Geraci's call sign*) your thoughts. Go."* Tom replied dryly.

"2-6, Roger 6. There is a bunch of banana trees in front of us. Go." I said, and then stopped.

"This is 6, banana trees? Good. Do you want to pick one? Go ahead and pick one, but keep moving. Go." Gaffney said, sarcasm dripping with every word.

"Uh, 2-6. No, but every time I see banana trees I get shot at. Go." I blurted it out all at once and then stopped.

"What? Keep moving! 6 out!" Gaffney exploded over the radio.

Only a couple seconds or so later bullets, a lot of bullets, from lots of machine guns, fully automatic AK-47s and more than a few RPG rockets added their own razor-sharp, steel-laced, tortures to the air all along the line.

By then, the Australian SAS led Mike Force to my right was in an open rice paddy; there was no place for them to hide there. So, they all immediately charged forward right into the gunfire.

My platoon was just inside a little village, right next to the banana trees. So we dropped behind what cover we could find, and the rest of the line disappeared into smoke, dust and bullets as they also returned fire all along the line.

Because I did not know where the Australian Mike Force had gone, I had one squad on the right side of my platoon hold their fire.

A minute or so later Gaffney walked up leading his little command group of his two RTO's, one radio to control the company, and one to talk to battalion. Also with him was the FO, Lt. Bob Richardson, his RTO, the First Sergeant, Bull Gergen, and the Company medic. I stood up when they got near me. Everybody but Gaffney, Bull Gergen and I immediately dropped to the ground when Tom stopped to talk.

"What the Hell is going on Lieutenant? Why aren't all of your men firing?" he asked pointing to the right side of my platoon.

"I told you we needed to stop. I don't know where the Aussies went. (Pointing to the right) They ran forward when the shooting started. That's why. They and the rest of the line disappeared when we got to the banana trees and everything broke loose. I don't want to shoot any of them by accident." I said angrily.

I did not have to say anything further. Tom had a temper, but he also always recognized a tactical situation immediately. Tom looked around. We were standing together in the middle of a cluster of three, grass roofed, mud and wattle huts right next to the three or four banana trees. Everybody else around us was down, laying on the ground behind what ever cover there was because there were still a lot of bullets flying around us, shredding the banana trees, cracking loudly as they went by, or thudding into the mud and wattle houses. Then, the VC mortars started in as well.

However, we knew that our gunships, already on station overhead, would take care of the mortars. That's what they were there for. So, although that distinctive "*thump, thump, thump*" sound of mortars firing is remarkably spine-chilling, we ignored them too.

Tom and I just stood there for a moment looking around. The beautiful "*world on line*" had completely disappeared into dense cloud of smoke, and dust, and bullets, lots of bullets. You could not see any of them. With the SAS led Mike Force somewhere in front, all of the other units were down and almost invisible in all the smoke and dust. It was a big mess, an ugly, loud, very dangerous, very big, mess.

Tom looked up as the gunships, call sign *Tiger Shark*, from the 192nd Assault Helicopter Company, opened up on the mortars with their rockets and mini-guns. The gunships could clearly see the arc of the mortar shells as they flew through the air. Tracing them back to origin was not difficult at all. They shut those VC mortars down almost immediately.

"Find the Australians. Then, clean this mess up Lieutenant." Tom said.

Then he and his little group walked away through the fire.

I motioned to Hall Dobie, my RTO, and we went looking for the Australians and their Mike Force. We went through the banana trees and then around some more trees looking for them. We found that they had charged forward to the next paddy dike in front of them and had stopped as soon as they had cover. That meant they were in front of us by about 40-50 meters, but except for being a little advanced, they were still in exactly their proper position to our right. The Australian SAS and their mountain tribesmen mercenaries were simply incredible warriors.

I blew my whistle to get his attention, and then motioned to my friend, the Mike Force commander, to stay there. Dobie and I went back to my platoon. By the time we got there, the VC had stopped firing.

I blew a long blast on my little green whistle. Everybody got up and the Australians and their Mike Force got back on line when we caught up with them. The world was back on line. It was all beautiful again. It all literally flowed forward. Cool.

"Alpha 2-6, this is 6. Go ahead".

"This is 2-6. Go."

"Really good job 2-6. Now let's keep this line moving. This is 6- out."

I hadn't really done anything though. The VC/NVA had just stopped shooting and then left as they normally did. If you were VC/NVA, it was always a good idea to leave before the Phantom jets could roll in with their bombs and napalm. So, they fired us up when they could and then usually pulled right out. As for the rest, everything is a lot easier to do when no one is shooting at you.

The VC/NVA were the ones that deserved Tom's praise if anyone did. However, this time I did not argue, I just took Tom's compliment and we moved out.

Three or four days later, during another attack, our then brand new battalion commander chewed me out over the radio because he said my line of attack was not straight enough for him. Although it was very difficult, I restrained myself that time. I did not tell him because he was so new.

While I would have told Tom, or even "*Mal Hombre*" (Lt. Col. Geraci) that the line that he was talking about was VC, not my guys at all. However, I was not sure of this new guy yet. So I didn't tell him.

In any event, I was already engaged in eliminating their line entirely. I was not going to straighten it out. I was working on blowing it up.

I think our new battalion commander figured that out when the artillery that I had called in through our FO, Bob Richardson, relentlessly hammered, one after the other, the VC positions that he had thought were mine.

The new battalion commander, flew away in his Huey without further comment.

I had learned early on in the Army that, as my daddy used to say:

"Sometimes you're the windshield, and sometimes you're the bug."

I knew from hard experience that it rarely pays to argue on either day. While that didn't always stop me from arguing, I did know it.

The World on Line had worked though, and it had been a really big deal. We kept it up all day, advancing, pausing, wiping out pockets of the enemy, and then advancing again and again. Getting better and better at it as we went. We had never done anything like it before, and we never did it again, but on that day, it worked, beautifully.

Geraci and Mairs had been right. We counted more dead VC/NVA and picked up more enemy weapons and equipment that day than any other day of the war.

I still don't like banana trees much though.

Sixteen

Leading a rifle platoon, or probably any kind of platoon, in combat is a very personal, some would say even a mystical, experience. Because we had trained together as a unit in the States before we left for Vietnam, it was even more so for us.

It is hard to express how close we all were without becoming cloying. Having said that, we learned repeatedly when the butcher's bill came due after each contact of the costs of such closeness. On the other hand this story is about positive side of training together until working together became second nature.

Infantry fighting is always team sport. This story is about that part of the Infantry at work.

The Attack At the Bridge

"I never knew why we're doing it, I just knew we had to do it, kill or be killed. The latter didn't happen."

tom croff
C Company, 3/506th Abn. Inf.
August 6, 2014 at 8:57 pm

Jim Schlax was the 1st Platoon Leader of Alpha Company, 3/506th from the time Alpha Company was formed at Fort Campbell, Ky., until he was wounded in Vietnam during Tet '68. We were both recent OCS (Officer Candidate School) graduates when we were assigned to Alpha Company.

However, Jim clearly out ranked me because his OCS class was commissioned a week earlier than mine. This was a fact that he never mentioned, but one that we both knew because junior second lieutenants keep careful track of such petty, but nonetheless important things.

When I first reported to Alpha Company, I was appointed as the Executive Officer (XO) since by then all of the platoons already had platoon leaders. While higher in position, after all the XO is second in command of the company; the XO's job was less desirable for a lieutenant than that of platoon leader.

Luckily for me, after another officer was relieved, Army-speak for fired, I took over the 2nd Platoon. I also continued as XO.

This curious situation, the most junior officer in the company being both second in command as XO and a fellow platoon leader produced some unusual conversations among the Alpha Company lieutenants. For example, Schlax and I might have a conversation as fellow platoon leaders of more or less equal rank, in the midst of the conversation I might act as XO for a while, therefore I was in charge of some things and might even give a couple of orders and then switch back to being just another platoon leader.

From time to time, but only for short periods, I might also act as the Commanding Officer of Alpha Company while the CO, Captain Tom Gaffney was away. Then, I would be giving the platoon leaders orders, but at least two of the other three Alpha Company platoon leaders, Jim Schlax and Joe Alexander, both clearly outranked me.

This is customarily very important stuff in the Army, but the question of rank never came up between us, only the job of getting Alpha Company ready for Vietnam mattered. Part of it was that the same people had trained us all and everyone recognized that had our positions been reversed, much the same orders would have been given. Still the complete lack of friction between us was extraordinary, particularly given the pressure we were all under getting Alpha Company ready for war.

My nickname for Schlax was "*Nasty little Man*", not because he was actually nasty, although he was physically short. I gave him the name because he was so effective, so dangerous, as a rifle platoon leader. He earned it many times over.

For reasons that only our CO, Tom Gaffney, could explain, the 2nd Platoon usually led any company movement in the field. Second Platoon was therefore the "*point*" platoon in that formation. If two platoons were up on-line, then the 2nd Platoon was the base platoon, the platoon that set the pace and the direction of march.

Alpha Company in Action

Lt. James Schlax with the interpreter in the upper right. Photo from James Schlax

First Platoon, Schlax's platoon, was almost always the next platoon in the Alpha Company line of march, or it would be the platoon moving on line on the 2nd Platoon's flank.

On the other hand, when Alpha Company stopped, it was the 1st and the other platoons that did almost all of the patrolling and night ambushes while the 2nd Platoon provided Company CP (Command Post) security and acted as a reaction force for the other platoons while they were operating away from the Company.

As a practical matter, what this meant was that Jim Schlax and I had to absolutely depend on each other all of the time. If the 2nd Platoon made contact, it was the 1st Platoon that would be maneuvering though the enemy fire to get us out of trouble. If the 1st Platoon made contact on a patrol or ambush, more often than not it would be the 2nd Platoon that arrived first to help. Because of experience over time in Vietnam, I came to believe that there was no trouble that the 1st Platoon, or it and the rest of Alpha Company could not get me and the 2nd Platoon out of, so I acted accordingly on point.

All of the Alpha Company platoon leaders were very aggressive, but this was not a competition among lieutenants, rather it was an expression of our shared confidence in the men of Alpha Company, and anyway, they were as aggressive as we were. Like every airborne soldier, we were all volunteers.

When there was contact with the enemy, at least until the situation stabilized a bit, Jim and I would pretty much direct each other at first depending on the tactical situation. I would tell Jim where I needed 1st Platoon, or he would do the same for me if he was the one in contact. Captain Gaffney would listen to these conversations, try to get more information about what was going on, and talk to battalion. If Captain Gaffney heard something we said that he did not like he would intervene, but usually he just asked for more information, lined up fire support and let the situation clarify before he gave orders.

Because of movies and television, people expect a flurry of orders immediately when the bullets fly. But all those orders have pretty much been codified into battle drills that each platoon has practiced until they are second nature. Therefore, the first part of any firefight is as nearly automatic as we could make it. It is really rare that any orders were given early in a firefight in a well trained platoon.

Our radio conversations during a firefight usually consisted of:

"What do you have?"

"What do you want to do?"

"What do you want me to do?"

"What do you need?"

"Do you have any casualties?"

And my personal favorite from Gaffney:

"I can get you some air support, do you need it, or will gun ships do? Artillery is on the way. Prepare to adjust fire."

There is just nothing like an F4 Phantom jet screaming in at about 400 miles an hour, dropping very accurate 750 pound, High Drag, bombs, or napalm, to create a positive attitude adjustment on the part of the enemy. Awesome, just total, beautiful, awesomeness.

People listening in on the *Charlie-Charlie* (Command and Control) radio frequency during a firefight often commented how mundane, even in the most extreme circumstances, these conversations sounded, except for the hard clatter of battle in the background.

For example, one day during Tet '68 Alpha Company was moving through the outskirts of Phan Thiet, RVN. We received heavy fire from an old, colonial French, steel-reinforced, concrete blockhouse next to a bridge across the Ca TY River. Since we had been told that the ARVN had all been pulled back to Phan Thiet, 2nd Platoon attacked immediately, and violently.

When we got to the river, across from the blockhouse I called Schlax on the radio and asked him to cross the river on the left while 2nd Platoon pinned the garrison down with fire. For some reason, he could not hear my radio transmission. So, the next thing I heard was Gaffney, I am not sure if he used the radio or not, yelling at 1st Platoon to attack left. Even so, it was not an "*order*" so much as: "*Go Left! Go Left!*" The attack part was understood.

The 1st Platoon immediately maneuvered left, forced a river crossing under heavy fire, and then attacked the blockhouse from another direction, all while the 2nd Platoon poured fire on the blockhouse. The 2nd Platoon laid down a particularly heavy base of suppressive fire, including all three M60 machine guns firing at full cyclic, 650 rounds per minute per gun, the entire time that the 1st Platoon was in the river.

While all that was happening, the 1st Platoon made a picture perfect, contested river crossing under heavy fire. Then, with the continued fire support of 2nd Platoon but still under heavy fire from the blockhouse, the 1st Platoon maneuvered to an assault position close to the blockhouse, and close to the 2nd Platoon's fire.

It was this complex, and very difficult infantry maneuver, under heavy fire from the enemy, and using, but never masking our supporting fire, that forced the blockhouse to surrender. During the whole attack, Schlax and I had been completely unable to communicate.

We made this two platoon, attack based entirely on relying on each other's training to know what to do, to know when to do it, and to execute.

If you are exceptionally observant, or you humped the "pig", you will have noticed the empty brass 7.62 mm shell casing flying to the right of gunner's shoulder. This photo was taken while under fire. Another cool picture by Jerry Berry, PIO 3/506th.

Otherwise, somebody, perhaps several somebodies, would die. Combat is not a game played with OD Nerf balls.

I really think our radios reacted more to enemy fire than we did. The number of times that the Army's PRC-25 (Personal Radio Communicator #25) was working fine until the bullets started flying and then stopped working, was astonishing. We never figured it out, but Hal Dobie, my first

RTO (Radio Telephone Operator) and then Ed Brady, my second RTO, almost habitually unfolded and attached the long antenna as soon as the first bullet cracked on its way by.

While both my RTO's recognized that the long antenna was sort of a big *"Shoot Me First"* sign over their heads, we really needed to be able to communicate. So, up it went.

In spite of all the bullets and other ordnance flying around, I do not think we suffered a single casualty from the attack at the bridge. The South Vietnamese Popular Force (*"PF"*) platoon in the blockhouse was not so lucky even though they were in solid French designed fighting positions protected by steel reinforced concrete.

They told our interpreter, named Bong, that they were firing at VC who were attacking the blockhouse from another direction and they were very sorry that they had also fired at us by accident. I think they were sorry, particularly the wounded ones, but I was angry by then, being shot at always made me angry. Although I was not very sympathetic, we did treat and medivac their casualties.

Looking back on it now, I think the PF platoon, equivalent to our National Guard but not nearly as well-trained or equipped, were just terrified at being left out there all alone during the most violent battle of the war. They could literally see, feel and hear, the Tet '68 Offensive exploding all around them. So, they were shooting at anything that moved. It was their bad luck that they shot at us.

What I remember most about that day was watching the 1st Platoon perfectly execute a difficult, a very complex, infantry maneuver, under heavy fire without once having ever trained to do anything like it. It was simply remarkable. Not only was it something we had never practiced; I think the only time I had only ever even seen it was watching old news reel footage of Allied attacks across the Rhine, or some other river in Germany from World War II on TV when I was a kid. However, I am not sure to this day that Schlax had ever even seen it done before he, and his rifle platoon, did it.

The 1st Platoon first had to actually maneuver under the 2nd Platoons' fire as they crossed the river and then out to the side of our fire right up next to where our bullets were landing in order to get to their assault position.

Schlax and his men accomplished all of this fluidly, moving under and then right around our gunfire as though they did it every day even though we could not communicate.

That remarkable display of courage in action and the 1st Platoon's absolute trust in the 2nd Platoon's fire discipline is what has remained with me for almost fifty years.

From right 1st Platoon Leader Jim Schlax, (WIA 2/19/68), 2nd Platoon Leader John Harrison, (WIA 2/2/68, 2/3/68 & 2/8/68) 3rd Platoon Leader Len Liebler, Weapons Platoon Leader Joe Alexander (WIA 2/19/68). Taken on the Mall with my camera, but not by me.

Seventeen

February 19, 1968 was the bloodiest day for Alpha Company out of the entire year we were there. Early on it was the 1st Platoon that suffered first. Nevertheless, it was the 3rd Platoon that bore the brunt of our losses that bloody day.

This is the story of that day from the perspective of the 2nd Platoon.

2/19/1968—The Day The Weapons Platoon Died

"When others run from the sounds of battle, I run towards it, where the fighting is thick, there I am, I am the INFANTRY! As a holder of a CIB(2nd Award) I read your story and visualized every detail as if I were feeding ammo to the M60 myself. I was in D Company 2/502 INF for over 6 years, I met LTC Hank Emerson (call sign "Gunfighter") when we dedicated the memorial to the Regiment in '87 for our Vietnam Brothers who passed. Thank you for standing your ground and setting the example for us to follow."

SFC (RET) Kevin DeVos
Vietnam Veteran
July 30, 2014 at 3:58 am

There is a certain smell to combat. Once smelled, it is never forgotten. Part of it is a harsh copper taste in the back of the mouth. Then, there is the stench of clotting blood and other bodily fluids. Fear produces a particularly pungent sweat, and the acrid smoke from fires with burning human and other kinds of bodies inside them can almost be tasted as well as smelled. While I have always liked the smell of cordite, or gunpowder, that is part of it as well. There is a certain smell to combat and sometimes, when it is going to be very bad, you can actually get just a whiff of it even before the action begins.

Not only that whiff, but there was already a surreal quality to 2/19/1968 at our base camp, LZ Betty just outside of Phan Thiet, RVN before the fighting started that day. LZ Betty was a fortified perimeter around a beautiful old

French Colonial airfield perched high on a bluff overlooking the South China Sea. At the gate to LZ Betty there was a colonial French, reinforced concrete, blockhouse, perhaps built by the French Foreign Legion, but more likely by a forced labor battalion.

The caption reads: Phan Thiet- Cpt. Thomas Gaffney's Company A crosses the Ca Ty River on the morning of Feb. 19, 1968 to block enemy forces attempting to escape the heavy fighting in the City of Phan Thiet. Lt. Joe Alexander's Platoon is seen crossing the river. (Feb. 19, 1968). Photo and caption by Jerry Berry, 3/506th PIO.

Around the perimeter of LZ Betty there were many more American built, sandbagged blockhouses every 30 or 40 yards or so. In between, the blockhouses were scattered infantry fighting positions to be used if the firebase actually came under attack. In an attack, the blockhouses were viewed as death traps by the troops because they were RPG rocket magnets.

There were also several 40 foot or so tall watchtowers, with sandbagged floors and walls, set on four black tar coated telephone poles and spaced around the perimeter. In front of the bunkers were ranks of barbed wire fences strung in echelon, tied with various noisemakers and with claymore mines carefully set, covering dead spaces where bullets could not reach.

There was a two lane dirt road all the way around the perimeter behind the blockhouses that the officer and sergeant of the guard used at night to check if the guards were alert. The perimeter road had also often been used as a late night improvised race-course when junior officers raced stolen jeeps on it.

The winner was usually the officer that managed to steal the Air Force's jeep because unlike the Army jeeps powered by engines with only four cylinders, the Air Force jeep had a much more powerful six-cylinder engine. Even with the heavy, $50,000 Air Force radio in back, that six-cylinder engine made it by far the fastest jeep on the base. But those races were over for a while, during Tet '68 the lieutenants were tired at night, not drunk, and with the recent casualty lists, the mood of even the most irrepressible junior officer was more somber than spirited.

As had quickly become a pattern, early in the morning of February 19, 1968 the paras of the 3rd Battalion, 506th Infantry Regiment (Airborne) lined up in front of the mess hall for breakfast, but the chow line was now tactically spaced because now and then rounds would crack overhead. Sometimes a green tracer flashed by, but no one ducked; they were too high to hit anyone; no one even bothered to look up.

It was the new normal, breakfast in the Mess Hall, chow line, tactically spaced, under random rifle and sometimes machine gun fire as well. Only one guy ever got hit. He died.

Inside the mess hall a typically good Army breakfast waited: eggs any way you wanted, crisp hash brown potatoes, creamy grits, crisp bacon and savory sausage, or dry cereal, fresh fruit, all the strong black coffee, milk and juice you could hold, and of course SOS, always Army SOS for the lifers. It was even served on clean, white china plates, stainless steel silverware, white folded paper napkins and with a brown plastic tray to carry it all. No one seemed to feel the obvious disconnect as they passed the salt and pepper.

During Tet '68, the doctors and medics really appreciated the cleaner wound channels because, even though there was all that food in the intestinal tracks, there was less dirt and crud carried into the wounds because of the showers the men took in the morning and the clean uniforms they put on, before breakfast, before battle.

After breakfast, usually just as dawn was breaking, the paras went to the Can Do pad to gun up, fill aid bags and canteens, draw ammo, grenades, smoke canisters, railroad flares, cigarettes, tooth paste, claymore mines and LAW (Light Antitank Weapon) rockets. Then, they loaded their rifle magazines and packed their packs for their day's expected business of war.

The caption reads: Phan Thiet- Co. A gears up on the "Can Do" Pad on LZ Betty for another combat assault (1968) Photo and caption by Jerry Berry, 3/506th PIO.

February 19th opened no different from any other day since Tet '68 had started. After beginning with a bang, no pun intended, the Tet '68 Offensive had continued around Phan Thiet long after it had stopped in most of the rest of Vietnam.

However, at Phan Thiet every time a Hardcore VC or Main Force NVA unit had run into the 3/506th they had been thoroughly bloodied. This was particularly of the NVA units that soon showed the effects of their newfound lack of local guides by running into 3/506th combat patrols regularly.

Often this had disastrous results for the unprepared NVA. But, the Hardcore VC and Main Force NVA around Phan Thiet were very experienced, veteran, units so they recovered quickly and often gave as good as they got thereafter. As a result, while the American casualties around Phan Thiet for any particular action had usually not been substantial, they were always a steady drain for all three rifle companies of the 3/506th.

The plan that day for Alpha Company was to simply walk out of LZ Betty, cross the Ca Ty River where it was shallow and assume a blocking position near the steel bridge down river across from Phan Thiet.

Meanwhile Bravo Company, most of Charlie Company and a Mike Force of hill tribesmen mercenaries led by Australian SAS would drive through downtown Phan Thiet, pushing the enemy into Alpha Company's blocking position on the other side of the Ca Ty River. We were walking that day because most of our helicopters had been shot up already and we were saving the remainder for Command and Control, and for Dust Off, or medical evacuation flights.

Alpha Company's part of the operation started first; led by the 2nd Platoon, Alpha Company walked right out the front gate of LZ Betty and down to the Ca Ty river's edge. There two 40mm Dusters waited to provide covering fire for the river crossing. The Dusters "*prepped*" the other side of the river for us by firing several hundred high-explosive, 40mm rounds at it. The 40mm guns started on the tree tops for spectacular air-bursts and then they worked down the river bank itself.

It was all very impressive unless you knew that the VC and NVA were infantry, very good infantry, and infantry being troublesome people were well used to hiding the folds of the earth from such violence, but could nonetheless emerge from their hiding places, unscathed, angry and well-armed at any time they wanted.

However, this was the first time I had seen the Dusters work and I was impressed. As we waited, the driver told me about the Army's M-42 40mm Self-Propelled Anti-Aircraft Gun, or "*Duster*," as it was called. He said it had started as a lightly armored, air-defense gun developed in the late 1950's.

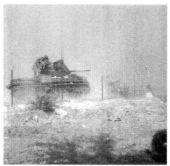

Phan Thiet: A 40mm M42 "Duster" from the 1st Plt., Alpha Battery. 4th Battalion, 60th Artillery. Feb. 19, 1968

This picture was actually taken that morning, February 19, 1968.

Photo and caption by Jerry Berry, 3/506th PIO.

The tank division of General Motors built it with part of an M-41 light tank. With a crew of six, it weighed almost 50,000 lbs., had a maximum speed of 45mph and a range of about 100 miles. It was armed with fully automatic, twin 40mm M2A1 Bofors cannons, with a total rate of fire of 240 rounds per minute, and a 7.62mm M-60 machine gun as well.

Even though the M-42 Duster was initially designed as an anti-aircraft gun, it had proved itself in Vietnam when used directly against the VC and NVA infantry, particularly on convoys. We had two Dusters at LZ Betty and two quad .50 caliber machine guns from the same unit as well. I never did find out where the name "Duster" came from.

I stood beside one of the Dusters watching the fireworks and smoking a cigarette as they lit up the other side of the river with hundreds of 40mm high explosive shells. After I patted the solid homogenous steel hull of the Duster the second time, the driver said:

"Not very thick."

I replied:

"Thicker than my fatigue shirt." And went back to my platoon.

When the Dusters were done playing, the 2nd Platoon started across the Ca Ty River. Out of no where, when the 2nd Platoon was about halfway across the river, the FAC fired over our heads and into the opposing river bank all of his smoke rockets that he usually used one at a time to mark targets for ground support jets. Coupled with the dust from the Dusters' 40mm cannon shells' explosions, the FAC's rockets gave us a good smoke screen to conceal our movement across the Ca Ty river.

222

However, no troops, particularly veteran troops, like fire from the rear. So the rockets were still a very unpleasant surprise no matter how well intended or useful.

As any Marine will tell you, there is no place to hide when you are knee deep in water and moving slowly, leadenly, because of the water. You can't run and you just can't hide when you are in water.

Walking slowly through water toward an unseen, armed enemy feels remarkably like being stark naked in a room full of clothed people who are pointing at your privates while they stare at you and smile knowingly. Meanwhile in the water, you must move forward or you will surely die, and fire from the rear is the last thing you want.

When we arrived at the other side of the river we set up a hasty defensive perimeter while the rest of Alpha Company followed us across. Other than the smoke rockets from the FAC, it turned out to be a quiet river crossing. As each platoon came across, the company defensive perimeter was simply expanded until everyone was across and in position.

Just before this operation, because of the continual drain of casualties suffered in the almost constant combat of Tet '68 around Phan Thiet, Alpha Company and the other companies of the 3/506th were reorganized into three rifle platoon companies rather than four platoon, three rifle and one weapon's platoon, companies. In spite of a spasmodic stream of casualty replacements, we simply did not have enough men, or unwounded officers, left in the 3/506th rifle companies to run four platoons.

While unwounded officers were becoming scarce, Sergeant First Class platoon sergeants were already a vanishing species in the battalion.

It seemed that the lieutenants in the battalion were all getting wounded but, the platoon sergeants were getting killed.

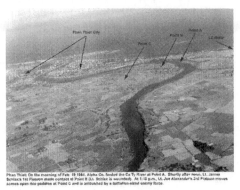

The caption reads: Phan Thiet. On the morning of February 19, 1968 Alpha Co. forded the Ca Ty River at Point A. Shortly after noon Lt. James Schlax's 1st Platoon made contact at Point B. Lt. Schlax is wounded. At 1:10 PM Lt Joe Alexander's 3rd Platoon moves across open rice paddies at Point C and is ambushed by battalion-sized enemy force. Photo and caption by Jerry Berry, 3/506th PIO.

Even with transfers of men from the eliminated weapon's platoon in the reorganization, and even with the addition of nineteen "*new-guy*" replacements on the day before, February 18th, my platoon, 2nd Platoon, still only had about thirty-four men ready for the field on 2/19/1968.

This was barely enough to carry our three machine guns and the 3,500+/-rounds of ammunition we were carrying for each machine gun. Since you really don't want to run out of ammo in a firefight, during Tet '68 each para, officers included, carried about 300 rounds of machine-gun ammo into battle in addition to what ever else they were carrying.

Some times during Tet '68 firefights we were resupplied with ammo two, or even three, times a day. While that sounds like a lot of ammunition to be blasting away, even 3,500 rounds of ammo only lasts about five and a half to six minutes at the full cyclic rate of fire for an M-60 machine gun. That is not very long in a street fight.

Although they were trying hard to hide it, this was these "*new guys*" first time outside the wire and they were showing it. Most of all they were still tentative, well trained most of them, but as yet unsure of what they were doing, so they did it all slowly, too slowly. They still had to think. There is a big difference between training, however realistic, and the real thing— combat with an armed and experienced enemy intent on killing you and the man next to you. That realization was sinking in fast for the new guys.

The 1st Platoon led the initial advance out from the perimeter beside the river. They moved across an open rice paddy and then through a grave yard and made initial contact with the enemy. A sharp, short, firefight ensued.

Just as the 3rd Platoon led by Lieutenant Joe Alexander, the last platoon in formation and mostly formerly the Weapons Platoon, finished crossing the river, battalion commander ordered an immediate advance. From his command helicopter, high over the battle, Lt. Col. Robert Elton, the brand new battalion CO, who was the second of three Battalion CO's that would command the 3/506th during the year we were there, managed the fight below.

Lt. Col. Elton could see what he thought to be VC or NVA troops one dike level up from where we were that appeared to him to be running away from the advancing 1st Platoon paras of Alpha Company. Therefore, he ordered an immediate advance by the rest of Alpha Company.

Tom Gaffney, Alpha Company CO, at first had ordered the 2nd platoon forward. However, when 2nd Platoon took too long getting back into formation, all those new guys were slow finding their positions in the column formation, Tom ordered 3rd Platoon, still pretty much in formation from crossing the Ca Ty River, to move up on line with 1st Platoon and to move out. While 1st and 3rd platoons moved out, the sergeants and I tried to sort 2nd Platoon and get it into a proper tactical platoon column formation to follow along.

Strangely for the 2nd Platoon, this time we would be bringing up the rear. Almost immediately firing broke out again, particularly in the rice paddy above us and to the left where the 3rd Platoon had gone. While not nearly as heavy as the firing had been on February 2, 1968, it was clearly a very serious firefight.

When the firing started, everybody in 2nd Platoon dropped where they were for the moment, bullets whistled and cracked overhead while grenades exploded in front. We could hear the pounding of several M-60 machine guns cutting loose on full cyclic. Leaving my platoon where it was, I moved up in front of my point man to see what was going on on the other side of that rice paddy dike.

Later some said the 3rd Platoon had run into an ambush. But, to me it was not an ambush because the killing zone was not closed. While that did not make it any less of a killing zone while you were in it; there was a way out and that is an important difference. It looked to me that if we could cover them and get them moving, there was a way out for the men still in the killing field; the back door was open.

What the battalion commander had actually seen was VC or NVA soldiers running from their secure, covered, positions where they had hidden from the Dusters' fire, to their fighting positions to get ready for our advance. These Mainforce VC/NVA definitely did not intend to run away.

In traditional tactical terms, what we had that day was a classic infantry movement to contact, with us engaging an entrenched, well-prepared enemy. Unfortunately, the VC/NVA were not only well entrenched, they had developed open, cleared, fields of fire right in front of their positions and from his helicopter high above the battle, Lt. Col. Elton had in effect, mistakenly ordered, 3rd Platoon, Alpha Company to charge right into those clear, fields of fire.

In no more than a couple of minutes of actual fighting the 3rd Platoon lost 8 men killed and about 20 wounded out of the 40 or so men that had started the day. Joe Alexander, the Platoon Leader was shot five times including being shot in his head, but he was still fighting what was left of his platoon. Bleeding profusely, he was trying to get his men, living and dead, out of that rice paddy and to set up some kind of fighting position with the men he had left.   Many of his men, although wounded, were nonetheless still fighting hard, still trying to get the rest of their buddies out of that bloody killing ground in front of them.

Some of the bodies lying in the killing field already seemed to be too quiet. They seemed already to be covered with that super fine, almost white, powdery dust of death.

However, a few of the men laying in that killing field, dusted or not, were not wounded; they were playing dead. Some were wounded; they too were playing dead, and some were dead.

The living played dead because the VC/NVA had the annoying habit of continuing to shoot wounded men in order to kill them, or even better, to attract someone to try to rescue them. Then, they could shoot the would be rescuers as well.

So wounded, or unwounded the men in the killing field laid there all day under the tropical sun, not moving. While the battle raged over them and all around them, bullets slashing within inches of their bodies, they laid there but they did not move.

Joe's Platoon Sergeant, SFC John Geffeller, had been killed in the opening salvo of the enemy. Geffeller had been getting his men to return fire. Of all of the Alpha Company platoons, at that point, other than one squad that had been loaned to 2nd Platoon for a while because of heavy casualties in 2nd Platoon, the 3rd Platoon, formerly the Weapons Platoon, had suffered the least combat so far during Tet '68.

Although they were veterans of many fire fights prior to Tet, the 3rd Platoon had not yet experienced the street fighting, infantry slugfest, all day, all night, battles that characterized much of Tet '68 in and around Phan Thiet for us. For example, in contrast to most past battles of Alpha Company with the VC/NVA that were usually over in minutes, this one lasted two full days.

While bloody, the 3rd Platoon's agony that morning was only the very start of this battle. Although the fierce enemy onslaught had stunned the 3rd Platoon for a moment, they soon shook that off, and fought back hard.

In spite of his five bullet wounds Joe Alexander repeatedly refused to be medically evacuated. Even after Lieutenant Len Liebler came to the field to take over the 3rd Platoon, Joe Alexander was still trying to get to his men that remained trapped in the killing ground in the rice paddy.

Finally, Joe had to be ordered from the field to have his wounds tended to. Lt. Len Liebler took over 3rd platoon for the rest of the battle. While it had started the day as the largest platoon in Alpha Company, by then the 3rd Platoon was by then down to about the size of a very large rifle squad.

At the beginning when I had first looked over the dike, I could see the back of one 3rd Platoon M-60 machine gunner just standing flat footed in the middle of that rice paddy, right in the middle of that killing zone, sweeping his machine gun, firing constantly at the full cyclic rate of 550- 650 rounds per minute, raking the enemy positions repeatedly and buying time for the rest of the platoon to seek cover and return fire themselves.

His assistant gunner ignored the bullets flying around as well, and kept slapping on more ammunition to the belt leading to that machine gun to keep those bullets flowing; to keep hosing the enemy with fire; to keep buying lives and time with bullets. That machine gunner saved American lives that day, at the cost of his own. His finger left the M-60 trigger when he died; he was shot in the head.

There were a lot of 3rd Platoon men shot in the head on February 19th. The NVA/VC were usually not such precise shots so there had to be at least one sniper working that morning as well as the dug in infantry.

In fact, one of the main differences between our American M-16 rifle and the AK-47 assault rifle they were using reflected this basic difference in battle tactics. The first detent of the selector switch on the American M-16 assault rifle is semi-automatic; you must pass through the semi-automatic detent to get to full automatic fire with an M-16. On the AK-47 assault rifle, these positions are reversed. The first detent on the AK-47 assault rifle is full automatic fire.

That difference is because the Soviet designer of the AK-47, Mikhail Kalashnikov, based his design on his experience in fighting Germans in WW II. Because of that, he believed that the side that achieved fire superiority won the infantry battle. The American military on the other hand, and particularly the Marines, have always preferred aimed fire to what we called the "*spray and pray*" approach.

In effect, this was an argument we had everyday in combat with the VC/NVA. Looking at the overall kill ratio for the entire war of about 16 VC/NVA dead for each American death, I would say that we won the argument. The VC/NVA would probably argue that we cheated by using the Air Force as much as we could, but, who said life was fair, much less war?

However, many of the men killed that morning in the 3rd Platoon were killed by single, precise, head shots. Such head shots were something new and dangerous in our battlefield equation around Phan Thiet. That meant a sniper was working, a good one.

As the battle unfolded, in effect Alpha Company sort of naturally moved into a modified perimeter defensive position with the 2nd Platoon holding the section facing the Ca Ty River. 1st Platoon was up one dike level and spread out in the graveyard, and the remainder of 3rd Platoon was set along the dike in front of the rice paddy looking over the killing field.

Periodically choppers would land, through heavy fire sometimes, in the center of the Alpha Company perimeter to pick up wounded and drop off ammunition. Except for Gaffney's small headquarters section, one entire side of the perimeter, probably the largest side and facing the direction we had come from remained entirely open. However, my men could cover that area with fire if necessary.

Overall it was not a great defensive position to fight from, but with entrenching tools, sweat, and filling and emplacing the three empty sand bags each man carried we were making it stronger by the minute. In a firefight, well trained infantry is either shooting, moving or digging. We were digging as well as shooting most of that day.

After I set up my platoon in position, I kept going over to 3rd Platoon to see if I could help, but I only succeeded in getting in the way. I really wanted to help. I really needed to help. I needed to do something. It was that bad.

The bodies and wounded being shipped back to the battalion aid station were our men. They were our friends. This was Alpha Company, my company and so far we had taken a shellacking; but I thought that if we could recover our wounded men from the killing field alive then it would not be as bad as it looked right then, and then we could start working on the enemy again; we could have our turn.

Finally, a couple of cases of LAWs came in on a chopper and I began to put them to use on the enemy positions we had identified on the other side of the killing field. We could not use close air support or artillery fire because of the 3rd Platoon men still lying in the killing field were in the open. We hoped at least some of them were still alive and we wanted them to stay that way.

However, with the LAWs I could shoot the enemy bunkers that I could see, and any blast from the LAW rocket strikes would be angled away from our men still in the killing field. At first the VC were very reliable. I would make a

LAW ready to fire, go stand in the open just into the rice paddy to the left of the killing field and the VC would shoot at me rather than at the 3rd Platoon.

When I could identify the position they were shooting at me from, I would fire the rocket. That way I shot off over a case and a half of LAW rockets at their bunkers and firing positions.

Even if I had known then about the sniper working I still would have done it that way. It is the best way to find out where they were. When they fired at you, you had both sound and movement, and sometime smoke or dust, to guide you to them. Otherwise finding their well camouflaged, fighting positions could be very difficult.

After a while I ran out of the easy to find targets. In addition, they soon pretty much stopped shooting at me when I appeared in the field with another LAW on my shoulder. So, I had to look for targets. Since their camouflage was excellent, finding good targets for the LAW rockets became much more difficult.

So, I tried shooting the rockets in an indirect fire role as well as direct fire. I was shooting them where I thought they might be hiding, and where I would hide if I was them.

That was fine until I began to drop a few rockets close to 1st Platoon's position. Lt. Schlax ("*Alpha 1-6*") got on the radio to complain about the rocket strikes, so Tom ("*Alpha 6*") told me ("*Alpha 2-6*") to:

"Cease fire."

However, by then I was consumed by anger. Every time I looked at the bodies still in the killing field I was in a rage against the dying light. I wanted to strike back hard those men that had hurt my friends.

So I said to Tom ("*Alpha-6*"):

"They can't be hitting close to where 1-6's men are, over."

Tom's deadpan reply in the middle of a fierce firefight was classic Gaffney. It stopped me cold:

"Well 2-6, since 1-6 is standing right by where they are landing, he probably knows more about where they are landing than you do, so cease fire, over."

Later, the 1st Platoon Leader Lieutenant Jim Schlax managed to get shot while he was aiming at a VC. I never heard if the same guy that Schlax was shooting at actually shot him, nor if Schlax hit his man. He probably did; Schlax was a good shot. In any event, a VC shot Schlax in the leg.

Schlax let the medic bandage it, but since he still had work to do, he ignored the suggestion that he ought to go get on a medivac and go to the rear for treatment of his bullet wound.

Schlax knew he had to move many of his men into better fighting positions before darkness fell. So he refused to be evacuated until that was done.

In combat, and particularly when under heavy fire, even veteran soldiers that are relatively safe in one position tend to want to stay in that position. However, it was Schlax's job to get them into mutually supporting, useful, fighting positions so that side of the perimeter could be held after nightfall.

Schlax stumped around to each position using his M-16 rifle as a cane and moved his men around into better fighting positions. Only when he was satisfied did he come down into the center area of the Alpha Company perimeter to be evacuated.

When he limped heavily through my platoon's area, pale faced, with black, dried blood, thickly caked, on his pant's leg, I had him picked up and carried to the Dust Off helicopter as a matter of respect. Smiling, I told him it looked like he had been shot in the ass to hide it.

While all of this was happening on one side of the perimeter, there was a full-scale battle underway in downtown Phan Thiet on the other side, the river side, the 2nd Platoon side. Bravo and Charlie Companies and the Mike Force were heavily engaged with the enemy and were pushing them our way. They pushed them all day and well into the night.

While Alpha Company had not quite made it to the blocking position we were supposed to be in, the 2nd Platoon could still control the bridge we were supposed to be blocking with machine gun, M-79 and rifle fire. Not perfect, but good enough, particularly since by being located on the top of a turn in the river meant we actually covered more of the river facing Phan Thiet than we would have if we were where we had been ordered to be.

Later, when the VC/NVA tried coming across the river in boats, they soon realized the strength of our position on a small bluff overlooking the river.
Another Lieutenant, John Ross, our XO, had come to the field to replace Jim Schlax as 1st Platoon Leader. In the meantime before Schlax left the field, Ross was standing in the open, in the middle of Alpha Company's defensive area, managing helicopter arrivals when a machine gun located across the river opened fire on him. I told one of 2nd Platoon's machine

guns to shut that machine gunner down with suppressive fire while I got a LAW ready to fire at him.

When the LAW was ready, I stood up and blew the machine gun and the machine gunner into the river with it. That permanently stopped that machine gun from firing at Lt. Ross. He was able to find a slightly more covered position to manage our helicopters from the 192nd Assault Helicopter Company coming in and out. But, covered or not he kept the helicopters moving in and out. They were our life line, our only lifeline, to the world.

Late in the day, two large boats, each full of 20-25 NVA or VC, left the other side of the river. They came toward us shooting all the way, trying to force a river crossing and get away from Bravo and Charlie companies and the Mike Force. I got two more LAWs ready and sank both of those boats with them.

At which point another enemy machine gun opened up, this time on me. He was firing from a large boathouse hanging out over the river on the other side. Since I was out of LAWs I ordered a nearby 90mm recoilless rifle to fire on the boathouse.

He literally dumped the whole thing in the river when the first 90 mm round hit the building. It was like he had hit what is called the "*Jesus nut*" on a helicopter, the one thing that holds it all together. The boathouse just exploded into fire and smoke, and then it all fell into the river, bodies flying everywhere.

It turned out that there had been a lot of VC/NVA in that building. They were now in the water learning to swim. Like the ones in the two boats, they seemed to be having trouble getting the hang of it.

Now and then fighting became general along the riverbank between the 2nd Platoon and the VC/NVA attempting to escape the pressure of Bravo and Charlie companies, and then it would just stop for a while. This battle had a rhythm of its own, totally unrelated to the other side of the perimeter, which still had its own battle going across the killing field. We were surrounded and heavily engaged in two directions most of the night.

The VC/NVA tried to push across the bridge only one time that day. Even though they pushed civilian refugees if front of them, it did not go well for those that tried. One of my jobs when we were training the 3/506th in the states had been to teach marksmanship to the entire battalion—the men of the 2nd Platoon, the teachers I used for the marksmanship class, could really shoot, particularly Sgt. Charles Hayes.

The VC/NVA were in olive drab green uniforms, the civilians mainly wore black, or black pants and white shirts or the women wore a white áo dài over long black pants. We shot the VC/NVA; the civilians ran through the fire. All night, we covered that bridge with fire and steel. All night, they probed for a way out of Phan Thiet. All night, we pushed them back.

When it was quiet for a while and almost dark Tom called me over to his CP (Command Post) and asked me to go down to the river and see if I could find a place that we could use to get Alpha Company back across the river after it was dark. He said that battalion was worried that they could lose an entire American rifle company that night if they did not get us out of there first. Battalion had ordered Tom to see if he could find a way to move Alpha Company across the Ca Ty River back to LZ Betty under cover of darkness. So, Tom sent me to the river to find a way across since he knew I had been a swimmer in college at UNC-Chapel Hill.

I walked out of the perimeter along the side of a large rice paddy down to the riverside with two riflemen as guards from 2nd Platoon. When we got to the river I took everything off except my pants and slowly walked into the cold water. Even though my men and I had just dumped a boat house and two boats full of armed men into that river only a short time before, since I was barefoot I was actually mostly worried about cutting my naked feet on some glass on the river bottom than I was about anything else.

As soon as I could, I lowered myself into the water and pushed along the bottom toward the middle of the river. I really wanted as low a profile as possible in that river. Since I could see pretty well in the short tropical twilight and from the ambient light of the tracers, the fires burning in Phan Thiet and the moon coming up, I knew that the enemy could see me pretty well too. So, I stayed low in that water. Soon it was clear to me that the Ca Ty River where we were now had a lot more water in it than it had in the section that we had crossed that morning. It was deep and it was running a strong current in the deeper parts.

When I went in the river, the only weapon I carried was my K-Bar knife. At first, I tried holding my K-Bar with my teeth in my mouth like a pirate. But, cold steel on teeth sucks big time. More important, I found out that you can't breathe and swim with a K-Bar knife in your mouth. So I switched it to my right hand and with my thumb folded over the knife handle and my palm open. I could swim with it that way, and I could breathe. If necessary, I thought I could fight too.

I set about swimming up and down the river looking for a more shallow crossing point where no one would have to swim since I was sure we had some non-swimmers in the company. While I was worried that I was going to lose track of my two protectors in the growing darkness, I still had to check out the river. So I kept swimming up and down the river, further and further, looking for a more shallow place to cross.

Although I found a couple of sandbars in the middle of the river, if there was such a shallow place to cross, I could not find it that night. The Ca Ty River had about a 5 foot tide at Phan Thiet at that time of year, and clearly the tide was in, most of the channel part of the river was at least 8 feet or more deep.

Luckily, I did not find any of the men I had dumped in the water earlier, but I did find my two guards when I was done. Better yet, they did not shoot me when I slipped silently out of the dark water right in front of them.
When I got back from the river, I told Tom simply,

"It's deep; swimmers only."

We were not going back to LZ Betty that night. We had to hold our position. Well, we were paratroopers. While we were surrounded again, and that is not fun, it is exactly what we do—as the saying goes, *"We are paratroopers, we are supposed to be surrounded."* Then, we hold until relieved.

That tradition for the 101st Airborne Division started at Normandy. It continued at Bastogne and it hadn't changed. The 101st Airborne Division was nicknamed the "*Battered Bastards of Bastogne*" because they had been surrounded in Bastogne. As a separate unit of the 101st Airborne in Vietnam, the 3/506th was nicknamed the "*Bastard Battalion*" and now, we too were surrounded, on our own, this time in Phan Thiet, RVN.

238

Just after total darkness, Tom called the platoon leaders together for a meeting. I asked about Gefeller, and the armorer Ratee, both were dead. Shot dead in the killing field.

So then, I stopped saying the names of my friends and just asked who else was dead or wounded. It took Tom Gentry, normally 1st Platoon Sergeant, but now acting as Alpha Company's First Sergeant a while to read all eight KIA names and then the twenty-two WIA names in the darkness. I knew all of those men. I had met most of their wives or girl friends. I couldn't cry— but I wanted to.

Tom asked us if we thought we could hold that night. I said yes that my platoon could hold the riverside and if necessary, the open side of the perimeter as well. Because of the way the land laid, most of my men could fire in either direction without leaving their positions. If I had to, I would have one man in each of my two-man foxhole positions fire in each direction. I pointed out that if anyone actually did penetrate the perimeter from the open side, because of that wide opening in the perimeter line, any enemy there would be in an absolute cauldron of gunfire because just about the whole company could shoot at them with little risk of friendly fire casualties. It was a strange tactical position, sort of a big "C" rather than a circle, but I thought it do-able.

In any event, we couldn't leave. While we simply did not have enough men left to cover all of the perimeter that because of the lay of the land we had to hold that night in a real sense that did not make much difference. Nor did it make any difference what I or the other platoon leaders thought, but Tom wanted to know. It was one of the things that made him a great combat leader—Tom Gaffney had no pride of authorship. He would listen, and he would take a good idea from anybody.

Particularly now that our former First Sergeant Bull Gergen had left on his way to promotion to Sergeant Major, Tom Gaffney, our company commander, was by far the most experienced soldier in the company. A true warrior he had received a battlefield commission in Korea, been RIFed back to sergeant in a Reduction In Force after the Korean War and had spent the intervening years in Special Forces.

Tom Gaffney knew war and he knew what was important. Having first learned his trade on the battlefields of Korea, Tom was very worried about that big gap in our perimeter. Ultimately, Tom's solution for the gap was that he would place his small headquarters section right in the middle of it. He would hold the gap; there was no one else.

Before the battle, that morning Lieutenant Len Liebler, formerly 3rd Platoon Leader had been dressed in starched new green fatigues with his rank, crossed rifles, Combat Infantry Badge, jump wings and screaming eagle patches all newly sewn on since we did not wear rank or badges in the field. Lucky Len was on his way to division to be reassigned to the rear area, probably to a staff job in another battalion. He had already packed his duffle bag, turned in his M-16 rifle and all of his field gear. However, when Alpha Company lost two platoon leaders that morning in a matter of minutes, Len was ordered back to the field to take over the former Weapons, now 3rd, Platoon.

When Len woke up that morning his tour of duty in the field as a platoon leader had been over. Against the odds for an infantry platoon leader he had made it—alive and unwounded. However, as we used to say in OCS, that was the "*word*", and then the "*word*" was changed.

So, instead of being on his way to a safe staff job for the remainder of his 12 month tour, almost all that day Len was walking his platoon's firing line in those clean, starched fatigues, with stiff, dark green, new field gear, but nobody mistook Len Liebler for an FNG, or a "f — — —g new guy".

He walked his line, ignored the gunfire directed at him, steadied his men after the slaughter in the morning and took control of what was left of the 3rd Platoon. We had all trained together in Alpha Company; even though Len had never led Weapons Platoon, now called 3rd Platoon, he still knew everybody's name. And, that safe staff job in the rear would just have to wait; Lt. Len Liebler, Alpha Company, 3/506th, had business to attend to first.

After Len Liebler reorganized 3rd platoon's side of the perimeter he came over to the meeting and said that he thought that he could hold as well. He might not have that many men left he said, but he did have three M-60 machine guns in good, strong, defensive positions, a lot of ammunition for each gun, and some guys looking for payback. Len said he was sure 3rd Platoon could hold their side of the perimeter.

Before the meeting, in the earlier darkness, Tom and Len had continued sending small volunteer groups that Joe Alexander had first used to slip in and out of the killing field to recover all of our dead and wounded. They got the last one out right before the meeting started.

One of the guys Len had on his line that night had laid in the killing field, under that broiling sun, all day. When the rescue group had tried to get him to move, although not wounded, he was so stiff from laying there all day that he couldn't move. So, they had dragged him out.

He had been shattered when they dragged him out of the killing field, but they made him some hot cocoa, spiked it with powdered coffee and lots of sugar. Now he was ready to fight again. Len and the survivors of 3rd Platoon would hold their side of the perimeter.

It was about 3:00 AM, when the last Dustoff chopper left, the battlefield was now clear and ready for the morning.

At first light in the morning, Charlie Company choppered in to reinforce us. One of the Charlie Company platoon leaders, my friend Lt. Bucky Cox, later the SAC (Special Agent in Charge) of the FBI's Los Angeles field office, was on the first chopper to arrive. Bucky was wrinkling his nose a bit as he got off the chopper and walked over to me.

I had caught a whiff of it too—that certain smell, of battle.

We went back to work, 2nd Platoon leading, Alpha and Charlie companies attacking, back into Phan Thiet.

This picture was taken in 2012. From right to left: Jim Schalax, 1st Plt; John Harrison 2nd Plt. & XO; Tom Gaffney CO; Len Liebler 3rd Plt; Joe Alexander Weapons & 3rd Plt. Photo by Michael Trant with my camera.

Given our jobs, given where we went, given what we saw and what we did, it is almost unbelievably unlikely that this picture could have been taken of the Alpha Company Commander Tom Gaffney and his four platoon leaders over 44 years after we left Vietnam. Tom is still showing the effects of a recent heart attack, and sadly, Len Liebler, our only unwounded platoon leader, passed away in 2014.

Eighteen

After I wrote this, *How To Hide Behind a Pebble,* several readers wrote to tell me that when they were new that they had been told by combat veterans that when they actually came under fire from the enemy, that they would intensely regret that the buttons on their shirts kept them from getting closer to the ground. I wish I had remembered that when I wrote this, because I thought the same thing the first time I was caught out in the open, under fire.

When I was first told that about the buttons I thought that it was the usual BS that you get as a new guy, but after I was shot at the first time, I found that it was true. Those buttons are way too big. You actually could be much closer to the ground.

So, this is yet another try at Infantry humor. . .

How To Hide Behind a Pebble*

"I was in Phan Thiet as an Infantryman in Dec – Jan '68 and agree with all. The thump, thump, thump was scary indeed until you heard the first round hit. The others tended to follow the first, so after the first one hit, you could crawl out of your helmet. For some reason, while waiting for that first tell tale explosion, I felt like I needed to crawl over to a different spot on the jungle floor although the odds of being hit there were the same in one's mind. I would like to add that, in my opinion, it is true that the buttons on your fatigues seem more like cinder blocks when you are trying to press Mother Earth."

LLC Thunderhorse
Vietnam Veteran
September 5, 2016 at 2:59 am

Every combat infantryman knows how to hide behind a pebble, but they also know it's not much use to do so. It is not that you can't conceal yourself behind one so much as it is that even though most pebbles are really hard, they still can't stop bullets. However, because they are so hard, pebbles make excellent secondary shrapnel should an explosion go off nearby. If you are an infantryman seriously considering hiding behind a pebble, a nearby explosion is almost a certainty.

Since a pebble is too small to protect you, but is solid enough to hurt you when it is driven into your body by an explosion, a good infantryman avoids them if possible. This is just one of the little things that you learn as an infantryman that serve to keep you alive in that place called battle.

This is pinned down, but given the need an infantryman could get even lower to the ground. If you look closely, you can see he is in a small depression. This is Edward Clark and was taken on February 2, 1968, near Phan Thiet, under fire. Another cool Photo by Jerry Berry, PIO 3/506th (ABN).

The question of hiding behind a pebble also points out the difference between what the Army called "*cover*" and what it called "*concealment*" when I was in the service. If you can find good "*cover*" then you are safe from enemy fire. They may know exactly where you are, in a bunker for example, but if you have good cover then you are protected from their fire.

On the other hand concealment is exactly that. The enemy cannot see you. In fact they may not even know you are there. It is their lack of knowledge of your position that protects you.

Since you can be killed just as dead by random as well as by aimed fire, most times cover is better than concealment; but there are some exceptions to this. A bunker is usually safe against the fire of an AK-47 for example, but a bunker is an absolute death trap if the enemy has a few RPG rockets. It is a much better idea in that case to simply hide.

If you can't be seen by the enemy, then the enemy can't find you, and better yet if they can't find you, they probably can't kill you. At least they can't kill you on purpose.

It was this simple rule that the VC, and the Viet Minh before them, used to fight armies far more powerful than they were for years. Therefore, if your cover can't protect you, then hiding from the enemy is a much better, much more effective, idea than staying where you are. Like most decisions, it all depends on the particular circumstances that you face.

So, if it is not useful, why then does every combat infantryman know how to hide behind a pebble? Simple, because something is always better than nothing, and if you are a combat infantrymen nothing is often all that you have in the world.

On the other hand, when you are talking about 2,000 pound, 16 inch naval gunfire, or a 750 pound Hi-drag bombs, there is no such thing as good cover. Only concealment and a little luck in being out of the blast range will work under those extremely challenging circumstances. Battle can be brutal.

I once told a civilian that I had often crawled into my helmet to hide while in combat. The civilian for some reason, doubted my story. He may have thought that he had a good reason for that doubt. I don't really remember. I had been drinking for a while that night before we spoke, so it is entirely possible that I was not as clear as I should have been in my description of how that could happen. However, I have no doubt that I did indeed hide deep inside my steel pot repeatedly in combat.

If you have ever heard the sound, "*thump, thump, thump*" then you know exactly what I am talking about. "t*hump, thump, thump*" is the sound that three mortar rounds make when they are fired from their tube. You hear that sound, and you wait. Just that sound concentrates and focusses the mind wonderfully.

You wait and you listen for the explosions that you know are coming. You listen carefully because, you know that if you hear the mortar rounds explode, that means you are still alive. You will never hear the one that kills you. On the other hand, hearing the one that maims you for life is probably at best small comfort.

As an American the good thing is, you will rarely hear more than three or four mortar rounds fired unless they are yours. One of the very real advantages of being born American is the amount of ammunition that we send to the battlefield, and that we have helicopter gunship pilots who think that it is great sport to track down and then fire up the firing positions of enemy mortar crews. These gunship pilots can do that because mortar shells are mostly visible in flight. So if you are up in the air over the battlefield you can see pretty quickly, where the mortar shells are coming from and then hone in on them.

The abundance of ammunition means that American artillery always loves to fire, and they have literally tons of ammunition available to do exactly that. They all think that what they call "*counter battery fire*" is great sport, and a fitting payback for anyone that fires at their American brothers. I always found massive American artillery fire to be very helpful on the battlefield.

Having gunships overhead also means that if the enemy mortar crew is not of the shoot and quickly scoot school of mortar crews, then that gun ship overhead will flat kill them with its first pass. The latter passes serve mostly to bust up their equipment, although it is said that some gunship pilots continue to fire purely for esthetic reasons. Not being a pilot I would not know, but I have always enjoyed watching that process unfold.

Before any of that happens though, other things occur. First you hear that "*thump, thump, thump*" sound. Then, your sphincter muscle tightens tighter than it ever has before in your life. It continues to tighten, or contract with each thump. According to doctors during contraction of a sphincter, or circular muscle, the lumen (opening) associated with the sphincter constricts or closes. This constriction is caused by the progressive shortening of the sphincter muscle itself. If the thumps continue, that sphincter muscle continues to shorten with each thump.

Again according to doctors, voluntary sphincters, like the one in the anus are controlled by the somatic nerves. That is, your brain actually orders the voluntary sphincter muscles in your anus to contract, or open, by a conscious command from your brain. However, I would love to see someone down range that hears that distinctive "*thump, thump, thump*" sound try to order their sphincter muscle not to contract. It simply can't be done.

249

Of course, some will say that they have known people, never themselves of course, that have reacted very differently when under mortar fire. They will say that these people, usually just acquaintances, not even friends, have experienced severe, multiple spasms rather than a single continuous, progressive contraction. Invariably these spasms would lead to unfortunate, dark brown, stains, some permanent, on their uniform trousers. However, this just proves the point that sphincter muscles are not always voluntary since no one would chose to spasm that way on purpose, or at least not on purpose when their pants are up, and their boots are bloused.

Therefore, no matter what the doctors say, sphincter muscles are not always completely voluntary, as anyone who has ever fully experienced explosive diarrhea can also attest. Sometimes even a good, otherwise reliable, sphincter muscle seems to just have a mind of its own.

It is the shortening of the sphincter muscle that allows one to fit into that helmet. As the firing continues, it continues to shorten. You can look this up in any medical textbook describing the operation of sphincter muscles. They will all say that the sphincter muscle constricts by "*shortening*".
When you are short enough, you will fit entirely into your helmet.

Case closed.

• Title created by the poet RonGFord. Used with permission. The rest is all my fault; don't blame Ron. You can read Ron's poem the *Wall* on my blog. Google "*johneharrison vietnam*" and it will be first up.

Edward Clark, Feb 2, 1968

Photo by Jerry Berry. Edward Clark made it home.

Nineteen

Another story about dealing with the flora and fauna of Vietnam. This time we meet an Indochinese tiger in its natural habitat. It was much closer than I ever wanted to be to a tiger.

The thing to realize about a full grown tiger is that it is huge, and very dangerous. Including the tail, it can be about 13 or more feet long and it can weigh well over 400 pounds. In short bursts, an Indochinese tiger can run about 40 miles per hour. That is a really big, really fast, really dangerous, hard to hit and harder to kill, wild animal.

It is also beautiful.

The Tiger That Tried To Join The Platoon Formation

"People back in the States thought we were making this stuff up about huge anacondas, gigantic centipedes, wild elephants and especially the tigers."

Lem Genovese

A lot of Vietnam is simply gorgeous, breathtaking and gorgeous. It was early in the morning and not very hot yet. Alpha Company was walking in platoon column formations through an emerald green, vast grassy area overlooking the South China Sea that could have easily been converted into a luxury, top flight, golf course simply by putting in the holes and placing the little flags on the greens. The sand traps were already in place as were these sort of nascent greens, fairways and rough. It was perfect, all just waiting for golf balls and golfers.

There is an actual golf course near there now, the *Ocean Dunes Golf Club, Phan Thiet* designed by Nick Faldo. It is reputed to be one of the finest golf courses in South East Asia and is located just northeast of Phan Thiet along the coast of the South China Sea, only a few miles away from where this action took place.

253

Ocean Dunes Golf Club, Phan Thiet

I was actually enjoying our early morning stroll when, suddenly as we walked along, I heard someone screaming from the radio handset behind me. I looked back to see Hal Dobie, my RTO, running up to give me the black plastic handset he was holding out in his right hand.

Then it sunk in, the voice on the radio had yelled:

"It's a lion! It's a lion! It's a fucking tiger!"

And then right before Hal got to me with the hand set, a perfect maelstrom of bullets arrived first. There were bullets flying everywhere, luckily no M-79 rounds were fired so no explosions, but lots of lead was flying all over, all around us and coming close too. It was as though you could hear each bullet cracking harshly as it broke the sound barrier on its way past us. Intense, agonizing, and fierce at the same time.

Then, I saw the enormous, orange and black, candy-striped, white-fanged, cat, running flat out in the space between my platoon and the following platoon's column formations. That cat was huge; including the tail it looked to be at least 14 feet long. It was running all-out trying to get away from the crazy humans with the black, bang sticks trying their best to hurt it.
It was a tiger, a very big tiger. A just a few feet away, tiger. No cage. No whip. No chair. No animal tamer. Thrilling? Yes, but in a really bad way.

Like everyone else in my platoon, I was dropping to the ground as fast as I could because the bullets kept pouring in from behind us as the following platoon tried its best to shoot that fleet footed tiger. I don't know how long it lasted, but the act of getting down on the ground was almost like being in some sort of scary cartoon horror movie where your feet come up, but you

254

stay right there, suspended in mid-air waiting for gravity to take effect while tracers flamed bright red as they flashed by way too closely. That part seemed to last forever as ever more bullets buzzed, cracked and whistled all around us.

Everybody missed the tiger. When last seen it was still heading northeast toward the South China Sea in the distance, still running flat out in spectacular leaps and graceful bounds across what still looked strangely like a well-manicured, gently rolling, golf fairway. . .

Although there is little worse for an infantryman than being fired on from the rear, I held my temper and complemented the following platoon leader, who will remain forever nameless, on the almost supernatural accuracy of his men in avoiding hitting any of my men when his platoon had opened fire on the tiger; and in the interest of future cooperation, I also did not mention the complete lack of any observable hits on the tiger.

Frankly though, thinking about it later, that lack of hits worried me even more than the tiger had. . .

Not as much as those bullets flashing by though, but that tiger, that tiger was something special. I can't forget that tiger.

While as far as I know, no animals were hurt creating this story, it was not for lack of trying. Afterward, well afterward, I for one, was glad that beautiful tiger got away.

Twenty

Now and then the Infantry always has to do real some Infantry things. Only the weapons change, the actual tactical business of the Infantry remains the same as it has been for centuries,. The Infantry's job is to close with and destroy the enemy. It is really that simple.

It is, and it always has been very dangerous work, even for those that can hack it. After Tet '68 we were still chasing Charlie, still doing that Infantry thing, all around Phan Thiet and up in the highlands. From time to time, we also worked further up that incredibly beautiful coast of the South China Sea at Nha Trang, and around Dalat as well. We were often so high up that the mountains were constantly misted. We were literally working above the clouds sometimes.

Our job as a unit was to be the Infantry fire brigade for most of II Corps. Even when we were not putting out fires though, we were always looking for Charlie and fighting him everywhere we found him. We found him quite a lot, particularly after Tet '68 because after Tet '68 most of the VC were wiped out and that cost the NVA their local guides.

This is about one of those Infantry meetings.

"Fix Bayonets"

"As I recall we did a couple of those charges. Bayonets or not, we must have scared the hell out Charlie.I always wondered what went thru their minds when they saw a bunch of screaming heathens looking like Vikings in steel pots coming at them."

Ron G. Ford, 2nd Platoon,
A Company, 3/506th Abn. Inf.
January 24, 2016 at 11:10 pm

If you want a chill to run up and down your spine, think of the order:

"Fix bayonets!"

Let that short phrase roll around in your brain for a while. It will pick up some speed as it does. Then, remember that an M-16 rifle is all of 44.25 inches long when it has an M-7 bayonet attached to its end. Said another way, it is a little less than four feet long.

If you do the math, and if you understand the function of a bayonet, you will also understand that the immediate reason for fixing bayonets is for you to put yourself, on purpose, within less than three feet of your equally well-armed enemy. At which point the idea is for you to shove all of the M-7 bayonet's 6.75 inches of solid carbon steel blade into the body of your enemy, preferably into his heart or some other vital, *i.e.,* blood drenched, organ.

Do you feel the chill yet?

The M-7 bayonet is based on several earlier bayonet designs, all of which are direct descendants of the World War II, M-3 Fighting Knife. Like the M-3 Fighting Knife, the M-7 Bayonet has a spear-point blade fully sharpened on one side and with a half sharpened, 3 inch long, secondary edge on the other. It can be a wicked weapon when sharp, even more so on the end of a rifle.

I have given that order, "*Fix Bayonets!*", only once in combat. Giving that order sent a chill right down my spine then, and every time since then, when I have just thought of those two words, it is the same chill. There are some things that you cannot forget.

After being out on a long search and destroy mission Alpha Company secured an extraction LZ early one morning in the dry rice paddies near Phan Thiet and near the South China Sea on the coast of South Vietnam. However, while the rest of Alpha Company choppered out of the field later that morning, the Second Platoon stayed behind.

We stayed behind to set up an ambush on the LZ that Alpha Company had just left. There was a stream bed on the southern border of the LZ. Like most stream beds everywhere in the world, the vegetation was much thicker there. So we literally just hid in the bushes along that stream, and waited.

We did not have long to wait. Two VC, both armed, both wearing black pajamas, tan ammo belts, and the tan, rice farmer's, conical, palm bamboo-plated, leaf hats strolled out into the LZ minutes after the helicopters had lifted off. Quietly, we got ready. I had prepared an M-72, LAW to fire at them as the signal for the rest of the platoon to open fire.

When they were about halfway across the LZ I fired the LAW at the rice paddy dike the two VC were walking just on the other side of. I intended for the 66 mm LAW rocket to detonate against the dike, and then the shrapnel from the rocket blast would blow through the dike and into them.

War is a mean business.

As soon as I fired the rocket and everybody opened up, I called for gun ship support, call sign "Tiger Shark" from the 192nd Assault Helicopter Company based at LZ Betty just outside of Phan Thiet. There was some return fire, but it stopped just before the gun ships arrived. The gun ships fired up the LZ with machine guns since they did not see a target worthy of their rockets, but they did a through job with those machine-guns for us. They knew as well as we did of the VC's seeming ability to hide under even a small leaf. So they shredded that rice paddy with bullets and then they did it again.

As soon as the gun ships were done firing we moved out from the protection of the creek bed to see what the result was of our stay behind ambush. Just on the other side of that rocket blasted paddy dike, we found a simple, white cotton, brassiere with a lot of blood on one side and some blood on the ground as well, but that was all we found. No bodies, no blood trail, but at least one somebody had been hit hard. The stay behind ambush had worked.

We looked around in expanding concentric circles to see if we could find a blood trail, but after a while we gave up. You always drop the rucks[1] as soon as the bullets fly because they get in the way. So, we were on the way back to the stream bed to pick up our rucks, when we were suddenly fired up from another stream bed to our right.

259

Second Platoon in an open column formation moving over a dry rice paddy outside of Phan Thiet, RVN. This was taken a month or so earlier. Even though I am up front and this is the last squad in the platoon, notice how everybody is looking in a different direction, carrying their weapons in their hands, well spread out, not all walking in a straight line, doing it right. These guys were real pros. Photo by Jerry Berry, 3/506th PIO

In response to the automatic rifle fire from our flank, the second platoon moved into an immediate action, battle drill and came up on a line firing together, everybody facing the enemies' fire.

I waited for a moment trying to figure out who had fire superiority, us or them. It seemed to me that we did, but then one of our M-60 machine guns unexpectedly stopped firing. I waved everybody down and ran down the firing line to see what was going on with that machine gun. They had not been shooting at us as much until that machine gun shut down, but their firing picked right up again when the machine gun went down.

I took the gun away from the gunner, opened the bolt and shook out the cartridge belt from the feed tray. The gunner poured some white LSA, a really incredible gun lubricant, all over the bolt and feed system and then replaced the cartridge belt carefully in the feed tray.

I jacked the charging handle. Then, I fired the M-60 on full cyclic for a full, hundred-round, belt of ammo. That took the M-60 about 10 seconds or less to fire. The machine gun worked fine for that, but immediately after that it jammed again when I tried firing, stopping, and firing again with a second belt of ammunition.

Bang, bang, jam. Not good. The first two bangs—gets their attention—makes them angry—tells them where you are—tells them that you are a machine-gun—tells them where to fire an RPG. Not good, but nothing I could do about it right now.

I told the gunner to clear the new jam and then wait for my signal. I ran back to the center of the firing line, blew my whistle and then gave the command:

"Fix bayonets!"

I was waiting for the machine gunner to be ready. Near me an F-N-G[2] rifleman turned to his fire team leader and said:

"Bayonet? I don't have a bayonet! Wait! What do I do? Wait!" the newly minted rifleman said.

"Don't worry, nobody has a bayonet. Just get ready to go." His fire team leader said.

"Charge!" I said.

Everybody got up, shooting fast, and screaming our heads off as we ran toward those bastards that were still shooting at us. That M-60 was talking lead again, full cyclic, trigger held down, assistant gunner slapping on more hundred-round, cartridge belts on the run. He knew he couldn't let it stop firing.

Damn their fire! We flat out charged their guns.

However, by the time we got to the stream bed they were firing from, the VC were gone. No bodies. No blood. No blood trails. No bloody clothing this time. Nothing.

Best of all though as far as I was concerned, there were no casualties for us either. A tripped ambush and a firefight in less than an hour, just another day in the boonies for the Second Platoon, Alpha Company, 3/506th (Airborne) Infantry, 101st Airborne Division.

It turned out that of about 34 men in the Second Platoon that day, there were only 2 or 3 bayonets in the whole platoon. For almost everything, except being stuck on the end of a rifle, a real knife is much more useful than a bayonet, so very few paras carried bayonets in the field. Line doggies[3] are utterly ruthless about the weight that we carry.

After we throughly checked out the stream bed, we headed back again for our rucks.

Probably in recognition of the success of the stay behind ambush, Alpha Company choppered out to the LZ several wooden ammo boxes full of cans of Coca Cola that had been ice cold when they left Phan Thiet. I got one. Everybody got one.

I enjoyed that Coke. I smoked a Pall Mall cigarette and sat there beside the stream in the shade leaning against my ruck. I drank the Coke slowly even though it was getting warmer all the time. I tasted that Coke like I have never tasted anything before or since. It surprised me how good it was.

Only afterwards, did I realize that I had never in my life truly tasted a Coca Cola before that one. That was one of many things that, prior to going to Vietnam, I did not know. Good to know, I guess.

Then, I wondered what sent a chill down a VC's spine? I expect there were lots of things, gun ships, F-4 Phantoms, M-60 machine guns, and probably most of all—us.

We scared 'em—you betcha.

(1) "*Ruck*" = ruck sack or back pack, aka our house on our back.

(2) "*F-N-G*" = F — — — — — New Guy.

(3) "*Line Doggie*". A nickname for an infantryman on the line in Vietnam. The nickname, "*Line Doggie*", probably relates back in some way to the famous Cheyenne Dog Soldiers of the Old West. They were ferocious fighters that fought as infantry usually. A "*Line Doggie*" is the opposite of a "*REMF*". ("*REMF*" = Rear Echelon Mother F — — — —, that famous, all purpose "F" word again.)

Twenty One

"*A Sad Story: the Soldier Who Would not Kill*" was very difficult to write, and it haunts me still.

Many who have read it think that this soldier should have been withdrawn from the field. However, this occurred right after the huge bloodletting that was Tet '68 and trained infantrymen, like him, were in very short supply all over Vietnam at the time. In addition, this young man wanted to be an infantryman, nothing else.

He was offered a position in the rear as a clerk, but he said he wanted to "*share*" the experience in the field. His mother's word and idea he said. His mother believed that one should "*share*" in the burdens of others, but that the taking of a human life for any reason was an absolute anathema to her. His father believed in always doing one's duty. I always thought that between their ideas, he was trapped.

He said that if he was pulled from the field he would request an immediate transfer to another unit as an infantryman. Given the severe shortage of infantrymen all over Vietnam at the time, he would have gotten that transfer in a flash.

People also tend to forget that we sent Conscientious Objectors to the field as medics all of the time without a weapon. They too are unable to defend themselves on the field of battle. There was also always the chance that simple self preservation, or even anger at being shot at, would finally kick in to change his mind.

Given all of that, under the rules and orders of the day, there was simply no way to pull him from the field. In any event, at that point as XO, I had to justify every day to the S-1 (the S-1 is a staff position responsible for personnel) every man that was not out in the field with Alpha Company. The Sergeant Major prowled the rear area, also every day, looking for more troops to send to the field. We were really that short of infantrymen for a while.

They were even pressuring the Battalion surgeon about giving out medical profiles that restricted field duty. It was an ugly time in that sense.

This is one soldier's story.

A Very Sad Story: The Soldier Who Would Not Kill

"I had a hard time making the decision to kill. When it was presented to me it was in anger as I had just lost two friends in the blink of an eye. I was in training for a door gunner in 15th Medevac, 1st Cav. He was the only person that I know that I killed."

"Even today I feel bad about that. On the other hand we saved an awful lot of our brothers. What is strange, I feel at peace with myself. Sorry about that young man. He had a tough job trying to please his folks."

Dave Parks
December 15, 2014 at 4:49 am

One of the bravest men I have ever known was also one of the most foolish. While this is not an unusual combination, he did it in a unique, a very strange, and a very senseless way. After being in the field as a rifle platoon leader for over seven months, I was finally reappointed and stayed mostly in the rear as Alpha Company's Executive Officer. In the normal course of things as XO, I assigned a young soldier as a replacement to the 2nd Platoon of A Company, my old platoon.

After making sure he was sufficiently trained, that is another sad story that I will tell some time, I sent him to the field. When he came back from the field the first time a couple of weeks later I found out that well trained or not, he would not fire directly at the enemy.

He fired over their heads on purpose, even on point. Since his platoon leader, platoon sergeant and squad leader had all tried talking to him about this to no avail, some of his fellow squad members, who liked him, asked me to talk to him as well since he was literally placing all of their lives as well as his own at risk.

I talked to him about it for a long time during the three days or so they were out of the field for a routine stand-down. He had thought about it a lot, but he came to a very different conclusion from me. His mother's training had made it impossible for him to participate in the taking of another human's life. His father's training on the other hand had made it impossible for him to try to avoid or evade in any way what he perceived to be his duty as an American citizen.

Therefore, he answered his country's call (a draft notice); he even volunteered for Airborne School; he was well trained in the art and craft of soldiering by the Army; and in fact, he was an excellent shot on a rifle range. However, I, and his squad members knew that when he ran into an enemy that could tell the difference between effective and ineffective fire that he and those around him would have a problem, a deadly problem. It is the way of war.

Unfortunately, when his platoon ran into such an enemy during Tet III late in the summer of 1968 he was killed in action. I was saddened because he was a truly wonderful young man, but I was not surprised.

Under the law at the time, and probably still today if they ever bring back the Draft, he really had little choice. His views did not meet the guidelines set for a Conscientious Objector, so he had to go anywhere the Army sent him. He was educated so he probably could have avoided the Infantry if he had really wanted to, but, probably because of his father's training, he elected not to.

During those three days, I used every argument an expensive Jesuit education had provided—unfortunately to no avail. He would not kill—not to save himself, not even to save his fellow squad members.

Although he literally endangered everyone's life, he was still well liked in the platoon. He really was just a nice kid; but he was also still a very young man that needed a little more exposure to life and then I think he would have made a better choice. It was just sad.

Some people really do have difficulty in "*pulling the trigger*" when doing so takes another human's life. I cannot bring myself to believe that is a bad thing, generally.

My own experience was considerably different, I found killing in a sense "*easy*," but also very costly over time. It is easy because the Army provided both excellent tools and excellent training to do exactly that because it is the job of the Infantry.

Originally, I had entered the Army expecting to make it a career. I left it because I liked everything about it — except killing people. Even when it is entirely necessary, and in every sense justifiable; even when it produces an importantly good result; it still hurts the killer to kill. Over time, it simply lacerates the soul to kill people. If you pause to think about it; it is a good thing that it does.

I do not have an answer for what an honorable man faced with this young man's kind of choice should do, but I consider that young man to be one of the bravest men I have ever met. I also consider him to be one of the most hardheaded and foolish.

Frankly, based on our discussions I blame now and I blamed then, his mother. She indelibly imprinted him with a view of life and morality that was romantic, utter nonsense, and it got her son, her only son, killed. However, when as Executive Officer I had to write her and her husband the "*letter*" after her son's death I did not tell her that. I told her and her husband the truth—that their son had been a brave, even a courageous, young man and that we were all very sorry that he was dead. The rest of the truth really made no difference anymore. He was, and would remain, dead.

Some who view the war in Vietnam think that the young soldier was playing in a rigged game that he could not win and that is answer enough for them. It is just another tragedy from a war that they believe never should have been fought.

However, that is too simplistic an answer for such an important question. In war, good war—bad war, it really does not make a difference, a soldier must kill with an absolute absence of hesitation. If he does not, the enemy will probably kill both him and his fellow soldiers at some point because they will not hesitate. Therefore, almost all infantry training is directed at achieving this result; taking a nice young American and turning him into a reliable, un-hesitating, killer of men. And, the Army does this at least in part for the soldier's own sake.

Based on my experience in the Army, it is clear that that good, realistic battle training can facilitate an appropriate, an infantry, response in combat. Strangely, probably the best, the most accurate description of the value of

269

such training that I have ever read is set forth in the book *"One Shot"* (*One Shot: A Jack Reacher Novel*, by Lee Child):

> *"James Barr was a sniper. Not the best, not the worst, but he was one of ours, and he trained for more than five years. And training has a purpose. It takes people who aren't necessarily very smart and it makes them seem smart by beating some basic tactical awareness into them. Until it becomes instinctive."*

Then, they become a soldier.

Except that the word *"smart"* is wrong. Good training teaches people the craft of the thing. Anyone, talented or not, can learn a craft, any craft. Only the talented that are fully versed in their craft can become brilliant, but anyone that knows the craft can beat even an otherwise brilliant player that does not know, or does not practice their craft.

When I was teaching in high school I compared this to the difference between two great basketball players, Michael Jordan and Allan Iverson. While Jordan is larger and you can't teach size, from a purely athletic perspective Iverson is probably more talented, but the real difference between the two is that Jordan was always relentless in the pursuit of perfection of his craft as a basketball player and that made him the greatest basketball player ever. While Iverson was always a performer, a brilliant basketball performer, he was never a true basketball player because basketball is a team sport not a showcase for an individual's talent.

Some jobs are inherently unforgiving. The Infantry is one of them. If all of the soldiers on your side are dead, it is hard to pretend that your side won the battle. In the best sense of the word this young man was a true gentleman, but that was just not enough this time.

Twenty Two

I had at least two great medics that I served with in the 2nd Platoon, John Melgaard and James Mezzetta. While I was leading another platoon, I believe that I also served with Al Thompson. Al is another combat medic of sterling reputation and a fellow author. Being a combat medic is to me the most difficult job in the armed services. The Army, or the Navy which produces corpsmen for the Marine Corps, gives you a few weeks of training and then you literally hold men's lives, perhaps even your best friend's life, in your hands.

There is no real way to prepare for that, but Dr. Andrew Lovy, our brilliant Battalion Surgeon did the best that he could. This was particularly true on the ship while on the way over to Vietnam. In that sense the stop in Olongapo, the Philippines, was a godsend for him because there were all sorts of cuts and contusions that needed stitching and setting, and there was also lots of bright red blood in his Operating Room for three full days. I never saw Doc Lovy happier.

Neither John, nor James nor Al was the medic in this story, but they and he exemplify why I, like most combat veterans, would rather been seen by a medic first if I was badly hurt, and only after that by a doctor.

Combat Medics are very special people.

Stick

"As a former combat medic with First Cav 66-67, good article. One point of contention, the idea that medics rotated out of combat after six months is a myth, at least in my assigned company. I had to chopper back to base camp with permission from our First Sergeant to personally get replacement medics waiting in the rear so that I and my best friend to this day, also a medic, could go back and rotate home."

"Our company was always short of medics, at times covering two platoons at once. I'm proud of my CMB (Combat Medic Badge) and prouder of the brothers who covered my butt and saved my life more than once."

Pete Van Til, Combat Medic
1st Cavalry Division

A Combat Medic's Badge is a very special, a very rare award. There is only one way to earn it, be a combat medic in a firefight. I never earned one. I had been a rifle platoon leader. While that was another position that also had a short life expectancy, combat medics and their badges are special for more than that.

I took a brand new medic to the field one day about halfway through my tour. Like platoon leaders, medics rarely spent more than about six months in the field. If they were not badly wounded or killed during that six months, they were rotated back to another job in the rear. The platoon's previous medic had just rotated back.

It was not that much of a firefight that day, just sort of a long-range rifle and machine-gun duel across a huge rice paddy to the North of Phan Thiet near the coast of the South China Sea. The new medic earned his Combat Medic's Badge on his first day in the field. He did his job as a combat medic, and I did mine as a rifle platoon leader, but partly because he was pushing me all the way.

The VC were in a copse of trees around a stream bed across several large, dry, rice paddies several hundred meters away from where we were. Unfortunately, we were out in the open, right in the middle of all those dry rice paddies.

The rice paddy dikes we were behind were good cover from their bullets, but we were not going anywhere until we could knock out their machine-guns and suppress their AK-47 fire. So, we traded bullets across the rice paddies while I tried to work something out.

The area on the bottom of the picture shows the huge area of dry rice paddies near Phan Thiet city shown on top of the picture split by the river. The blue is the Ca Ty River flowing into the South China Sea. If you look closely at the rice paddies you can see lots of small round white

I was waiting for the FAC (Forward Air Controller) to show up because I never sent a man where a bomb could go first. Until that happened we were trying to keep the enemy pinned down in their position. Find 'em, fix 'em, get the United States Air Force to blow them up was my tactical ideal for a good firefight.

We had one guy wounded already and I was arranging a Dust Off (Medical evacuation) for him as well. However, because of the heavy enemy fire and our wide-open position in the middle of all those rice paddies, we needed the air strike from the FAC before the Dust Off chopper could safely come in.

Just the usual helicopter gun ships accompanying the Dust Off would not be enough firepower. There were too many VC and they had too many machine-guns and automatic weapons in those trees and bushes by the creek bed for us to even move on the ground, much less to get a Dust Off chopper safely in and out.

I had the radio handset to my ear trying to arrange the air strike and the Dust Off when I felt someone tugging on my arm. It was my brand new medic, his first day in the field, his first casualty and he looked worried. I took the handset down from my ear.

"He won't let me bandage him Sir."

"What?" I said.

"He won't let me near him."

274

"What?" I said.

"He won't let me touch him. He says he's going to shoot me."

"His gun's broken." I said.

"That's what he says." replied the medic.

I looked over at the wounded soldier. He was lying on his stomach behind the same rice paddy dike I was behind. His pants were pulled down to his knees, his shirt was pulled up, his naked butt was sticking up and there was a little blood, not much, bubbling out of his ass and dribbling onto the ground.

I already knew that he had been shot right in the asshole, right in his anus. No exterior wound that the medic could see, really hard to bandage but, a perfect bull's eye.

I had his M-79 grenade launcher on my lap with the round stuck in the barrel that he had been leaning over, trying to clear, when he got shot. He had fired the weapon but the 40 mm, high explosive grenade, round was defective. It got stuck in the barrel when he fired.

"He's bleeding internally Sir. We've got to get pressure on the wound."

"What's the stick for?" I asked.

He was holding a short stick in his hand. Bullets from the VC cracked, buzzed and slashed overhead constantly.

"I was using it to apply pressure to the bandage. It's all I could think of."

"They're moving Sir. Over there." My RTO (Radio Telephone Operator) Hal Dobie said and pointed.

I blew on my whistle; pointed to Edwards, an M-60 machine-gunner, and with Ed Blanco his assistant one of the best M-60 machine-gun teams in the business. Then, all I had to do was point at his new targets and the steady, sustained fire of his M-60 machine-gun stopped that movement cold.

"We have to stop the bleeding Sir."

"Alpha 2-6, this is Jack Sprat. What do you have, over?" the black radio handset squawked loudly from my lap.

I was *"Alpha 2-6"* or the Second Platoon, platoon leader of Alpha Company. *"Jack Sprat"* was the radio call sign of our FAC.

"This is 2-6. We have gooks in the open. I think about a big squad or a platoon. I am popping smoke." I pulled the pin and tossed a smoke canister in front of me on the other side of the dike.

"Jack Sprat. I identify purple smoke 2-6."

"2-6, roger, purple smoke Jack Sprat. Do you see the tree line, 270° about 300-350 meters from my smoke, over?"

"Roger, I have Phantoms inbound, ETA 5-6 minutes. I'll let you know what they have on board when I find out, over." (ETA, Estimated Time of Arrival)

"Keep an eye on their back door please. I don't want them to leave this party, over."

"Roger, 2-6. Jack Sprat out."

"Sir, he's bleeding."

"What?"

"He's bleeding. We need to stop the bleeding. We have to get pressure on the wound."

He was still holding the stick and he had a bloody, OD green, bandage in his other hand. Staying below the top of the dike, I crawled over to the troop lying on his stomach.

"Shot in the ass." I said to him.

He smiled and nodded. His pupils were dilated from the morphine, but he was awake, alert.

"Well, let's see what's happening."

And I leaned over and pulled his cheeks apart to look at his asshole. The medic was right. I couldn't see anything except a small stream of blood bubbling out of his anus. But, the whole area was turning purple. Even I knew that meant he was bleeding internally.

"Sir, Jack Sprat." And the radio handset was shoved in my face.

"This is 2-6, over." I said.

"This is Jack Sprat. You want it all in those trees, right? Over?"

"2-6, Trees are good and then maybe strafe the whole creek bed with 20 mike mike, over?"

"Roger that, a flight of Phantoms is almost on station, we will start with napalm, then they each have a couple of 500 lbs. slicks and then finish with the 20 mike mike. I'll mark them with smoke first, over."

"Roger, good to go. 2-6 out."

The translation is that the two F-4 Phantoms, still coming up fast on afterburners, were going to drop their two napalm bombs each, follow that with their two 500 pound slick, or unguided, bombs each and then strafe the resulting mess with their Vulcan 20 mm cannons. The FAC was going to mark the enemy position with smoke rockets from his spotter plane as soon as the Phantom jets arrived. He would let the jet jockeys have a look at their target and then send them in. It was going to be beautiful, at least from our perspective.

"He's not going to jam that stick up my ass again Sir."

"We've got to stop the bleeding." I said.

"They're moving again L-T!"

"God damn it!"

I blew my whistle again, this time to get every bodies' attention. Just like in the Superbowl, no matter how noisy it gets, you can always hear a whistle. Unlike a radio, a whistle always worked, and never needed new batteries. I liked whistles. The Army gave me a dark green one which I had attached to my shirt.

"Fire!" I yelled and the whole platoon opened up.

"Dobie, give me that roll of electrician's tape." I said to my RTO Hal Dobie.

"Here, stick your butt up in the air." I said to the trooper.

I blew my whistle again just before the Phantoms roared in, one after the other, a little above tree top level.

"Cease fire!" I yelled. *"Get down. Everybody get down! Air strike coming in."*

Then, I grabbed the roll of tape from Dobie.

"Here push his cheeks together really hard. Like this. . ."

"Get the fuck away from me!" the troop yelled at the medic as he moved over to push.

"Shut up! We need to do this. No stick this time, but this will probably hurt. Get ready."

"Jesus. I am glad I'm not in those trees." Said Hal Dobie my RTO as the two strikes of napalm bombs flared off in the copse of trees.

279

One of the napalm bombs skipped and flared further down the creek bed. But the other three napalm bombs had really torched that little copse of trees. The Phantom jets circled for another pass.

"OK, push."

As the medic pushed the troop's butt cheeks together I pulled a long strip of black plastic electrician's tape from the roll and taped his cheeks closed.

We continued to do that, pulling each strip of tape as tight as we could from hip to hip, completely covering the crack of his ass with overlapping strips of black plastic tape, putting pressure on the wound to stop the bleeding inside or, at least to slow the bleeding down. The one inch wide, black plastic tape was sticking good to his skin, but, to keep it tight we made five or six passes with the tape all the way around his body as the medic held the troop's genitals out of the way. The kid groaned a few times, but he held steady for us as we taped him up.

I heard some metal pounding on metal after the forth pass, the second set of two 500 pound bombs going off. I looked over a couple of feet away from where I had been sitting to see my new platoon sergeant, Manfred Fellman, pounding away with his entrenching tool. He had the handle of one entrenching tool jammed down the barrel of the M-79 and he was pounding on it with another entrenching tool trying to drive the stuck shell out of the barrel.

I was actually glad to leave Sergeant Fellman with the wounded troop, the medic, and that dud 40 mm M-79 round, while I took the rest of platoon forward to clear the copse of trees after the Phantoms left. When we finished that I called in the Dust Off and then we moved on down the creek bed since we found nothing useful in what little was left of the copse of trees, no bodies, no body parts, no blood trails, no weapons, nothing except three Ho Chi Minh sandals and a brand new, folded up, brown plastic, VC poncho. At least one of the sandals had some blood on it though.

Just another day at the Infantry office for me and my new medic is the way I remember it. He did his job, and I did mine. In combat you do what you need to do. Those 40 mm grenade shells have a casualty-producing radius of 15 meters, so we were all right in the middle of that radius if the dud had gone off while Sergeant Fellman was pounding on it. However, we needed that M-79, so Sergeant Fellman had pounded the dud shell out. Then, he fired the M-79 to make sure it worked.

We needed to stop the bleeding, so we taped the trooper's butt shut. I knew my RTO Hal Dobie had the electrician's tape; the medic did not know that. You work together; you find a way to do what needs to be done; then you do it; rank does not matter; only results matter. That night, after we had set up an ambush position on a nearby trail the medic came over.

"He's going to be all right, L-T. Doc Lovy says he was lucky." He said. Dr. Andrew Lovy was our battalion surgeon.

"Good." I said and stuffed some C-Ration white bread smeared with some jam in my mouth.

You can't eat hot food, even C-Rations, on an ambush. You can't eat canned white, C-Ration bread without something on it. The jam was almost all sugar, not much fruit but it did improve the white bread.

"How are his balls?" I asked.

281

"Doc says he thinks they will be fine. The bullet went in his ass, hit his pelvis, turned and went down his right leg next to the bone. Stopped just above his knee. Other than his first, and probably second, dump being a bear, there shouldn't be a problem."

"He might have stabbed you. I don't think he would have shot you. You never know though, he did still have his .45. I forgot about his pistol. Sorry." I said.

Most M-79 gunners carried a .45 caliber automatic pistol, the venerable John Browning designed Colt, Model 1911 for when it was too close to fire their M-79. It had been sitting right next to him along with his K-Bar fighting knife and the rest of his gear. The pistol was probably loaded, cocked and locked, since it is not much use to an infantryman any other way.

Now the platoon would trust him, maybe even when he had crazy ideas about the use of sticks, because he saved lives. He was a combat medic. I gave him the rest of my can of jam. I already knew he liked it. I hated that jam, it was way too sweet, but a little of it did make the white bread edible. He ate it with his index finger, right out of the can.

"Doc Lovy said the electrician's tape was a great idea. Doc said the pressure of the tape and the blood expander I gave him probably kept him alive. Kind of hard on his pubic hair though when they pulled all that tape off." He said.

And, we both crossed our legs.

Twenty Three

There are somethings that you really cannot forget. They engage too many basic emotions, for too long a time. It is a combination of intensity and violence that sears them in the mind's eye.

This story covers two of these times for me. You will understand after you read it. There is memorable, and then there is powerful. There is a difference. Here is one of each that are strangely, tied together.

A Way You'll Never Be

"We (Charlie Company) were about 4 klics north of LZ Betty when we saw the explosions. I swear the biggest one looked like a tactical nuke. Best firepower demonstration ever. but it forever ruined 4th of July's for me."

"We thought LZ Betty was wiped out!"

John A. Barber
C Company, 3/506th Abn. Inf.

There are few things as boring as sitting on an ambush all day. You can't eat. You can't smoke. The smells of each would alert the enemy. You can just sit there. That's all. Sometimes watching the sweat bead up and then run down my arm was the most interesting thing around. So, we would read, or we would very quietly tell each other stories. We would do almost anything, that was quiet, to make the time pass.

Even for Vietnam that day was hot. Of course, that may be what brought the story to his mind.

"Well," I heard a nearby troop begin a story, *"Minnesota can get cold like you would not believe, but that never stopped anything. We had an oil pan heater, and a battery heater in the pickup, so that was no problem.*

And my mother had bought me this huge down coat that went all the way to my knees. That coat was so warm.

"So, I took the pickup and went to Julie's to pick her up for the Prom. She was so pretty. She had a sexy strapless dress and everything."

"My mom had bought me a corsage. The kind you pin on. Not a wrist corsage like I had asked her to get. She was smiling when she gave it to me."

"I said: 'But mom, but, but, I'll have to touch her, to touch her boob mom.' My mom said it was 'OK', and that even her father would not object. Besides they were out of wrist corsages, so it was this one or nothing."

"Man I was so excited when I got to Julie's. I took that flower box and walked up to Julie in her living room. Julie smiled as I reached in to pull her dress out a little to pin the corsage on her, but all of a sudden I had to fart. I'd had tacos and refried beans for lunch. All at once it hit me so hard ."

"Her parents were standing there. They were smiling just like my mom had said they would, and I had to fart so bad. But I held it in. And I gently pulled the top of her dress out just enough and pinned the corsage just like my mom had taught me so it wouldn't stick her. It was the first time I ever did that."

"And then of course they wanted to take pictures. So I had to take my big coat off and I really had to fart by then, but we stood there smiling in front of their fireplace. They had a really big fire going too."

"Then Julie took forever putting on her coat because of the flowers. Her coat was also a big down one like mine. And I was watching her, standing there on one foot and then on the other. Her dad sort motioned to me silently, kind of like asking if I had to go, but I shook my head 'No'. I just wanted to get out of there. Now, right now. Please. It was all I could think about."

"We finally got outside, and I put Julie in the pickup and then I walked around the back. Her parents went back inside as soon as I put Julie in because it was so cold. You have no idea how cold it can get in Minnesota. As I was walking around the back of the truck right after they shut their front door, I let that big fart rip. Man did that feel good. I just let'er rip."

"I got back in the truck smiling big. I was so proud of myself. Of how I'd handled it all, the flowers, touching her boob, the fart. So adult and everything. Julie had sort of slid a little over to the middle after she got in. I thought, man this is going to be so great. My first Prom, my first date really. I had been so scared when I had asked Julie. I was so surprised when she said 'Yes.' It was all turning out so perfect. Better even than I ever thought it could be."

"It was just a little later, we were not even out of her driveway when I smelled that fart easing its way out of my coat. I just ignored it. But man, it stunk. It was so bad. I mean, I am a farm boy and I never smelled anything like that. And that down coat had held it all in. Saved it up, and then sent it up, really. There is not that much room inside a pickup truck, so that smell filled it up pretty quick. The fan on the heater was going full blast blowing it around."

"I was almost gagging. I was afraid to say anything. Julie had stopped talking. It seemed like she might have even stopped breathing."

"All of a sudden, like we did it on a signal, cold or no cold, we both reached for those window crank handles at the same time. Man, we ripped those windows down. That ice cold, stink free, air filled that truck, but I yanked the zipper down on my coat anyway. There was still more of that fart inside. Julie started laughing and then pounding my coat to get it out, I started laughing too."

It had gotten absolutely silent as he told the story. Then, everybody was laughing at it. It was way too loud for an ambush, but worth it I thought. He got a little angry.

"Hey, that was the best fucking night of my life. . . And, and all of it because of that fart." Then, he too started laughing.

Two days later we were back at LZ Betty (Landing Zone Betty) on a short stand down. We had issued two beers and two Cokes per man. It does not sound like much, but it surprises a lot of people to learn that probably about a quarter of the guys, paratroopers and elite warriors all, did not drink, and a few more generally liked a cold Coke better than beer. In any event, everybody liked Coke. So, depending on the market, on a trade you could get one, or most times two, beers for each cold Coke.

That was enough for a very relaxed mood for everybody except my new Platoon Sargent, SFC Manfred Fellmann. As a former member of the German Wehrmacht in World War II at eleven years old and a holder of the Iron Cross no less; he did not just like beer; he loved beer. So he always made his own, more extensive, arrangements.

After the beer and a barbecue, we were at the company headquarters building that evening. Tom Gaffney, the Alpha Company CO (Commanding Officer) and I were sitting in our office drinking when we heard the first of the three mortar rounds hit up the hill, near the Battalion Headquarters.

This was the battalion headquarters building. The roof was holed in several places. The front of the building was partially blown in even though it was not facing the explosions. Although old, the building was solid concrete block and steel reinforced concrete construction but it still partially blew apart. Photo by Jerry Berry 3/506th PIO.

We had not even heard the thump when the mortars were fired, but we sure heard the little explosions when they went off. By the time we got outside we could hear Tiger Shark, our gunships, already winding up their engines on the tarmac getting ready to go mortar hunting. It was easy at night to see the flash when the mortars fired, and gunship pilots loved hunting and killing mortar teams.

After the mortar explosions there was a fire burning up just beyond battalion headquarters that we could see the light from it in the dark sky, but the first few secondary explosions were not much. Then, a big one detonated.

Tom started yelling to set up a perimeter around the company headquarters. He was worried about VC sappers infiltrating the LZ Betty's perimeter in the confusion. He was standing in the Orderly Room doorway, yelling, but still holding his fifth of Jack Daniels Black Label open in one hand. Then we heard the blast from the next explosion that was even bigger than the last one.

I got my platoon digging their foxholes and connecting them with 1st and 3rd platoons positions. We made a large company perimeter around our HQ building entirely inside the LZ Betty perimeter. When I finished setting the troops' positions, I walked back along my line as they dug in.

The next explosion was simply unbelievable. There are some sounds that are so loud that you cannot hear them. You feel them instead. I immediately dropped down in a foxhole beside of one of my troops, who had also dropped down in his half dug foxhole as the sound waves shattered the night above us.

After the explosions died down again, I got up and continued to walk my line. I had taken only about three steps when there was an even bigger explosion. It was like nothing I had ever heard. It was so large, so loud, so powerful, but first, it lit the entire night sky like day.

When I saw that, I dove back to my troop's foxhole, landing on his back with a thud and digging my steel pot into his back. We actually felt the explosion's sound as it rolled over us in violent waves of perfect noise, and then we felt it again as it rumbled though the ground underneath us. The concussion made you feel dizzy like you had been drinking.

Initially I felt really bad about hitting him so hard in his back when I had landed on him, but I needed that cover too. It turned out that I had hit him hard enough when I had landed on him that he had farted. I hadn't heard it, but I did smell it.

Then, I realized that the troop I had just landed on was also the one who had told the story at the ambush, and I remembered that he had really emphasized the shear power of his farts. The smell seemed to be trapped down in the foxhole, just like it had been trapped in this coat. He was right. It was powerful.

It was bad, really bad. So, I started laughing. Explosions still pounding us and all, and I was laying on top of him, trying to crawl entirely inside of my steel pot, laughing.

After the big one, there were secondary explosions going off, some quite large as well. So we stayed down and waited. Some of them were even going off in the air, probably cannon shells after they had been blown up there by another explosion.

Shrapnel was flying everywhere and there I was, laying on this soldier's back, giggling about a long ago fart in Minnesota. I could not stop laughing. His farts did have real staying power I thought, and then I started laughing again.

When the explosions finally died down some, he asked if I was all right. I told him I was and I apologized for landing on him so hard. He said that was all right because he was glad to have me, or anything really, on top of him for cover, and then he started laughing too.

I was glad to know that my body, being at least as useful as a couple of three or four sandbags as overhead cover for him had made up for the way I had arrived as far as he was concerned.

Then, there was another big explosion. So we both ducked back down again. When that had ended he asked:

"What were you laughing at Sir? When the bombs were going off?" he was looking at me more than a little strangely when he asked the question.

We were sitting facing each other on opposite sides of his foxhole. We were mostly reading lips in the bright moon light. Our ears were still shot and we were also still too dizzy from the explosions to stand up.

"That story you told about the magnificent fart." I said and then I laughed a little again thinking about it.

"Oh, that. I had thought that I was plenty scared then too, particularly when I asked Julie to go to the Prom. But back then, back then I really didn't know nothing about what real scared could be." he looked around, and then he began to dig again, still sitting down.

The explosions kept coming almost all night, some big, some little. We found out later what had happened. One of the three mortar rounds had hit the ARVN's Binh Thuan Province Ammo dump just outside and a little on the other side of the hill LZ Betty was on. It had started a fire in the ammo dump and that was what set off the explosions. Some of the explosions were so huge that people had heard, watched and some had even felt them for miles around LZ Betty.

Bravo and Charlie Companies, out in the field, had seen them. They had thought that LZ Betty and all of us were just gone. They could not see how anyone could live through what they had seen, and Bravo Company at least had also heard the explosions as they watched them light up that night sky. After they found out that we were all right, I don't believe there were any American fatalities, they all said that LZ Betty blowing up had really looked spectacular.

By unanimous agreement, it was the most incredible fireworks display that any of them had ever seen. At that point I always replied that my eyes had been squeezed shut tight, most of that night, and that I would have much preferred to have watched it from their perspective.

The front gate of LZ Betty was near the ARVN ammo dump. It had started the night with a sand bagged watch tower set on four big telephone poles and then down below, a steel reinforced concrete bunker built by the French to protect the gate.

This is what was left of that steel reinforced concrete bunker built by the French. Even though it was low to the ground because it was partially dug in, it was still destroyed by the explosions. It only stood about 3 or 4 feet above the ground on the side facing the ammo dump. As you can see it was not hit by anything except repeated shock waves from the explosions, but it was still essentially blown apart. There had been a triple sandbag thick fighting position built on top of

the bunker before the explosions, and two rows of sandbags stacked in front of the bunker. They were mostly gone in the morning. Photo by Jerry Berry 3/506th (ABN) PIO.

When I walked over to the front gate the next day to look around I could see that the watch tower was gone too. It had been completely obliterated by the explosions. There was not even a trace left. I had already heard that the guards in the tower had just jumped down after the first small explosions. The tower had been about 40 feet tall. Then, they ran into the concrete bunker below.

After the first big explosion they decided that even a steel reinforced concrete bunker was not enough so they and the guards from the bunker had just started running. It was well they did because a later explosion, perhaps the next one, had wrecked that concrete bunker as well. The power of those explosions was just incredible.

These are before and after pictures of the front gate, and importantly the picture on top is after the engineers had cleaned up the road and bulldozed the road and area around the gate. You can see the debris pile in the back. The gate on the bottom is the repaired gate, and that is about what it had looked like structurally before the explosions. The building in the center of the bottom picture is about where the French blockhouse used to be, commanding the entrance to LZ Betty. Photos by Jerry Berry 3/506th (ABN) PIO.

In a very real way the two tower guards were lucky that they were paratroopers. The landing might have killed a leg (non-Airborne), but not jumping, or being incapacitated by a hard landing, would certainly have killed them when the next explosion detonated.

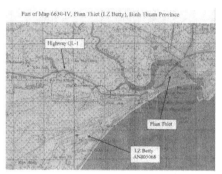

Map showing LZ Betty and the length of the runway.

For just one example of their power, the explosions had blown artillery shells all the way to the other end of the air field and scattered them all along its length, including some 200+ pound 8" howitzer shells as well as 155mm shells and lots of 105mm shells. All those artillery shells were now considered to be unstable. According to the engineers, just walking up to them could possibly send enough of a vibration through the ground so that you risked setting them off and if one went off, others would surely follow.

On the other hand the runway had to be cleared and cleared fast. The ARVN needed an emergency resupply of ammunition. The engineers went to work.

They soon had enough of the runway cleared that they were landing and unloading Air Force C-123s one after the other. At first, even before they had cleared the entire runway, these planes would hit the top of the runway and then go into a full emergency stop mode. That was interesting to watch all by itself. It seemed that those planes could land and stop in little more than their own length. This went on all day. Those Air Force pilots were real pros.

We went back out to the field the day after the big explosion, our stand down was cut short. In the field, I put my CP near the troop's foxhole a few times. I was hoping for another good story, but all he ever talked about was cows.

Author's Note

No, after almost 50 years I do not remember which troop it was that told the story. I wish I did. If someone can identify who it was, I'll put it in. To me that part of the story is almost Holden Caulfieldish of *Catcher in the Rye* fame.

Twenty Four

Coming home from Vietnam was unlike coming home to America from any other war. This is that story for me.

It still hurts.

The Time America Forgot

"Ditto my Vietnam experience Lt. I was with the 327th and was wounded 3 weeks in country. 1969 proved to be a very bad year for our battalion, in particular, in the A Shau valley where I was wounded."

"Coming home and landing at Fort Lewis at 2:00 AM, we found ourselves being bombarded with the f-bombs and assorted hippy liberal bullshit from beyond a fence by the tarmac. It was a shock to all us coming down the stairs off the aircraft. It broke my spirit."

"It became an awakening as to how America was treating Vets coming back from Nam. I swore to myself to never treat anther human being as we were subjected to during that ugly part of my life. . ."

Larry Pretzer
Vietnam Veteran
December 26, 2016 at 4:35 pm

Finally my war was over. That plane was so quiet on takeoff, but when those wheels came up, pandemonium reigned. I've been in firefights that weren't as loud. Then, that 7-0-quick, freedom bird, flew us home.

Everyone that was there has their own story of what it was like to return to America from the Vietnam War. But, the big thing is, one minute you are there, in country and then suddenly, you are home. Or, at least in California, and on the way. There was no transition, no time at all for decompression, and usually all of the people you came home with on the plane were strangers.

This was a great day. I am Infantry, but I am sitting down. My rifle and my radio are in easy reach. I am in a war zone, but no one is shooting at me. Life was good, but it was also a very unusual day for us. Photo by Jerry Berry, 3/506th Abn. Inf. PIO

After my tour I came back in late 1968. I flew into San Francisco, caught a ride from the military airport to the spectacular Mark Hopkins Hotel sitting magnificently on top of a hill overlooking downtown San Francisco and the Bay beyond. That was where my Uncle John picked me up. I was standing there in front of the hotel in full dress khaki uniform, brand new ribbons pinned to my chest and all, but I had been sitting on a plane for about sixteen hours and I looked like it.

No one spit on me, but no one said, "*Welcome home*" until my Uncle said it, and then he hugged me. I don't remember him ever doing that before, or since.

Pretty much everybody else had completely ignored me standing there in front of one of the finest and busiest hotels in America in my still shiny, black Corcoran jump boots, with a hard to miss, powder blue infantry cord, and then a big, bright Combat Infantry Badge over three rows of colorful ribbons pinned above silver Airborne wings. They all really stood out on those rumpled dress khakis. There was also a big, stuffed, Army OD green, overseas service, duffle bag sitting there right beside me on the curb.

As far as being noticed by the people of San Francisco, I could have been a tree, but I had a big smile on my face. I was really glad to see me back home in America, even if no one else seemed to notice, much less care. I was home!

According to my Uncle everything was fine until after dinner that first night back from the war when I leaned back in my chair and it just kept going until I hit the floor. It might have been jet lag, but I think it was much more likely related to the impressive amount of Jack Daniels, Black Label, sour mash, Tennessee sipping whiskey, that I had consumed before, during and after dinner.

That was also my Uncle's guess. He and my cousin Nancy put me to bed. It was the first time that I had slept between real sheets in about a year, but unfortunately I was way too drunk to notice.

While I had only been gone one year many things, some very important to a young man, seemed to have changed in America during that year. Now, after some bra burning that I had missed, women suddenly had nipples poking out, one on each side of their chest, and, with their girdles gone as well, they now had two round buttocks instead of just one large one. It was all quite startling for a young man fresh from a war zone.

I no longer knew what the rules were. I did not know whether I was supposed to notice these changes, or not. I wanted to act correctly, and to throughly explore both topics, but that would have to wait until I got home to Washington, D.C. First though, I felt a real need to reconnect with both my extended family, and my country.

I was back, and I needed to see them both. San Francisco was only the first stop on my return tour through America and my family that I had very carefully planned as my trip home from war.

My Uncle John was by then a Navy Captain and was the Director of NCIS. I called him "*Spy*" because he had actually been one in Turkey right after World War II. He was working on his third war as a naval officer.

He invited me to lunch the day after I got back. I had a real bad hangover from all of that Jack Daniels, but I joined him at the Condor Club in North

Beach. My aunt dropped me off at the door to meet him there. She was smiling, but she did not come in.

We were met at the door by a very pretty young lady about my age who was topless, and who was wearing the shortest, black leather, miniskirt I have ever seen. I got a good look at her face because I was trying very hard not to stare at her exposed breasts. However, I did notice that she had nipples. Two of them. One on each side. I counted them carefully as I ignored them completely.

I did not know what to say:

> "Nice skirt." seemed forced, given the circumstances and the size of the skirt.

> "Neat nips." seemed flippant, and perhaps too personal as well?

So, I did not say anything. She smiled at me. She seemed truly glad to see me. While I was wearing civvies, clearly out of date style wise, as well as being rumpled from being stuffed in that   Army OD green, duffle bag, neither seemed to bother her. Nor did my very short, also very out of style, Army haircut.

She was the very first person that I met in America, other than my family, that had showed any interest in me as a person. I liked her immediately.

As we were seated at a small round table inside the club, Carol Doda descended to the stage on top of a brilliant, shiny, white grand piano. You could say that she was wearing that piano since, other than a small black sequined G-string, that was all she was wearing. This was not a strip joint —they appeared stripped. Her two huge breasts were already famous as

302

the "*Twin Peaks*", or "*Twin 44's*" of San Francisco, but I actually preferred the smaller, perky ones on the pretty, young lady that had greeted us at the door.

During that long, liquid lunch with my uncle I found out that the "*hair of the dog*" does indeed work. Although that first drink goes down a lot more like medicine than like a proper drink would. On the other hand, the second drink and those that follow are, fine.

We were served by another young lady who I noticed immediately was also topless. Her's split the difference between Carol Doda's and the young lady's at the door, and like her pert, blond pony tail, they bounced a little as she moved. I liked our waitress too.

She was also dressed in an equally short, black leather, miniskirt. Just like the girl at the front door. That completely improbable black leather skirt was their uniform I finally figured out. That black leather skirt and equally black, high heal shoes was also their uniform, all of their uniform. I thought that both were a real improvement over the Army's shapeless uniforms that I was more used to, but I doubted that the Pentagon would ever approve such a change.

Several times as we sat there drinking quality American whiskey, in short, thick American glasses with lots of American ice, I noticed that my face actually hurt from smiling so much. Really, the muscles in my face hurt. I have never felt that before, or since.

There were several waitresses moving around the room serving drinks mostly and as I watched them I tried to get that big smile off of my face. I tried to relax my face, but it would not relax. I was so glad to be home and it was so much fun each time to order more booze from our ever more beautiful waitress. We took a cab home, I think.

After a few days with Spy and family in San Francisco, I went to LA to see my Aunt Elizabeth. I took the train down the coast from San Francisco to Los Angeles. It is a spectacular way to travel the West Coast. I had bought some new civilian clothes from the Presidio PX with Spy. So other than my short, obviously military, hair, I no longer looked so out of place sitting in the observation car, drinking alone, with only my big, stuffed, duffle bag sitting on the seat beside me to keep me company.

The bartender on the train was a man. So it was not as much fun to order as it had been at the Condor Club, but I overcame that and noticed that he had a delightfully heavy hand with the whiskey. He was the only person I spoke to on the train but then, other than ordering a drink or three, we did not speak.

Then it was on to Dallas, Texas to see my father and the Texas side of the family. No "*welcome homes*" so far anywhere, except from family. I was still carrying that big, Army OD green, overstuffed, duffle bag whenever I travelled, but both it and I were apparently invisible to everybody we met.
In addition, other than one time, there was no interest from anybody, including family, about what had happened in Vietnam, or what I had done there, or what was still going on there. Silence ruled.

Nor were there any more topless bars. While well covered nipples were in evidence everywhere, I think air conditioning helped that, evidently topless bars were a San Francisco thing. I regretted that, but I continued to drink whenever it was offered, and it was offered regularly. So, I was still mostly smiling.

When we visited my father's job in Dallas we learned that the son of an associate that worked there with him had been killed in Vietnam the day before I visited. So that part of the visit was quiet. No smiling by anyone. However, other than with my family, that was the only time that even the word "*Vietnam*" came up from people that I met during my extended trip home.

Finally, it was on to DC and home. I was surprised when I got home a little after lunch that day to find the front door of our house was locked. In all the time that we had lived there the front door had only been locked after the last person came in at night and when we were out of town. The back door to our house had never been locked—nobody ever had a key to the old fashioned lock on that door.

Now there were heavy locks and bolts on every door into the house. There had been riots in DC and many other cities after Dr. Martin Luther King had been murdered in Memphis while I was in Vietnam. Then, in a Los Angeles hotel kitchen Senator Bobby Kennedy had also been murdered while I was gone. So now we locked all our doors at night, and even during the day as well.

One of the first things my Mother did was to give me the two keys that I needed to open the front door of our home. Having a key felt so strange. Before I went to Vietnam, I had never needed, nor ever had, a key to our home.

My Mother also gave me back a .22 caliber rifle of mine that she had taken out during the riots and loaded, but did not know how to unload. She thought you had to shoot it to unload it and she did not want to do that in the house. Even after I explained the process, she still told me to take it outside to unload it.

That first night my Mother told me about a couple of friends that had died in Vietnam while I was there. One of them, a Marine named Tom Fleming, had been a very close friend. He had been killed by a mortar round. My brother said his casket was very light. They had decided not to tell me about Tom and the others until I returned.

Like several of my friends, our family dog had also died while I was in Vietnam. They did not tell me that either until I got home. I missed that dog. I had really been looking forward to seeing her again. Her name was Penny. She was a beautiful, pure bred, collie. Actually she was my little sister's collie, but she was our dog and now she was gone too.

I was beginning to feel as though it was dangerous to ask any questions about what had happened at home while I was gone. There was no good news.

Stranger still though, other than just once, and telling me about my friends' deaths, nobody talked about Vietnam. It was on the news every night, but nobody talked about it. Other than my closest family and then only when we first met, nobody seemed to care that I had just returned from a war zone, from a still very active war zone where Americans were killing and dying everyday, but nobody seemed to care.

However, even in the family all was not entirely well about my tour in Vietnam. One time, I was asked by one relative when I first saw her:

"So, how many people did you kill?"

I guess I should have been angry, or insulted, or something, but it was the first real question about the war, about my war, and as it turned out; it was also the only question from anybody about what I had actually done while I was in Vietnam. While I was there, fighting for them. So, I answered it as honestly as I could:

"More of them than they did of me."

However, now I am not so sure that is true. What with Agent Orange waiting in the shadows and killing more of us every year, with flashbacks and demons in the dark of night, I am not even sure sometimes that the Vietnam War is over.

After I got back I made two promises to myself. I vowed, never again. Pregnant women and little children would go before I would fight for these people again. Next time, if there ever was a next time, that I would only fight for myself and my family if I ever fought again at all, and that I would vote in every election.

I've kept both promises.

Twenty Five

The Vietnam War continued long after we Currahees had all returned from our various wars over there. For some, this continuation was a good thing, for most others it was not good at all. We could not get away from it even after we returned. Some also carried death with them when they returned in the form of Agent Orange. So their war really never ended at all.

When we returned and for a long time thereafter we Vietnam veterans, at least socially in America, were pariahs of the worst sort. After many years, we began to be honored for our "*service*", even if our war was still not honored at all. After so many years, it was difficult for many veterans to accept the profound change in public attitude toward them, and many vets kept the persona of outlaws that they had adopted when they had first returned to ridicule, or spit.

These Vietnam veterans preferred remaining as an outlaw to the glib phrase: "*Thank you for your service.*" These veterans still lived by the much harder phrase we often used in Vietnam: "*It don't mean nuthin.*" That one they understood.

They had given their service there without expecting any thanks, since that was exactly what they got, it came as no surprise. They could ignore what was said about them, it was the studied insults to their friends that did not come home that hurt even the strongest of them. That has been impossible for many of us to forget, or forgive.

Now, some study the Vietnam War in college courses, and there are even Vietnam War re-enactors in England I am told. Although exactly what they are re-enacting there remains pretty much a mystery to me, and perhaps to them as well.

308

In all of the important ways, the Vietnam War will only really end when we, the veterans of that war, end. This is the story of one such ending.

Brothers then, Brothers now

"This unadorned-by-any-jewelry-except-a-CIB straight-leg grunt appreciates your work a great deal. My single-malt-aided discussions with my late brother-in-law attorney (a former Navy Lt. Cdr. who did FO duty with the the Marines on the beach) help me understand a bit of this story beyond what you wrote."

Bill Johnson
Vietnam Veteran
June 26, 2016 at 11:43 pm

Once when we were in Vietnam we found several hundred pounds of marijuana. Like the American Army did with beer, apparently the VC/NVA handed out marijuana to their troops as a morale booster.

According to one of my soldiers who said he was in a position to know, this was:

"Good shit. Really good shit, L-T."

We burned all of it on top of a mountain near Dalat. Alpha Company was in a 360°, all around, defensive perimeter, but when we burned the marijuana the down wind side of the perimeter seemed to be especially well defended to me. So, I went to the up wind side.

I was not being virtuous, I thought that at least it could warn the rest even if I was shot. Anyway marijuana had never appealed to me because I was afraid of getting hooked, like I was already hooked on cigarettes. It wasn't virtue that kept me away from the burning marijuana, it was fear. The fact that I liked smoking cigarettes did not change that I recognized that I was also hooked on them too.

On that hill top near Dalat was the first time I ran into marijuana in a professional sense. After I got back from Vietnam several years later I was a partner in a local law firm and that was when I ran into it again, professionally speaking.

Almost all law firms do some form of *Pro bono* work. That means doing free work for some clients as a matter of professional responsibility. Some law firms take impact cases as a form of *Pro bono* and also for the free advertising it generates for the law firm, but you do need to win those cases for that to really work, and the bigger the impact, the better the publicity, the harder they are to win. Anyway, I never thought "*impact cases*" were real *Pro bono*. So, we did not do them.

What my law firm did was that we would reduce our fee to our cost for middle income folks' personal cases. The rich get any lawyer they want since they can afford to pay for it. There are many free legal services for the poor, but there is pretty much nothing for a middle income person in legal trouble.

Lets say your kid gets charged with marijuana possession, or some other crime, even reckless driving. You could be looking at paying a substantial legal fee or risk watching your child go to jail, or even to prison; particularly in Virginia where we mostly practiced.

If a case is criminal, the entire fee must be paid up front before the lawyer even lifts a pencil. It can devastate even an upper middle class family's finances. For example, the up front fee for a felony could easily be the same as a full year's tuition at a good university. A major felony indictment would be much more, still paid up front. Most people find it hard to just write a check for that kind of money.

So, that was one thing we did. The other *Pro bono* work we did was we would take any former enlisted airborne soldier's case for free. I owe enlisted airborne soldiers a lot and that was one way I could recognize that debt.

Somehow, John Powers*, a former member of the 173rd Airborne Brigade (Separate) in Vietnam, had heard of us and had asked for our legal representation. We said yes.

John was a highly decorated former Staff Sergeant who had served in the 173rd Airborne Brigade (Separate) in Vietnam twice, two full tours. He had earned the Bronze Star for Valor with two Oak Leaf Clusters meaning that he had three of them, three Purple Hearts as well, a couple of Air Medals, an Army Commendation Medal with a "*V*" device and an Oak Leaf Cluster for that medal as well.

For those that have not been in the military, that's a lot of medals. He also had all of the usual service and campaign ribbons, topped of course by a Combat Infantryman's Badge and with sterling silver jump wings under the ribbons, on the bottom.

Most veterans know that the awarding of medals often has more to do with who lives after a particular action rather than what happened. It is not that the medals awarded are not deserved so much as it is that there are often many more men that deserve medals but do not receive them because everyone that saw the deed is dead, or because there is no one left alive that can write well, or even because the person that earned but never received a medal was not particularly well liked in the unit.

In addition, an officer is likely to get a Silver Star for the same things that an enlisted man might get a Bronze Star with a "*V*" device for doing. Generally as well, the more elite the unit, the harder it is to win any particular medal. It's not fair, but that is the way it often works. The only exception is the Medal of Honor, everyone is equally unlikely to get that medal.

Most important for a former Airborne trooper, John's wings, his silver Parachutist Badge, had a little bronze star right in the center. That meant he had made what we called a "*combat blast.*" He had been a member of the 173rd Airborne Brigade (Separate) when they parachuted into combat in Vietnam. The 173rd was the only large American unit in the Vietnam War to make a combat jump and John had been there, done that. For an Airborne man that is truly special.

Jumping, on purpose, out of a perfectly good airplane in flight according to my brother the former Marine is simply stupid. However, landing by parachute among the enemy is the dream of men that jump out of perfectly good airplanes on purpose. John was such a man.

Even without the combat blast, how many jobs as a part of the job description require you to "*close with and destroy*" an enemy that may be shooting at you with a machine gun or two while his buddy also tosses hand grenades at you? How many require you to charge up a hill when there are people with automatic weapons, grenades, mortars, rockets, *etc.*, that do not want you to join them on that hilltop? How many such jobs are there?

It is important to recognize that closing with and then killing a well armed, well trained enemy is just part of the job of being infantry. While it does not happen every day, doing this is not special. You do not get a medal for this;

this is what you are supposed to do every time you run into the enemy. It is your job.

Given this, given these kinds of medals, particularly for an enlisted man from an elite Airborne unit meant that someone had done something truly special, probably truly dangerous as well. Clearly, it was John that had done something "special", something probably incredibly dangerous as well, many times over.

John also had cancer, liver cancer. He had a particularly virulent, very aggressive form of liver cancer that had a less than an 8% survival rate at the time. He was in a special trial program at *Walter Reed Army Medical Center* but still, he had a prognosis of less than a year to live when he asked for our representation. Today we would know it was Agent Orange, back then nobody knew, or if they did know, they were not telling. However, since John had still been in the Army when it started, *Walter Reed* had included him in the program.

Actually, John was special period. He was tall, well over six feet. He was thin, "*raw boned*" they called it in his native Texas. He had pale blue eyes and a shock of blond hair that according to some pictures I saw, he kept neatly trimmed when had any hair at all. At the time I knew him, because of his chemo treatments, John was bald and wore a hat all the time. But, most of all John was just a laid back, nice guy.

One of the things that chemo does besides treating the cancer and killing all of your hair follicles is that it gives you nausea. It can give you nausea so bad you can't eat, and even if you force yourself to eat like a good patient, the nausea may make you throw it all up. That is why so many of the patients were dying in John's program at *Walter Reed*; in part because of the heavy duty chemo, they were literally starving to death under some of the best medical care in the world.

All of them except John Powers that is. Except for the liver cancer, John was doing well, better than anybody else in the program. John was eating well, and he was keeping it down. In contrast to many of the others in the program, his weight was stable. As far as John knew, no one in the *Walter Reed* program had ever connected it to marijuana.

Remember this was in the 1970's. According to John, the *Walter Reed* doctors assumed that his and a few others lack of a nausea response to the brutal chemical medications they were giving them was genetic; but it was not genetic in John's case, it was marijuana, lots and lots of really good, really potent, marijuana.

Then and now marijuana was completely illegal in Virginia and the laws were enforced vigorously. John was not about to tell anybody that he was a user, a pot head and a grower, so the doctors either did not know that John was using, or, more likely, they turned a blind eye.

No reputable doctors at the time prescribed marijuana to treat their patients. In fact, Federal law defined marijuana as an illegal, useless, drug, and found as a matter of law that it had no therapeutic effect whatsoever. However, though the law said that marijuana had no therapeutic effect, even the law cannot make the untrue, true.

Besides everything else, John Powers was a masterful marijuana grower with a very green thumb. He grew marijuana in his back yard. He had a townhouse in Fairfax County near Washington, D. C. It was an end unit with a much larger yard than most. He grew a lot of marijuana in that yard, for years.

Getting the munchies regularly and the heavy duty chemo he was receiving at *Walter Reed* was what was keeping John alive. The combination was the only thing that was keeping him alive.

You could almost sum up John when I met him in one long sentence: he had cancer mostly in remission; he drove an old, beat up, but bright yellow, bath tub, Porsche convertible usually very fast, summer and winter, with the top down, and he grew a lot of really good marijuana in his back yard. He also liked to read.

All was fine until a Virginia State Trooper living next door to John noticed the marijuana plants. When the trooper saw the plants peaking over John's fence he arrested John. In fact, he dragged John, just returned from a stay in the hospital, out of his townhouse in handcuffs.

I met John in the prisoners' library at the Fairfax County Jail two days after his arrest. All of the interview rooms were in use so the Deputy Sheriff let me use the prisoners' library to interview John. He told me his history. He said that he never sold marijuana. The closest he would come to that was now and then he would trade seeds with other growers. Because of the high level of THC in his marijuana plants, John's marijuana seeds were sort of celebrities in the local world of marijuana growers, but they were still a rarity, because he refused to sell to anybody.

His legal trouble started when his plants grew taller than the fence in his backyard. When that had happened in the past he had just topped the plants to keep them below the fence. However, his most recent relapse and subsequent hospital stay had been poorly timed. His stay in *Walter Reed* that time started in late April, lots of rain, leading into May with lots of sun that year. His plants in his back yard had just exploded while he was in

316

Walter Reed for a relapse, and his Virginia State Trooper neighbor had no sense of humor at all.

There was more pot in the attic in three large, steamer trunks, dried and ready to smoke. Counting the steamer trunks, what was drying in John's two otherwise unused upstairs bedrooms and what was growing in the back yard, the Virginia State Police seized about 200 pounds of pot. That alone made it a really significant pot bust.

Virginia's laws on pot possession at the time were especially stringent. For example according to courthouse scuttlebutt, there was already one unlucky soul in the Virginia State penitentiary system for his tenth year. His crime? Possession of three marijuana cigarettes.

However, because of the very generous amount of marijuana in the home rolled joints, they met the total weight requirement of the presumptive intent to distribute standard in Virginia at the time. The judge in Richmond had maxed this unlucky man's prison sentence out to an incredible total of thirty years. John was in trouble, big legal trouble.

The first thing I did was talk to John's doctors at *Walter Reed*. They said that John had a year to live, at most. Actually they said that he should already be dead. John was one of their program's few stars and they did not want to lose him from their medical trial. Besides that, they just liked him.

I got John's course of treatment from the *Walter Reed* doctors and filed an emergency motion in the Fairfax County Circuit Court to require the Sheriff's Department which ran the jail to continue the cancer treatments while John was in custody. These treatments were quite extensive, and quite expensive as well. That was the opening shot of our defense.

Naturally, the Fairfax Circuit Court judge turned it down. Anything that is likely to cost the taxpayers of Virginia a lot of money is even more likely to be turned down by a Virginia state court judge.

However, I never really expected to win there. What I expected, and got was the Assistant Commonwealth Attorney's immediate agreement on a substantial reduction in John's bail. That way John would be out of jail and could continue his treatment on the U.S. Army's dime at *Walter Reed*. The Assistant Commonwealth Attorney did not want to risk that I would win the motion if I refiled it, this time as a *Writ of habeas corpus* in Federal Court in Alexandria, Virginia.

John was out of jail until trial. Round one for us.

Then I got a copy of John's DD-214 form which listed his medals, and all of the places he had served. I also found as well as copies of all of the official citations describing what John had done to win those various medals. Finally, I got the doctors at *Walter Reed* to write a diagnosis and a prognosis for John.

From the standpoint of what I was trying to do, the prognosis was wonderful; from John's standpoint it was awful. According to the doctors John was sure to die, quite painfully, in less than a year, and under any standard, he was a certifiable war hero with an extraordinary record of personal heroism in America's service.

I got it all together and took it to the then Fairfax Commonwealth Attorney, Robert Horan. I knew Bob Horan to say hello to in the courthouse, but nothing more. However, I was counting on his reputation as an old school, a true, Virginia Gentleman.

318

That really was all I had. If Horan was less than that, then John would surely die in the Fairfax County Jail probably long before he ever got to a Virginia state prison.

All I wanted, all I hoped for was an agreement that the case would be continued for at least a year, because I expected that John would probably die by then. In the meantime he could continue treatment at *Walter Reed*. He could live in his home.

I wanted it because John was a good man and a hero, a true American, Airborne hero, and paying or not, he was my client. Therefore, it was also my duty as his lawyer.

There were no great legal theories to justify what I was asking for, only compassion, a little common sense and a sense of real justice. All of which are unfortunately in very short supply in most courthouses.

He is retired now, but then Bob Horan was known as a tough prosecutor and in conservative Virginia that meant something. The Commonwealth Attorney, or state prosecutor, is an elected position in Virginia and when other prosecutors in the Commonwealth had a difficult case that they were afraid they would lose, they would call on Bob Horan to win it for them. They called on him often. He was that good.

When he tried a case he would usually sit at counsel table alone during motions and trial, no bevy of assistants, not even any worker bees outside the courtroom doing the grunt work to get the case ready for trial. Most times he prepared his own cases. He did his own legal research. He tried his own cases, and he usually won them as well. His office also would try any case where he thought the defendant was guilty, whether they thought they would win or not.

All of this is very unusual for a chief prosecutor. It is almost unheard of for an elected chief prosecutor. But, Bob Horan was so good that he could be different. That was exactly what I was counting on.

Sometimes I think:

"How am I still alive? Given what I have done and where I have been, how could I still be alive?"

I have not come up with an answer except that in Vietnam my rifle platoon kept me alive and ever since then I have been equally lucky.

Only the luck of having some very good, very tough, young paratroopers around me had saved me in Vietnam, and luck along with the equally excellent Montgomery County, Maryland Police Department had also kept me alive as the target of an honest to God hit man after Vietnam.

(For that story see: https://johneharrison.wordpress.com/2014/06/02/have-you-ever-been-the-target-of-a-hit-man/).

My life, that is what I think I owe the paratroopers that I served with in the 101st Airborne Division, just my life. That is why I took John's case. Now I had to do something with it. I had a plan, but that was all I had so far. I gathered all of the documents together and made an appointment with Bob Horan.

I was ready with a real tear jerker of a spiel, but I never got to say any of it. When I arrived at his office, Bob's secretary asked me to leave my materials. She assured me that Bob would review them himself and that he would call me before the end of the week.

Not a good start I thought. The plan was not working.

I was wrong. On Friday afternoon Bob Horan himself called me at my office. With little preamble he told me he had reviewed my materials and that he was willing to drop the charges entirely, but he had not talked to the state trooper yet. As a matter of courtesy, almost all prosecutors will talk to the arresting officer before they drop a case. However, he said that regardless of what the trooper said, the case against John would go away. He promised that.

I called John Powers and told him the good news. Then I went home for what I thought was a well deserved, great weekend with my kids.

On Monday it all turned to shit. That is a technical legal term, "*turned to shit.*" You could look it up in Black's Law Dictionary.

The state trooper was enraged when Horan told him that he was dismissing the case. The problem was that the trooper had lived next door to a man that grew, and had in his house one of the largest marijuana seizures in Fairfax County history up to that time.

After congratulating him the trooper's boss had later figured out that the trooper had lived next door to the grower for about three years and that during all of that time marijuana, a lot of marijuana had been grown right under his trooper's nose in John's backyard.

Worse, almost every morning for those three years the trooper had eaten in a breakfast nook, bump out, in his kitchen that overlooked John's backyard. However, the trooper had not noticed the bumper crop of marijuana, mixed in with tomato plants, the several rows of corn and other vegetables that John grew there every summer.

Although his boss did not know it, it had been the trooper's daughter that had precipitated the discovery of the pot in John's backyard. She had asked her father what the plants were that were hanging over the their backyard fence. She thought that they were weeds growing in John's garden. She wanted to get rid of them for her friend, the neighbor who gave them tomatoes every summer. The one who was very sick and was just back from the hospital.

The trooper really looked at the plants for the first time. He said one of those technical legal terms quite loudly and promptly went next door to arrest his neighbor.

According to Horan, in our awful Monday morning telephone call, now the rest of the troopers in the State Police sub-station were asking the trooper things like:

"*How can you tell if a bank is being robbed?*" or,

"*What does a speeding car really look like?*"

However, both the trooper, and his boss, were having a lot of trouble seeing the humor.

Since the marijuana was also a Federal offense, the trooper said if Horan dropped the case, he would go to the United States Attorney, the

322

federal prosecutor. Since it was so much marijuana, and since it was such an easy conviction given the facts, Horan thought that the U. S. Attorney would take the case in a heartbeat.

We had to do something or John was on his way to a federal prison. It was Horan's idea. He had made a promise, and he intended to keep it. He said that to quiet the State Trooper, he would keep the charges pending in Fairfax. It would all be there, the two hundred or so pounds of weed that the state police had taken out of the yard and the upstairs bedrooms, and the three large chests of marijuana from the attic, the years of growing it in his backyard, everything.

If the feds ever tried to do anything Horan said he would call me and I would bring John in to plead guilty, but to a misdemeanor charge as minor as Horan could talk the judge into, and he would request a sentence of *"time served"*. Until then, the case would just sit there. You could count on Bob Horan.

Even the Feds can't trump double jeopardy. While technically, it would not actually be double jeopardy because there are two sovereigns, the Commonwealth of Virginia and the Federal government, still, trying John twice for exactly the same thing was practically impossible.

I told John what had happened and he was satisfied. That would normally be the end of our work together. The case was over.

However, about a week later John called me in a rage. He wanted to hire me again. He said that the Virginia State Police would not give him back his marijuana or even his seeds. In fact, they told him that they had already burned almost all of it. John said that it was his best crop ever, and that they had even taken the seeds that he thought that he had well hidden in his townhouse.

He had nothing left. He wanted justice. He wanted his marijuana back, and in fact he probably needed it to keep living. He demanded that I file suit immediately.

He was even more enraged when I told him that he could not win such a lawsuit. In legal terms, his marijuana and the seeds were contraband. In actual terms, they were already gone. The state police had "*seized*" them, not "*stolen*" them.

He would not shut up. John was still yelling at me when I finally just hung the phone up. Among other things, I was no longer his favorite "*L-T*", but there was nothing legally that could be done that I could see.

That was the last time I heard from John until I saw in the *Washington Post* a little over a year later that he had died. He was buried with full military honors in Culpepper National Cemetery between his father and his younger brother. After John's brother Tom had been killed in Vietnam he had been buried next to his father who was a World War II veteran, but they had left a space between them for John.

Bob Horan was there at John's funeral. We nodded. The State trooper did not show, but his daughter was there with her mother. They had liked John too. John was special.

*John Powers is not his real name. He was my client, and dead or not, I cannot use his name. jeh

324

Afterward

Our war is over. If there is one thing I am proudest of other than all of the men in my own platoon and the rest of Alpha Company, it is the way that the Vietnam Veterans as a group, both in and out of uniform have ensured that America never again turns its back on its soldiers, Marines, airmen and sailors returning from a war they did not chose to fight.

Never again. Currahee!

Although not noted as "WIA" Ron Ford, second row from the top, fourth man in from the left, and perhaps more were also wounded, some of us were wounded more than once, but this was the best that my friend Jerry Berry could validate. We really did our best for you America. Airborne!

ALPHA COMPANY, SECOND PLATOON (Revised 3/16/08)

Ft. Campbell, Ky. just prior to leaving for Vietnam, 10/2/1967.

ROW ONE (Bottom - L To R):

1. 2Lt. John E. Harrison, PL (WIA 2/2/68, WIA 2/3/68 & WIA 2/8/68)

2. SFC James Albert Bunn, PSG (KIA 2/2/68)

3. SSG Ulysses Pulley (WIA)

4. Sgt. Harvey Mathis, Jr (DEROS)

ROW TWO (L To R):

1. Pfc. Guadalupe Aguero (WIA 1/31/68)

2. Pfc. Christopher P. Adams

3. SP4 Emett E. Clark (WIA 2/2/68)

4. SP4 Dennis L. Sutton (WIA)

5. Pfc. Jackie Walker (WIA 2/6/68)

6. SP4 Emory L. Georgia (WIA 2/2/68 & WIA 2/8/68)

ROW THREE (L To R):

1. Pvt. Edgar A. Campbell (KIA 12/19/67)

2. SP4 Gary L. Gressett (WIA 2/2/68)

3. SP4 Francis G. Edwards

4. Pfc. Edward E. Brady (WIA 5/14/68)

5. SP4 Vaughn R. DeWaay (WIA)

6. SSG Jearl D. Keefer (WIA 12/19/1967)

7. SP4 Dennis W. Owen (WIA 2/8/68)

8. Pfc. Jackie Walker (WIA 2/8/68)

ROW FOUR (L To R):

1. SP4 James L. Philyaw (WIA 2/3/68)

2. Pfc. David R. Stiles

3. Pfc. Joseph R. Stephenson (WIA)

4. SP4 Ronald G. Ford (WIA 2/6/68)

5. Pfc. Dennis R. Craig (WIA 2/2/68)

6. SP4 Biven B. Patterson

7. Sgt. Charles L. Hayes

8. Sgt.. John L. Matkin (WIA 1/31/68)

ROW FIVE (L To R):

1. SP4 James Guymon (WIA)
2. Pfc. Andrew James Daniels (KIA 2/2/68)
3. SP4 Wally D. Couch (SIW)
4. SP4 George C. Payton (DEROS prior to Tet '68)
5. Pfc. Eugene C. James (WIA 7/17/68)
6. SP4 Harold M. Dobie
7. SP4 George R. Schultz (DFW 2/22/68)*
* Schultz died in Japan from wounds received on 2/2/68.

WIA = Wounded in Action
KIA = Killed in Action
DFW = Died from wounds
SIW = Self Inflicted Wound
DEROS = Date Estimated Return from Overseas Service

Made in the USA
Middletown, DE
29 March 2018